About the Authors

Among the best known and most respected gardening experts on the prairies, Hugh Skinner and Sara Williams bring decades of gardening experience to *Best Groundcovers and Vines for the Prairies*, a follow-up to their previous book, *Best Trees and Shrubs for the Prairies*.

Hugh Skinner holds a B.S.A. in horticulture from the University of Manitoba and has been active in the nursery industry for thirty years. He grows a wide variety of hardy plants and maintains a large collection of trees in the Frank Skinner Arboretum near Roblin, Manitoba, the result of ninety years of plant collecting, testing, and breeding, first started by his father, Frank Skinner. His garden is home to a wide variety of vines and groundcover plants.

credit: Michael Skinner

Hugh Skinner

Sara Williams has retired as the horticultural specialist at the University of Saskatchewan. She is the co-author of *Perennials for the Plains and Prairies* and author of the award-winning *Creating the Prairie Xeriscape*, as well as *In a Cold Land: Saskatchewan's Horticultural Pioneers*. She holds a B.Sc. and M.Sc. in horticulture from the University of Saskatchewan. Sara has led garden tours to England, Ireland, Scotland, and elsewhere and now spends much of her time in her five-acre garden near Saskatoon when not giving a wide array of gardening workshops.

credit: Darlene Polachic

Sara Williams

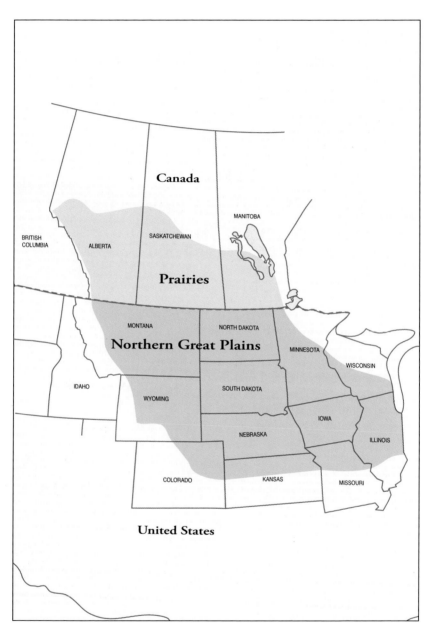

The groundcovers and vines described in this book are recommended for gardens in the Canadian prairies and the northern Great Plains of the United States.

Best
Groundcovers and Vines
for the Prairies

HUGH SKINNER & SARA WILLIAMS

FIFTH
HOUSE

Cover and interior design by Brian Smith / Articulate Eye
Cover photographs by Sara Williams: top: *Asarum canadense*; second row: landscape with vines and groundcovers; third row (left to right): *Clematis viticella* 'Mme. Julia Correvon'; *Aurinia saxatilis*; *Ajuga reptans* 'Chocolate Chip'; bottom: *Carex muskgingumensis*
Map by Brian Smith / Articulate Eye
Edited by Lesley Reynolds
Copyedited by Geri Rowlatt
Proofread by Joan Tetrault
Scans by Keith Seabrook and Rob Corbett / ABL Imaging

A Note on the Type:
The type in this book is set in Adobe Garamond Pro.

The publisher gratefully acknowledges the support of The Canada Council for the Arts and the Department of Canadian Heritage.

Canada Council   Conseil des Arts
for the Arts   du Canada

We acknowledge the financial support of the Government of Canada through the Book Publishing Industry Development Program (BPIDP) for our publishing activities.

Printed in China

11 10 09 08 07 / 5 4 3 2

First published in the United States in 2008 by

Fitzhenry & Whiteside
311 Washington Street
Brighton, MA 02135

Library and Archives Canada Cataloguing in Publication

Skinner, Hugh, 1951–
  Best Groundcovers and Vines for the Prairies / Hugh Skinner and Sara Williams.

Includes index.
ISBN 978-1-894856-80-5

  1. Ground cover plants—prairie provinces. 2. Climbing plants—prairie provinces.
1 Williams, Sara, 1941– 11. Title.

SB432.S55 2007   635.9'6409712   C20006-906386-9

Fifth House Ltd.
A Fitzhenry & Whiteside Company
1511, 1800-4 St. SW
Calgary, Alberta T2S 2S5

1-800-387-9776

www.fitzhenry.ca

Contents

Acknowledgements vi
Chapter One   INTRODUCTION 1
Chapter Two   GROUNDCOVERS AND VINES IN THE LANDSCAPE 3
     Designing by Habitat 3
     Designing by Function 6
       Groundcovers 6
       Vines 24
Chapter Three   PURCHASING, PLANTING, AND MAINTAINING
              GROUNDCOVERS AND VINES 27
     Getting Ready 27
       How Do Groundcovers Cover Ground? 27
       Preparing the Planting Site 28
       Spacing 29
     Purchase and Planting 30
       Groundcovers 30
       Vines 32
     Propagating Groundcovers and Vines 32
       Seed 33
       Suckers, Divisions, and Layers 33
       Hardwood and Softwood Cuttings 35
     Maintaining Groundcovers and Vines 36
       Mulching 37
       Pruning 37
       Fertilizing 38
       Pest and Disease Control 39
Chapter Four   GROUNDCOVERS AND VINES FOR PRAIRIE GARDENS 41
     Groundcovers 44
     Vines 195
Glossary 213
Bibliography 217
Index 221

Acknowledgements

People have contributed to this book in many ways. We wish to acknowledge their generosity, support, expertise, and encouragement. We thank Brian Porter and Philip Ronald for their in-depth review of the text and provision of their expert opinions with regard to the content of the work. Others who have reviewed the work and provided comments are Wendy Mackie and Rick Durand.

For use of photographs in the book we thank Brian Baldwin and Lesley Reynolds, and for the photos of the authors we thank Diane Polachic for the photo of Sara and Michael Skinner for the photo of Hugh.

Thank you to the editorial team at Fifth House: Meaghan Craven and Lesley Reynolds for refinement of the manuscript to its printed form, Geri Rowlatt for copyediting, and Joan Tetrault for proofreading. Thanks to Mike McCoy and Brian Smith at Articulate Eye in Saskatoon; they did wonderful work on the design of the book and cover.

To these and to the many individuals who have provided advice and insight we acknowledge our gratitude.

[1]

Introduction

There are times in our gardening lives when preconceptions get in the way of creativity and "definitions" impede a more imaginative use of plants in our landscapes. This book is our attempt to redress these issues by broadening the definitions of groundcovers and vines and exploring the many and varied applications of these versatile plants in prairie gardens.

Mention the term "groundcover" to most gardeners and they visibly tense as images of goutweed and ribbon grass come to the fore. But what about a carpet of thyme or white-flowered dwarf veronica setting off a lichen-covered rock or a birdbath in a small urban courtyard? Or an enormous bed of blue lyme grass or tawny daylily acting as a transition area between a carefully tended rural garden and the prairie beyond? What about using vines such as Virginia creeper or golden clematis to clothe a sun-baked slope or bank or hide your neighbor's ugly shed? Expand your groundcover repertoire with *Waldsteinia ternata*, *Paronychia capitata*, or our native strawberry, *Fragaria virginiana*.

Funk and Wagnalls Standard Dictionary defines a vine as: "Any of a large and widely distributed group of plants having a slender weak stem that may clasp or twine about a support by means of tendrils, leaf petioles, etc." Although the selection of hardy vines is more limited than that of ground-covers, there are, for example, many lovely

Virginia creeper (*Parthenocissus quinquefolia*) makes an effective groundcover for large, difficult areas.
(Sara Williams)

yet sadly underused clematis hybrids that will survive our prairie winters without fuss, muss, or protection, but are in great need of a publicist. We've happily taken on that role. If you've had problems with the more tender larger-flowered hybrids, you'll never regret purchasing a 'White Swan', 'Blue Bird', or 'Ruby'. Gardeners seeking hardy climbers should also keep in mind that although roses may not actually "climb," given the support of a trellis or obelisk, there are some that visually fill the role of vines. No garden should be without 'Prairie Dawn' or 'John Cabot'.

Groundcovers and vines can function in many ways in our landscapes, regardless of property size. Among them are plants that are adaptable to all of the varied habitats the prairie region offers, from sheltered bogs to windswept, gravelly berms, from moist, shaded woodlands to dry, south- or west-facing areas under an overhang of a building. What's more, the number from which to select is enormous. We've included over 200 species and 160 varieties of hardy groundcovers and 19 species and 23 cultivars of hardy vines suitable for prairie gardens.

But what do we really mean by the word "groundcover"? Groundcovers are relatively low-growing plants that cover the soil surface, preventing soil and water loss and controlling weeds. Although gardeners often limit their definition of groundcovers to those plants that are only a few centimetres in height, most are taller, generally 30 to 90 cm (12 to 36 in.). They are generally characterized by overlapping foliage that is dense enough to exclude light and a root system that is vigorous enough to outcompete other plants for soil moisture and nutrients dissolved in the soil water. They spread horizontally by means of suckers, rhizomes, or stolons. Depending on their spacing and the vigor of an individual species or cultivar, they physically take up space and exclude other plants within two to three years. There is no such thing as a completely "no-maintenance" groundcover, but once established, they require little maintenance.

Although we usually think of groundcovers as herbaceous perennials, a variety of plants will do the job: evergreen perennials, dwarf deciduous shrubs, evergreen shrubs, ornamental grasses, and even vines.

We trust you will discover myriad new and different ways to use these many hardy groundcovers and vines in your own prairie landscape, delighting in each new plant that becomes your own.

Groundcovers and Vines
in the Landscape

Designing by Habitat

As you observe your landscape, learn to think like a plant in terms of habitat requirements. Is a particular area sunny or shady? Moist or dry? For simplicity's sake, we've divided the groundcovers and vines into four categories: plants for dry sun, moist sun, dry shade, and moist shade. These are relative terms but they provide a starting point. More detailed information is available under individual plant descriptions.

Keep in mind that vines and groundcovers grown primarily for their flowers, such as daylilies, may grow well in shade but bloom less than if planted in a sunny situation.

If not listed under one of these specific habitats, the groundcovers and vines mentioned in this book may be assumed to require average moisture and garden conditions.

Dry Sun

Groundcovers
Achillea spp. (yarrow)
Antennaria spp.
(pussytoes)
Arabis alpina (rock cress,
mountain rock cress)
Artemisia spp. (artemisia,
wormwood, ghost plant,
silver sage)
Aurinia saxatilis
(perennial alyssum,
basket-of-gold, madwort)

Various sedums used as pavement plantings direct traffic and add color and texture. (Sara Williams)

Bergenia cordifolia (heart-leaved bergenia, pigsqueak)
Bouteloua gracilis (blue grama grass)
Bromus inermis 'Skinner's Golden' ('Skinner's Golden' brome grass)
Campanula spp. (bellflower)
Caragana spp. (caragana)
Carex pennsylvanica (sun-loving sedge)
Cerastium tomentosum (snow-in-summer)
Coronilla varia (crown vetch)
Cytisus decumbens (prostrate broom)
Dianthus spp. (pinks)
Diervilla lonicera (diervilla, dwarf bush honeysuckle)
Dracocephalum spp. (dragonhead)
Dryas spp. (mountain avens)
Elymus arenarius (blue lyme grass)
Euphorbia cyparissias (cypress spurge)
Festuca glauca (blue fescue)
Fragaria virginiana (wild strawberry)
Gypsophila repens (dwarf baby's breath, creeping baby's breath)
Heliopsis helianthoides (false sunflower, rough heliopsis)
Heuchera Morden hybrids (coral bells, alumroot)
Iberis sempervirens (evergreen candytuft)
Juniperus spp. (juniper)
Nepeta x 'Dropmore Blue' ('Dropmore Blue' catmint)
Paronychia capitata (whitlowwort, nailwort)
Potentilla spp. (potentilla)
Prunus tenella (Russian almond)
Rosa spp. (rose)
Saponaria ocymoides (rock soapwort)
Sedum spp. (sedum, stonecrop)
Sempervivum spp. (hen and chicks, houseleek)
Solidago hybrids (goldenrod hybrids)
Sorbaria sorbifolia (Ural false spirea)
Spiraea spp. (spirea)
Stachys lanata (woolly lambs' ears)
Symphoricarpos spp. (snowberry)
Symphytum officinale (comfrey)
Veronica spp. (speedwell, veronica)

Vines
Humulus lupulus (hops)

Moist Sun

Groundcovers
Ajuga reptans (bugleweed, carpet bugle)
Andropogon gerardii (big bluestem)
Carex muskingumensis (palm sedge)
Diervilla lonicera (diervilla, dwarf bush honeysuckle)
Dracocephalum grandiflorum (bigflower dragonhead)
Erigeron speciosus (Oregon fleabane)
Eupatorium maculatum (Joe Pye weed, boneset)
Filipendula spp. (meadowsweet)
Fragaria virginiana (wild strawberry)
Hemerocallis spp. (daylily)
Physostegia virginiana (obedient plant)
Rosa spp. (rose)
Schizachyrium scoparium (little bluestem)
Spiraea spp. (spirea)
Stachys grandiflora (big betony)

Dry Shade

Groundcovers
Anaphalis margaritacea (pearly everlasting)
Anemone spp. (windflower)
Aralia nudicaulis (wild sarsaparilla)
Bergenia cordifolia (heart-leaved bergenia, pigsqueak)
Cornus canadensis (bunchberry)
Euonymus nanus var. *turkestanicus* (dwarf Turkestan burning bush)
Geranium macrorrhizum (bigroot perennial geranium)
Mahonia repens (creeping Oregon grape)
Microbiota decussata (Russian cypress, Siberian cypress)
Omphalodes verna alba (creeping forget-me-not)
Smilacina stellata (star-flowered Solomon's seal, false Solomon's seal)
Symphoricarpos spp. (snowberry)
Viola canadensis (western Canada violet, wood violet)
Waldsteinia ternata (Siberian barren strawberry)

Vines
Clematis tangutica (golden clematis)
Humulus lupulus (hops)
Parthenocissus quinquefolia (Virginia creeper)

Moist Shade

Groundcovers
Aegopodium podograria 'Variegatum' (goutweed, bishop's goutweed)
Ajuga reptans (bugleweed, carpet bugle)
Alchemilla mollis (common lady's mantle)
Asarum canadense (Canadian ginger, wild ginger)
Astilbe spp. (dwarf astilbe)
Brunnera macrophylla (alpine forget-me-not)
Convallaria majalis (lily-of-the-valley)
Cotoneaster horizontalis 'Perpusillus' (ground cotoneaster)
Filipendula spp. (meadowsweet)
Geranium x *cantabrigiense* (hybrid geranium)
Hemerocallis spp. (daylily)
Hepatica spp. (liverleaf, hepatica)
Hosta spp. (hosta)
Lamiastrum galeobdolon (yellow archangel)
Lamium maculatum (spotted dead nettle)
Matteuccia struthiopteris (ostrich fern, American ostrich fern)
Pachysandra terminalis (Japanese spurge)
Paxistima canbyi (cliffgreen, paxistima)
Phalaris arundinacea 'Picta' (ribbon grass)
Polygonatum spp. (Solomon's seal)
Pulmonaria spp. (lungwort)

Designing by Function

GROUNDCOVERS

Groundcovers have many functions in both urban and rural landscapes. They can act as lawn replacements; beautify small, inaccessible, or inhospitable areas; hold slopes and banks; unify shrub beds; delineate space and define property lines; break up large expanses of lawn; form transition and back-lane plantings; direct traffic; accent focal points; screen unsightly objects; and form an understory beneath trees. It is easy to unify the various areas of your landscape through controlled repetition of favorite groundcovers that have proven themselves in your yard.

Lawn Replacements and Small, Inaccessible, or Inhospitable Areas

For centuries, lawn grasses have been selected and hybridized to create a near-perfect living surface on which to play, go barefoot, sit, or lie. Soft and

Best Groundcovers & Vines for the Prairies

resilient, lawns allow a toddler to toddle and fall down unharmed. They also act as "negative space" in our landscapes, highlighting and accentuating trees, shrubs, and flower borders.

Lawns make up one of the largest components of a conventional landscape. They are also one of our highest consumers of water and demand high inputs of environmentally unfriendly machinery, gas, electricity, fertilizer, and pesticides. As well, lawns require a great deal of labor over your lifetime and the lifetime of your lawn.

Much lawn area exists by default, quite possibly because we could not visualize alternatives. Think about your existing lawn and how it is used by members of your household. How much of it is actually used in an intimate manner to sit, lie, play, or go barefoot on? What parts of your lawn act as negative space to show off other plantings? What parts of it are odd strips or corners that you never venture onto unless you're pushing a lawn mower? Which of these areas would be better served by low-maintenance groundcovers that require fewer resources and little labor once established?

Keep in mind that few groundcovers can function as true lawn substitutes. They do not tolerate being walked on and are too uncomfortable to sit on. In addition, a single groundcover may not be an aesthetically pleasing alternative to a huge area of grass, although several groundcovers in combination may work. However, where lawn is unnecessary or impractical, they are an attractive alternative to conventional grassed areas.

Many front gardens, and some back gardens in older neighborhoods, include a long, narrow strip of lawn between a driveway and a parallel sidewalk. The space is too narrow to be used as lawn, and as negative space serves only to emphasize the adjoining cement. Although wider, the space between two houses is another problem area that often remains a no-man's-land, with neither homeowner taking responsibility for developing or maintaining it. Areas close to house foundations also present challenges. The space beneath the building overhang often found in split-level homes is permanently shaded if on the north side or in hot sun and glare if on the south or west side. These areas are too small for a lawn and present an extreme and inhospitable microclimate for many plants. Think groundcover!

Groundcovers may be used to accent trees and define a sitting area. (Sara Williams)

The accompanying lists include many varied groundcovers to suit specific habitats and gardeners' preferences.

Groundcovers for Lawn Replacement

Ajuga reptans (bugleweed, carpet bugle)
Antennaria spp. (pussytoes)
Arabis alpina (rock cress, mountain rock cress)
Arctostaphylos uva-ursi (bearberry)
Artemisia stelleriana 'Silver Brocade' ('Silver Brocade' artemisia)
Asarum canadense (Canadian ginger, wild ginger)
Aurinia saxatilis (perennial alyssum, basket-of-gold, madwort)
Campanula cochlearifolia (dwarf bellflower, fairy thimble)
Carex pennsylvanica (sun-loving sedge)
Cerastium tomentosum (snow-in-summer)
Convallaria majalis (lily-of-the-valley)
Dianthus spp. (pinks)
Dryas spp. (mountain avens)
Fragaria virginiana (wild strawberry)
Gentiana spp. (gentian)
Geranium spp. (perennial geranium)
Hosta spp. and hybrids (hosta)
Juniperus horizontalis (creeping juniper)
Lamiastrum galeobdolon (yellow archangel)
Lamium maculatum (spotted dead nettle)
Lysimachia nummularia (creeping Jenny, moneywort)
Pachysandra terminalis (Japanese spurge)
Paronychia capitata (whitlowwort, nailwort)
Paxistima canbyi (cliffgreen, paxistima)
Phlox borealis (arctic phlox); *P. subulata* (dwarf phlox)
Potentilla anserina (silverweed)
Sedum spp. (sedum)
Sempervivum spp. (hen and chicks, houseleek)
Silene acaulis (moss campion)
Thymus spp. (thyme)
Veronica spp. (speedwell)
Vinca herbacea (herbaceous periwinkle)
Waldsteinia ternata (Siberian barren strawberry)

Groundcovers for Small, Inaccessible, or Inhospitable Areas

Achillea spp. (yarrow)
Ajuga reptans (bugleweed, carpet bugle)

Anaphalis margaritacea (pearly everlasting)
Anemone spp. (windflower)
Antennaria spp. (pussytoes)
Arabis alpina (rock cress, mountain rock cress)
Arctostaphylos uva-ursi (bearberry)
Arrhenatherum bulbosum 'Variegatum' (variegated tuber oat grass)
Artemisia stelleriana 'Silver Brocade' ('Silver Brocade' artemisia)
Asarum canadense (Canadian ginger, wild ginger)
Aurinia saxatilis (perennial alyssum, basket-of-gold, madwort)
Bergenia cordifolia (heart-leaved bergenia, pigsqueak)
Bouteloua gracilis (blue grama grass)
Bromus inermis 'Skinner's Golden' ('Skinner's Golden' brome grass)
Campanula cochlearifolia (dwarf bellflower, fairy thimble)
Campanula glomerata (clustered bellflower, Danesblood bellflower)
Campanula persicifolia (peach-leaved bellflower)
Carex pennsylvanica (sun-loving sedge)
Cerastium tomentosum (snow-in-summer)
Chelone spp. (turtlehead)
Chrysanthemum zawadskii 'Clara Curtis' ('Clara Curtis' chrysanthemum)
Convallaria majalis (lily-of-the-valley)
Coronilla varia (crown vetch)
Cotoneaster horizontalis 'Perpusillus' (ground cotoneaster)
Dianthus spp. (pinks)
Dracocephalum spp. (dragonhead)
Dryas spp. (mountain avens)
Erigeron speciosus (Oregon fleabane)
Euphorbia cyparissias (cypress spurge)
Festuca glauca (blue fescue)
Fragaria virginiana (wild strawberry)
Gentiana spp. (gentian)
Geranium spp. (perennial geranium)
Geum urbanum (Siberian avens, wood avens)
Gypsophila repens (dwarf baby's breath, creeping baby's breath)
Hemerocallis spp. (daylily)
Heuchera Morden hybrids (coral bells, alumroot)
Hosta spp. and hybrids (hosta)
Iberis sempervirens (evergreen candytuft)
Juniperus spp. (juniper)
Lamiastrum galeobdolon (yellow archangel)
Lamium maculatum (spotted dead nettle)
Lysimachia nummularia (creeping Jenny, moneywort)
Lysimachia punctata (yellow loosestrife)
Mahonia repens (creeping Oregon grape)
Matteuccia struthiopteris (ostrich fern, American ostrich fern)
Microbiota decussata (Russian cypress, Siberian cypress)

Monarda hybrids (monarda, wild bergamot, bee balm, Oswego tea)
Nepeta x 'Dropmore Blue' ('Dropmore Blue' catmint)
Omphalodes verna alba (creeping forget-me-not)
Pachysandra terminalis (Japanese spurge)
Panicum virgatum (switch grass)
Paronychia capitata (whitlowwort, nailwort)
Paxistima canbyi (cliffgreen, paxistima)
Penstemon spp. (penstemon)
Persicaria affinis (Himalayan fleeceflower)
Phalaris arundinacea 'Picta' (ribbon grass)
Phlox borealis (arctic phlox); *P. subulata* (dwarf phlox)
Physostegia virginiana (obedient plant)
Polygonatum spp. (Solomon's seal)
Potentilla anserina (silverweed)
Pulmonaria spp. (lungwort)
Salix spp. (willow)
Schizachyrium scoparium (little bluestem)
Scutellaria spp. (skullcap)
Sedum spp. (sedum)
Sempervivum spp. (hen and chicks, houseleek)
Silene acaulis (moss campion)
Spiraea spp. (spirea)
Stachys spp. (woolly lambs' ears, big betony)
Thymus spp. (thyme)
Tradescantia virginiana (spiderwort)
Veronica spp. (speedwell)
Vinca spp. (periwinkle)
Waldsteinia ternata (Siberian barren strawberry)

Slopes and Banks

Groundcovers work well to cover slopes and banks, areas where lawns are difficult to establish and maintain. They hold the soil and prevent wind and water erosion, yet avoid the costly construction of walls or terraces. Their pattern, color, and texture add year-round interest to an otherwise dull and vulnerable area of our landscapes.

Groundcovers for Slopes and Banks

Achillea millefolium (common yarrow)
Aegopodium podograria 'Variegatum' (goutweed, bishop's goutweed)
Andropogon gerardii (big bluestem)
Artemisia ludoviciana 'Silver King' (artemisia, wormwood, ghost plant, silver sage)

Bouteloua gracilis (blue grama grass)
Bromus inermis 'Skinner's Golden' ('Skinner's Golden' brome grass)
Caragana arborescens 'Pendula' (weeping caragana)
Carex pennsylvanica (sun-loving sedge)
Cerastium tomentosum (snow-in-summer)
Clematis spp. (clematis)
Coronilla varia (crown vetch)
Cytisus decumbens (prostrate broom)
Diervilla lonicera (diervilla, dwarf bush honeysuckle)
Dracocephalum spp. (dragonhead)
Dryas spp. (mountain avens)
Elymus arenarius (blue lyme grass)
Euonymus spp. (burning bush)
Euphorbia cyparissias (Cypress spurge)
Fragaria virginiana (wild strawberry)
Geranium spp. (perennial geranium)
Gypsophila repens (dwarf baby's breath, creeping baby's breath)
Hemerocallis fulva (tawny daylily, orange daylily)
Juniperus spp. (juniper)
Lamiastrum galeobdolon (yellow archangel)
Potentilla spp. (potentilla)
Prunus tenella (Russian almond)
Rhus glabra (smooth sumac)
Rosa spp. (rose)
Saponaria ocymoides (rock soapwort)
Schizachyrium scoparium (little bluestem)
Sedum spp. (sedum)
Sempervivum spp. (hen and chicks, houseleek)
Solidago hybrids (goldenrod hybrids)
Sorbaria sorbifolia (Ural false spirea)
Symphoricarpos spp. (snowberry)
Symphytum officinale (comfrey)
Thymus spp. (thyme)

Vines for Slopes and Banks

Parthenocissus quinquefolia (Virginia creeper)
Vitis riparia (riverbank grape, Manitoba grape)

Groundcovers add color and texture to a slope while reducing erosion. (Sara Williams)

Unifying Shrub Beds

Groundcovers unify shrub beds and borders, especially when these beds are newly planted and the shrubs are still small and seemingly very far apart. Select a groundcover that ties the permanent plantings together and visually complements rather than competes with them.

Junipers are here used as a lawn replacement adjacent to a public walkway. (Sara Williams)

If the shrub bed or border contains dwarf evergreen shrubs, consider a groundcover with a very delicate, airy appearance, such as lady's mantle, or one with neutral silver or green foliage, such as thyme, speedwells such as *Veronica whitleyi* and *V. pectinata*, pussytoes, snow-in-summer, or 'Silver Brocade' artemisia.

Deciduous shrubs are more variable than evergreens and it may take more care to select an appropriate groundcover that complements both foliage and flowers. Gray pussytoes or snow-in-summer are neutral and work well with most shrubs. For deciduous shrubs with gray foliage, consider bright green dwarf phlox or blue-purple 'Chocolate Chip' bugleweed.

If the bed is small, you may wish to use only one species of groundcover for the entire bed. In a larger bed or border, think about using several different groundcovers, each within its own grouping.

Groundcovers for Unifying Shrub Beds

Ajuga reptans (carpet bugle, bugleweed)
Alchemilla spp. (lady's mantle)
Antennaria spp. (pussytoes)
Bergenia cordifolia (heart-leaved bergenia, pigsqueak)
Campanula cochlearifolia (dwarf bellflower, fairy thimble)
Cerastium tomentosum (snow-in-summer)
Dianthus spp. (pinks)
Fragaria x 'Pink Panda' ('Pink Panda' strawberry)
Lamiastrum galeobdolon (yellow archangel)
Lamium maculatum (spotted dead nettle)
Lysimachia nummularia (creeping Jenny, moneywort)
Nepeta spp. (catmint)
Omphalodes verna alba (creeping forget-me-not)
Sedum spp. (stonecrop)
Thymus spp. (thyme)
Veronica spp. (speedwell)

Vinca herbacea (herbaceous periwinkle)
Viola canadensis (western Canada violet, wood violet)
Waldsteinia ternata (Siberian barren strawberry)

Delineating Space and Defining Property Lines

Groundcovers can replace more obtrusive hedges or fences to differentiate areas or "rooms" within a landscape or to define property lines in urban areas. Keep scale in mind. To separate larger areas, use substantial plants such as savin junipers, the tawny or lemon daylily, dwarf burning bush, or 'Karl Foerster' feather reed grass. To delineate smaller areas, use shorter groundcovers like bergenia, perennial geraniums, or hostas.

Groundcovers for Delineating Space and Defining Property Lines

Achillea millefolium (common yarrow)
Aronia melanocarpa (black chokeberry)
Astilbe spp. (astilbe)
Bergenia cordifolia (heart-leaved bergenia, pigsqueak)
Calamagrostis x *acutiflora* 'Karl Foerster' ('Karl Foerster' feather reed grass)
Campanula glomerata (clustered bellflower, Danesblood bellflower)
Campanula persicifolia (peach-leaved bellflower)
Caragana spp. (caragana)
Chrysanthemum zawadskii 'Clara Curtis' ('Clara Curtis' chrysanthemum)
Cytisus spp. (dwarf purple broom, prostrate broom)
Diervilla lonicera (diervilla, dwarf bush honeysuckle)
Erigeron speciosus (Oregon fleabane)
Euonymus spp. (burning bush)
Eupatorium maculatum (Joe Pye weed, boneset)
Filipendula spp. (meadowsweet)
Genista lydia (Lydia broom)
Geranium x 'Johnson's Blue' ('Johnson's Blue' geranium)
Geranium macrorrhizum (bigroot perennial geranium)
Heliopsis helianthoides (false sunflower, rough heliopsis)

Groundcovers, such as this bergenia, can be used to separate two areas of a landscape. (Sara Williams)

Hemerocallis fulva (tawny daylily, orange daylily)
Hosta spp. (hosta)
Juniperus spp. (juniper)
Lamiastrum galeobdolon (yellow archangel)
Lamium maculatum (spotted dead nettle)
Lysimachia punctata (yellow loosestrife)
Matteuccia struthiopteris (ostrich fern, American ostrich fern)
Microbiota decussata (Russian cypress, Siberian cypress)
Monarda hybrids (monarda, wild bergamot, bee balm, Oswego tea)
Nepeta x 'Dropmore Blue' ('Dropmore Blue' catmint)
Panicum virgatum (switch grass)
Persicaria affinis (Himalayan fleeceflower)
Phalaris arundinacea 'Picta' (ribbon grass)
Physostegia virginiana (obedient plant)
Polygonatum spp. (Solomon's seal)
Potentilla fruticosa (shrubby cinquefoil, potentilla)
Pulmonaria spp. (lungwort)
Ribes spp. (currant, gooseberry)
Rosa spp. (rose)
Salix repens var. *argentea* (dwarf silver willow)
Spiraea spp. (spirea)
Stachys spp. (woolly lambs' ears, big betony)

Breaking Up Large Expanses of Lawn

If you find large expanses of lawn boring, consider creating informal island beds or borders of groundcovers to break up the lawn area. Groundcovers establish quickly, providing color and texture with little maintenance. For a more refined look in sunny areas near the house, consider lady's mantle, coral bells, 'Skinner's Blue' fescue, 'Dropmore Blue' catmint, bergenia, or the lemon daylily. For shaded areas, try hosta, bergenia, lily-of-the-valley, dead nettle, or archangel.

Groundcovers for Breaking Up Large Expanses of Lawn

Achillea millefolium (common yarrow)
Alchemilla spp. (lady's mantle)
Anemone spp. (anemone, windflower)
Arrhenatherum bulbosum 'Variegatum' (variegated tuber oat grass)
Bergenia cordifolia (heart-leaved bergenia, pigsqueak)
Calamagrostis x *acutiflora* 'Karl Foerster' ('Karl Foerster' feather reed grass)
Campanula glomerata (clustered bellflower, Danesblood bellflower)
Campanula persicifolia (peach-leaved bellflower)
Caragana spp. (caragana)

Best Groundcovers & Vines for the Prairies

Chrysanthemum zawadskii 'Clara Curtis' ('Clara Curtis' chrysanthemum)
Convallaria majalis (lily-of-the-valley)
Diervilla lonicera (diervilla, dwarf bush honeysuckle)
Erigeron speciosus (Oregon fleabane)
Euonymus spp. (burning bush)
Eupatorium maculatum (Joe Pye weed, boneset)
Festuca glauca (blue fescue)
Filipendula spp. (meadowsweet)
Genista spp. (broom)
Geranium spp. (perennial geranium)
Heliopsis helianthoides (false sunflower, rough heliopsis)
Hemerocallis fulva (tawny daylily, orange daylily)
Heuchera Morden hybrids (coral bells, alumroot)
Hosta spp. (hosta)
Juniperus spp. (juniper)
Lamiastrum galeobdolon (yellow archangel)
Lamium maculatum (spotted dead nettle)
Lysimachia punctata (yellow loosestrife)
Monarda hybrids (monarda, wild bergamot, bee balm, Oswego tea)
Nepeta spp. (catmint)
Panicum virgatum (switch grass)
Persicaria affinis (Himalayan fleeceflower)
Phalaris arundinacea 'Picta' (ribbon grass)
Physostegia virginiana (obedient plant)
Potentilla fruticosa (shrubby cinquefoil, potentilla)
Pulmonaria spp. (lungwort)
Rhus glabra (smooth sumac)
Ribes spp. (currant, gooseberry)
Rosa spp. (rose)
Salix repens var. *argentea* (dwarf silver willow)
Solidago hybrids (goldenrod hybrids)
Spiraea spp. (spirea)
Stachys spp. (woolly lambs' ears, big betony)

Bergenia in a more formal setting. (Sara Williams)

Drought-tolerant Transition Plantings

On large, rural landscapes, there is often a need for transition plantings between the more manicured portion of an acreage or a farmyard and the bush or non-irrigated bunch grass or pasture beyond. Transition areas usually can't be watered, so plants are on their own once they are established. This is where the more drought-tolerant and aggressive groundcovers are useful. The lack of water generally limits their aggression and, in any case, they're being placed where it may not matter if they spread unduly.

Groundcovers for Drought-tolerant Transition Plantings

Achillea millefolium (common yarrow)
Aegopodium podograria 'Variegatum' (goutweed, bishop's goutweed)
Artemisia ludoviciana 'Silver King' (artemisia, wormwood, ghost plant, silver sage)
Bergenia cordifolia (heart-leaved bergenia, pigsqueak)
Bromus inermis 'Skinner's Golden' ('Skinner's Golden' brome grass)
Campanula glomerata (clustered bellflower, Danesblood bellflower)
Diervilla lonicera (diervilla, dwarf bush honeysuckle)
Elymus arenarius (blue lyme grass)
Hemerocallis fulva (tawny daylily, orange daylily)
Juniperus spp. (juniper)

Nepeta spp. (catmint)
Potentilla spp. (potentilla)
Prunus tenella (Russian almond)
Rhus glabra (smooth sumac)
Ribes spp. (currant, gooseberry)
Rosa spp. (rose)
Solidago hybrids (goldenrod hybrids)
Sorbaria sorbifolia (Ural false spirea)
Symphoricarpos albus (common snowberry)
Symphytum officinale (comfrey)

Vines and groundcovers beautifying a back lane. (Sara Williams)

Drought-tolerant Back Lane Plantings

Often ugly and sterile, urban back lanes present a problem for homeowners. We want them to look nice but are reluctant to invest much time or money in their beautification. We rarely look at our own side of the back lane and plantings placed there may be subject to theft, intentional vandalism, or accidental injury by vehicles. As in transition plantings in large landscapes, back lanes are a good place for groundcovers that tend to be invasive given better conditions. In a back lane, even goutweed and ribbon grass might function well and not "get away" on you.

Groundcovers for Drought-tolerant Back Lane Plantings

Achillea millefolium (common yarrow)
Aegopodium podograria 'Variegatum' (goutweed, bishop's goutweed)
Anemone spp. (windflower)
Arrhenatherum bulbosum 'Variegatum' (variegated tuber oat grass)
Artemisia ludoviciana 'Silver King' (artemisia, wormwood, ghost plant, silver sage)
Bergenia cordifolia (heart-leaved bergenia, pigsqueak)
Bromus inermis 'Skinner's Golden' ('Skinner's Golden' brome grass)
Campanula glomerata (clustered bellflower, Danesblood bellflower)
Cerastium tomentosum (snow-in-summer)
Convallaria majalis (lily-of-the valley)
Coronilla varia (crown vetch)
Euphorbia cyparissias (Cypress spurge)
Fragaria virginiana (wild strawberry)
Geranium spp. (perennial geranium)
Heliopsis helianthoides (false sunflower, rough heliopsis)
Hemerocallis fulva (tawny daylily, orange daylily)
Lamiastrum galeobdolon (yellow archangel)
Lamium maculatum (spotted dead nettle)
Nepeta spp. (catmint)
Phalaris arundinacea 'Picta' (ribbon grass)
Potentilla spp. (potentilla)
Prunus tenella (Russian almond)
Rhus glabra (smooth sumac)
Ribes spp. (currant, gooseberry)
Rosa spp. (rose)
Sedum spp. (stonecrop)
Sempervivum spp. (hen and chicks, houseleek)
Solidago hybrids (goldenrod hybrids)
Symphytum officinale (comfrey)
Viola canadensis (western Canada violet, wood violet)
Waldsteinia ternata (Siberian barren strawberry)

Directing Foot Traffic

Groundcovers can be used to direct traffic within your landscape by defining walkways in a subtle manner or by providing more substantial barriers.

Pavement plantings are placed among and beside the flagstones or bricks that make up the pathways through your garden. They are small in stature and provide visual interest through their flowers, foliage, and texture. The human eye is attracted by them and our feet follow. If they are occasionally tromped on, they recover quickly. Groundcovers can also be used to prevent shortcuts across urban corner lots. If the groundcovers employed are tall enough and the planting bed wide enough, they are usually effective.

Sometimes traffic direction needs to be less subtle—that's where groundcovers function as barrier plantings. In rural landscapes, there is sometimes a need to discourage younger children from wandering into potentially dangerous places, such as the pump-out into the septic field. Here's where the negative impact of prickly foliage or thorns may be the lesser of two evils.

Groundcovers for Directing Foot Traffic

Pavement Plantings
Achillea tomentosa (woolly yarrow)
Antennaria spp. (pussytoes)
Arabis alpina (rock cress, mountain rock cress)
Aurinia saxatilis (perennial alyssum, basket-of-gold, madwort)
Campanula cochlearifolia (dwarf bellflower, fairy thimble)
Cerastium tomentosum (snow-in-summer)
Dianthus gratianipolitanus ('Tiny Rubies', Cheddar pinks)
Festuca glauca (blue fescue)
Nepata (cat mint)
Paronychia capitata (whitlowwort, nailwort)
Penstemon spp. (penstemon)
Phlox spp. (phlox)
Sedum spp. (sedum)

Sempervivum spp. (hen and chicks, houseleek)
Silene acaulis (moss campion)
Thymus spp. (thyme)
Veronica spp. (speedwell)
Vinca herbacea (herbaceous periwinkle)

Cutting Corners
Calamagrostis x *acutiflora* 'Karl Foerster' ('Karl Foerster' feather reed grass)
Campanula glomerata (clustered bellflower, Danesblood bellflower)

A double border of cat mint (*Nepata* 'Dropmore Blue') is here used to direct traffic. (Sara Williams)

Veronica repens 'Alba' as a pavement planting in partial shade. (Sara Williams)

Diervilla lonicera (diervilla, dwarf bush honeysuckle)
Euonymus nanus var. *turkestanicus* (Turkestan burning bush)
Eupatorium maculatum (Joe Pye weed, boneset)
Geranium spp. (perennial geranium)
Heliopsis helianthoides (false sunflower, rough heliopsis)
Hemerocallis spp. (daylily)
Matteuccia struthiopteris (ostrich fern, American ostrich fern)
Monarda hybrids (monarda, wild bergamot, bee balm, Oswego tea)
Persicaria affinis (Himalayan fleeceflower)
Polygonatum spp. (Solomon's seal)
Spiraea spp. (spirea)
Stachys spp. (woolly lambs' ears, big betony)

Barrier Plantings
Caragana pygmaea (pygmy caragana)
Diervilla lonicera (diervilla, dwarf bush honeysuckle)
Euonymus spp. (burning bush)
Juniperus spp. (juniper)
Potentilla fruticosa (shrubby cinquefoil, potentilla)
Prunus tenella (Russian almond)
Rhus glabra (smooth sumac)
Ribes spp. (currant, gooseberry)
Rosa spp. (rose)
Sorbaria sorbifolia (Ural false spirea)
Symphoricarpos spp. (snowberry)

Accentuating Focal Points

A focal point is an object in our landscape or a portion of our yard to which our eye is immediately drawn. It can be a particularly attractive plant, such as a weeping birch or flowering crabapple, or a part of the hardscape, such as a birdbath, sundial, statue, pergola, pond, or bench.

Groundcovers can enhance and accentuate these focal points. When making your groundcover selection, consider scale, color, and the formality or informality of the focal point. A European weeping birch is a large but informal focal point. The attractive white, peeling trunk is as much a part of its loveliness as its delicate foliage or graceful form. By underplanting it

Groundcovers and Vines in the Landscape

with windflowers, one achieves not only informality but also a groundcover in scale with the focal point being accented and a color echo of the white trunk with the white, nodding blooms of the anemone.

For a more formal but smaller focal point, such as a sundial, consider using a more compact juniper such as *Juniperus communis* 'Effusa'. For an informal birdbath, why not try 'Johnson's Blue' perennial geranium, hostas, or the evergreen bergenia?

Groundcovers for Accentuating Focal Points

Achillea tomentosa (woolly yarrow)
Ajuga reptans (bugleweed, carpet bugle)
Alchemilla spp. (lady's mantle)
Anemone spp. (windflower)
Antennaria spp. (pussytoes)
Arabis alpina (rock cress, mountain rock cress)
Arctostaphylos uva-ursi (bearberry)
Asarum canadense (Canadian ginger, wild ginger)
Astilbe spp. (astilbe)
Aurinia saxatilis (perennial alyssum, basket-of-gold, madwort)
Bergenia cordifolia (heart-leaved bergenia, pigsqueak)
Campanula cochlearifolia (dwarf bellflower, fairy thimble)
Carex muskingumensis (palm sedge)

'Johnson's Blue' perennial geranium (*Geranium* 'Johnson's Blue') serves to accentuate a sundial. (Sara Williams)

Cerastium tomentosum (snow-in-summer)
Chelone spp. (turtlehead)
Convallaria majalis (lily-of-the-valley)
Cotoneaster horizontalis 'Perpusillus' (ground cotoneaster)
Festuca glauca (blue fescue)
Fragaria spp. (strawberry, 'Pink Panda' strawberry)
Galium odoratum (sweet woodruff, bedstraw)
Genista lydia (Lydia broom)
Gentiana spp. (gentian)
Geranium spp. (perennial geranium)
Geum urbanum (Siberian avens)

Heuchera Morden hybrids (coral bells, alumroot)
Hosta spp. (hosta)
Juniperus spp. (juniper)
Lamiastrum galeobdolon (yellow archangel)
Lamium maculatum (spotted dead nettle)
Lysimachia nummularia (creeping Jenny, moneywort)
Matteuccia struthiopteris (ostrich fern, American ostrich fern)
Microbiota decussata (Russian cypress, Siberian cypress)
Molinia caerulea variegata (variegated moor grass)
Nepeta spp. (catmint)
Omphalodes verna alba (creeping forget-me-not)
Pachysandra terminalis (Japanese spurge)
Paxistima canbyi (cliffgreen, paxistima)
Penstemon spp. (penstemon)
Persicaria affinis (Himalayan fleeceflower)
Phlox spp. (phlox)
Polygonatum spp. (Solomon's seal)
Potentilla spp. (potentilla)
Primula spp. (primrose)
Pulmonaria spp. (lungwort)
Rosa spp. (rose)
Salix spp. (willow)
Scutellaria spp. (skullcap)
Sedum spp. (sedum)
Sempervivum spp. (hen and chicks, houseleek)
Spiraea spp. (spirea)
Stachys lanata (woolly lambs' ears, big betony)
Thymus spp. (thyme)
Tradescantia virginiana (spiderwort)
Veronica spp. (speedwell, veronica)
Vinca herbacea (herbaceous periwinkle)
Viola canadensis (western Canada violet, wood violet)
Waldsteinia ternata (Siberian barren strawberry)

Screening

From decaying tree stumps near the cabin at the lake to the dying foliage of spring bulbs, groundcovers can hide as well as accentuate. If the objects to be hidden are taller, employ larger spreading groundcovers such as the tawny daylily, common yarrow, 'Johnson's Blue' perennial geranium, Siberian catmint, 'Skinner's Golden' brome grass, alpine currant, Russian almond, 'Aurora' false spirea, or western snowberry. For hiding the dying foliage of spring bulbs, select something shorter and more delicate: lady's mantle, perennial alyssum, 'White Nancy' or 'Beacon Silver' dead nettle, or golden creeping Jenny.

Groundcovers for Screening

Achillea millefolium (common yarrow)
Andropogon gerardii (big bluestem)
Astilbe simplicifolia 'Sprite' (dwarf astilbe)
Bromus inermis 'Skinner's Golden' ('Skinner's Golden' brome grass)
Caragana spp. (caragana)
Diervilla lonicera (diervilla, dwarf bush honeysuckle)
Eupatorium maculatum (Joe Pye weed, boneset)
Filipendula ulmaria 'Flora Plena' (European meadowsweet)
Galium odoratum (sweet woodruff, bedstraw)
Geranium spp. (perennial geranium)
Heliopsis helianthoides (false sunflower, rough heliopsis)
Hemerocallis spp. (daylily)
Lamiastrum galeobdolon (yellow archangel)
Lamium maculatum (spotted dead nettle)
Matteuccia struthiopteris (ostrich fern, American ostrich fern)

Nepeta spp. (catmint)
Potentilla fruticosa (shrubby cinquefoil, potentilla)
Prunus tenella (Russian almond)
Rhus glabra (smooth sumac)
Ribes spp. (currant, gooseberry)
Rosa spp. (rose)
Solidago hybrids (goldenrod hybrids)
Sorbaria sorbifolia (Ural false spirea)
Symphoricarpos spp. (snowberry)
Symphytum officinale (comfrey)

Creeping Jenny (*Lysimachia nummularia*) grows well in shade as an understory to large canopy trees. (Sara Williams)

A Shady Understory

Large mass plantings of informal, shade-tolerant groundcovers can be used to emphasize the trunks, branches, and architecture of a grouping of similar trees or more simply as a woodland understory. For areas where moisture can be supplied, use bugleweed, windflower, hostas, Solomon's seal, lily-of-the-valley, archangel, or dead nettle. In dry shade where irrigation is not available, consider the western Canada violet, false Solomon's seal, bergenia, the double windflower, or Siberian barren strawberry.

Best Groundcovers & Vines for the Prairies

Groundcovers for a Shady Understory

Aegopodium podograria 'Variegatum' (goutweed, bishop's goutweed)
Ajuga reptans (bugleweed, carpet bugle)
Anemone spp. (windflower)
Aralia nudicaulis (wild sarsaparilla)

Windflowers (*Anemone sylvestris*) form an informal understory to a birch while echoing its white bark. (Sara Williams)

Arctostaphylos uva-ursi (bearberry)
Arrhenatherum bulbosum 'Variegatum' (variegated tuber oat grass)
Asarum canadense (Canadian ginger, wild ginger)
Astilbe spp. (astilbe)
Bergenia cordifolia (heart-leaved bergenia, pigsqueak)
Brunnera macrophylla (alpine forget-me-not)
Campanula persicifolia (peach-leaved bellflower)
Chelone obliqua (pink turtlehead)
Convallaria majalis (lily-of-the-valley)
Cornus canadensis (bunchberry, dwarf dogwood)
Diervilla lonicera (diervilla, dwarf bush honeysuckle)
Euonymus nanus (dwarf burning bush)
Filipendula spp. (meadowsweet)
Galium odoratum (sweet woodruff, bedstraw)
Gentiana acaulis (stemless gentian)
Geranium spp. (perennial geranium)
Hepatica spp. (hepatica, liverleaf)
Hosta spp. (hosta)
Lamiastrum galeobdolon (yellow archangel)
Lamium maculatum (spotted dead nettle)
Lysimachia nummularia (creeping Jenny, moneywort)
Mahonia repens (creeping Oregon grape)
Matteuccia struthiopteris (ostrich fern, American ostrich fern)
Omphalodes verna alba (creeping forget-me-not)
Pachysandra terminalis (Japanese spurge)
Paxistima canbyi (cliffgreen, paxistima)
Persicaria spp. (fleeceflower)
Phalaris arundinacea 'Picta' (ribbon grass)
Polygonatum spp. (Solomon's seal)
Primula spp. (primrose)
Pulmonaria spp. (lungwort)
Scutellaria spp. (skullcap)
Smilacina stellata (star-flowered Solomon's seal, false Solomon's seal)

Symphoricarpos spp. (snowberry)
Tradescantia virginiana (spiderwort)
Vinca herbacea (herbaceous periwinkle)
Viola canadensis (western Canada violet, wood violet)
Waldsteinia ternata (Siberian barren strawberry)

VINES

Clematis provides color while breaking up a large expanse of fence. (Sara Williams)

In nature, vines grow at the edge of the woods, with roots in shady soil beneath a tree or shrub and tops climbing up into the light. The mechanics of climbing and the vigor and size of the vine determine the support needed to elevate a particular species or cultivar. Some, such as honeysuckle (*Lonicera* x *brownii* 'Dropmore Scarlet Trumpet') and American bittersweet (*Celastrus scandens*), climb by twining around the stems of the supporting tree or shrub. Virginia creeper (*Parthenocissus quinquefolia*) climbs by thin tendrils that curl around branches or other supports, while its near-relative Engelmann's ivy (*Parthenocissus quinquefolia* var. *engelmannii*) has adhesive discs at the end of tendrils and can cling to a wall without support. Many of the clematis climb by twining leaf petioles, as well as by twining of the stems. They require support but can be quite at home climbing through the branches of a tree, as well as a trellis or fence.

Like groundcovers, vines play a number of roles in our landscapes, some aesthetic and others more environmental. They can also serve many of the same landscape functions as groundcovers.

Aesthetically, one of the most important functions of vines is to tie a house or other building to its surroundings and make it an integral part of its setting. By clothing it with foliage, vines visually lower a structure into the landscape, so that it no longer stands out like a sore thumb. Vines are particularly effective when used on a two-story or other large building.

Like the sky or trees, but on a smaller, more intimate scale, vines also provide us with a garden ceiling. Trained on an arbor, trellis, pergola, or roof overhang, they add flowers, scent, and even fruit to our outdoor experience, as well as the pattern and texture of their foliage and branches. As they age, the gnarled and twisted trunks of some vines, such as Manitoba grape (*Vitis*

Best Groundcovers & Vines for the Prairies

Clematis used to soften an otherwise stockade-like fence. (Sara Williams)

Virginia creeper (*Parthenocissus quinquefolia*) tying a building to its landscape. (Sara Williams)

riparia), 'Dropmore Scarlet Trumpet' honeysuckle, or 'Rosy O'Grady' clematis lend an old-world ambience.

Vines can also be used to break up a large expanse of wall or fence. They soften long extents of wood, siding, masonry, or bricks by providing color, texture, and patterns. If occasional maintenance of the wall is required, such as painting or cleaning, consider the installation of a moveable trellis that is hinged to the building at its base and hooked to the building at its top. The vines can be left in place on the trellis and the trellis itself unhooked and laid on the ground to allow access to the wall.

In much the same way as groundcovers do, vines accent the positive features of a building or a focal point in a garden. They can be trained on a pillar fronting a porch or deck, a chimney, a rural mailbox, a lamp post, or a sundial. Take care to select vines that are in scale with the object being accented. If too large in size or heavy in texture, they may very well hide rather than accent once they reach maturity.

The heavy texture of the vine frames the garden and separates it from the patio in the foreground. (Sara Williams)

Screening is also an important function of vines. Like groundcovers, they are useful plants to delineate areas of a garden. They lend seclusion to porches, decks, or verandas or to a romantic spot in a garden. They can provide a sense of greater privacy between two adjoining urban properties

Want to screen an old building? Use Virginia creeper! (Sara Williams)

where back entryways, decks, or sidewalks are only a short distance away. Trellised vines can define property lines. Bylaws often limit the height of fences but there are seldom restrictions on a trellis supporting a vine that extends above the level of the fence.

Vines are extremely useful for hiding unsightly objects or less-than-lovely areas of a garden. As Tovah Martin wrote, "Thank heavens for vines . . . They cover a multitude of sins." Among these may be a neighbor's shed, a decaying garage, junked cars, utility poles, storage areas, or a dog run. They can even clothe a back-lane fence. It takes little effort to plant a Virginia creeper and it is amazingly effective in this capacity.

Environmental modification is another role to which vines are well adapted. Use Manitoba grape or Virginia creeper to provide shelter from wind. All vines provide shade when grown over an arbor, pergola, patio, or deck. They can also act as groundcovers, especially on a slope or bank, preventing soil erosion and suppressing weeds.

Through all of these roles, remember scale. Vines vary considerably in height, spread, texture, and physical weight. Ensure that the one you select for a particular situation is in proportion to its job. Is its climbing support strong enough to hold its volume and weight? Is the support appropriate to the way (tendrils, adhesive discs, twining stems) in which the vine climbs and attaches itself? If an arbor, is it wide enough to accommodate the vines and the people walking through it? Allow an extra 30 cm (12 in.) of arbor width for the vine itself on each side of the path.

Finally, as with groundcovers, remember the idea of unity through repetition. By informally repeating a few favorite, best-performing vines in various parts of your garden, you can achieve a sense of unity throughout your entire landscape.

This large, two-and-a-half story building is effectively tied to its landscape by vines. (Sara Williams)

Best Groundcovers & Vines for the Prairies

[3]

Purchasing, Planting, and Maintaining Groundcovers and Vines

Getting Ready

HOW DO GROUNDCOVERS COVER GROUND?

A variety of plants can be used to cover the soil surface. Although lawn grass is most widely used for this purpose, there are many effective alternatives that quickly cover the soil surface, suppress weed growth, and protect the soil from erosion. Look for plants that provide aesthetic appeal and are adapted to the particular microclimatic, soil, and light conditions of a planting site.

When planning for groundcovers in the garden, it is also helpful to consider the growth habits of various groundcover plants. How do plants spread to cover ground? Some increase by self-seeding, but most spread vegetatively. Plants that sucker are effective at sending up shoots to fill space. A sucker is a shoot that originates from a below-ground root or a stem that is away from the main stem of the plant. Suckers usually originate from rhizomes, stolons, or roots.

Rhizomes are underground root-like stems that produce roots from the lower surface and send up shoots from their upper side in the same way that a stem produces branches. Some plants, such as quack grass, send out long rhizomes that shoot up a meter or more from the original plant in one season. Plants that are too aggressive are considered weeds, but in a more restrained manifestation this habit is very effective in covering ground. Hostas, lily-of-the-valley (*Convallaria majalis*), and cliffgreen (*Paxistima canbyi*) are examples of plants that spread by rhizomes. Blue grama grass (*Bouteloua gracilis*) and lungwort (*Pulmonaria* spp.) develop short rhizomes that give them a dense, clumped appearance.

Stolons are slender stems that run above or below ground and develop shoots, as well as roots, at their tips or at nodes along their length. The quintessential example is the strawberry plant (*Fragaria* spp.). Other examples are dwarf Turkestan burning bush (*Euonymus nanus* var. *turkestanicus*), carpet bugle (*Ajuga reptans*), and bishop's goutweed (*Aegopodium podograria*).

Some plants grow roots wherever their stems touch the soil. Plants that spread by naturally layering in this way include bearberry (*Arctostaphylos uva-ursi*), creeping juniper (*Juniperus horizontalis*), and mountain avens (*Dryas octapetala*). These quickly form mats that are very effective in holding soil on slopes.

PREPARING THE PLANTING SITE

Careful preparation is important to the successful establishment of groundcover plants. If they get a good start, they will form a dense mat of foliage that prevents weed seeds from germinating and becoming established. The roots of vigorous groundcover plants hold the soil on slopes, while the foliage shades the ground and conserves moisture. Groundcover stems and foliage also hold snow to protect bulbs and perennials in winter.

In contrast, if weeds get a head start before groundcovers are well established, they will be difficult to control and will compete with the plants for water and nutrition. Likewise, good site preparation gives vines a head start to become established and thrive.

The first step in establishing a new planting is to remove existing vegetation. Perennial weeds such as Canada thistle, quack grass, brome grass, or dandelions should be eliminated before planting as they will be difficult to remove once groundcovers or vines have rooted in place. Weeds can be removed by the use of chemical weed killers or by mechanical means, such as a tiller or hoe. Lawn grasses can be killed by applying chemicals, by covering with thick layers of mulch such as newspaper, or by stripping sod.

Soil can then be tilled and evaluated for its suitability for growing plants. In some instances, poor soil should be removed and replaced or better soil should be added to improve drainage or tilth and create level planting beds. Most soils can be improved by the addition of organic matter. The best strategy is to add amendments and good soil to the entire planting bed and work them in. The practice of adding good soil only in the planting hole around the roots can create a "pot" effect where roots have difficulty penetrating the surrounding soil, resulting in a stunted plant.

Most prairie soils are basic, with a pH of 7 to 8, a range in which all of the plants mentioned in this book will grow. A soil test will indicate the pH and nutrient level of the soil, which helps the gardener choose appropriate plants for the area and indicates the measures required to prepare the planting site. If nitrogen is low, add composted manure, rich compost, or a fertilizer with a relatively high first number. If phosphate is low, plants will benefit from the addition of bonemeal or a high-phosphate transplant fertilizer (with a relatively high second number). Although it is seldom necessary to adjust the pH of prairie soils, digging in some sphagnum peat moss will lower the pH of basic (alkaline) soils, while soils that are very acidic may be improved with dolomitic limestone.

The addition of organic matter improves aeration in heavy soils and contributes to the water- and nutrient-holding capacity of sandy soils. A 5-cm (2-in.) layer of compost or peat moss, thoroughly incorporated into the existing soil, significantly improves most soils.

In sunny, open locations, the soil should be well worked to a depth of 20 cm (8 in.), for most perennial groundcovers and even deeper for shrubs. To limit the damage to tree roots, cultivate soil only to a depth of 5 to 10 cm (2 to 4 in.) when planting under trees. Once the planting bed is prepared and a planting plan developed, you are ready to start laying out the site for planting.

SPACING

Before purchasing, determine how many plants are required to adequately fill your planting space. Groundcover plants should be spaced to give quick coverage to the area. Depending on growth rate, the form of the plant, and your budget, spacing may vary from 15 to 60 cm (6 to 24 in.). Staggered row-planting patterns give the best coverage and appear the most natural when the plants are mature. The accompanying diagram and chart should help you calculate the number of plants you will need.

The number of vines required will depend on the type of vine and the area to be covered. Check the spread of the vine in the individual plant descriptions in Chapter Four or on the plant tag.

	Staggered groundcover row-planting design	

this:	x x x x
	  x x x x
	x x x x
	  x x x x
		not this:

		x x x x x x x x x x x x x x x x

Number of groundcover plants required to cover a given area at various spacings

Distance between plants	Number of plants to cover 1 square meter (1.2 yd²)
10 cm (4 in.)	100
20 cm (8 in.)	25
30 cm (12 in.)	9
40 cm (16 in.)	6
50 cm (20 in.)	4
75 cm (30 in.)	2
100 cm (40 in.)	1

Purchasing and Planting

GROUNDCOVERS

Groundcover plants are usually planted in quite large quantities in order to give good coverage to an area as quickly as possible. This makes it important to consider the economics of the various sizes and types of planting material available. For some groundcovers, you can choose among bare-root plants, container-grown plants, or plugs (grown in trays similar to those used to produce forestry trees) of various sizes. Alternatively, some gardeners prefer to start plants from seed, divisions, cuttings, or layers.

Bare-root Plants

Bare-root plants are only available in spring or late fall. Cultivars that are traditionally used as hedge and shelterbelt plants are commonly available as bare-root plants from mail-order nurseries. These firms also sell a variety of flowering perennials in bare-root form. When you receive these plants, it is important to protect the roots from drying out until they can be planted. If plants are shipped in the mail, the roots are usually protected by moisture-retaining material such as peat moss or moist, shredded paper. If you are picking up plants at the nursery, take plastic bags (garbage bags work well) and moisture-retaining material such as paper, wet straw, or shavings to keep the roots moist. If the planting site is ready, retain packing material around the roots and protect the roots from sun and wind as you plant. If you aren't ready to plant, plants can usually be kept for a few days in a cool, shaded place, provided the roots do not dry out. To keep plants longer, they should be heeled-in in a sheltered place in the garden. If plants are dry when they arrive, put the roots in a bucket of warm water overnight to rehydrate them before planting.

When you are ready to plant, dig a hole large enough to spread out the roots. Hold the plant at a level that is about 2.5 cm (1 in.) below where it was originally planted (usually there is a change in bark or stem color at the soil line) and backfill around the roots. Firm the soil around the roots and add more soil if necessary. Water the plant well to settle the soil around the roots. Regular watering is important until the plant re-establishes its roots, but don't overwater it. Usually, it is better to give a plant a thorough soaking once a week than to water less thoroughly. Roots need air both for growth and to take up water and nutrients. Too much water or too frequent watering restricts air from getting to the roots and, paradoxically, produces similar symptoms to underwatering. If the soil is too wet, the roots cannot take up water. Mulching after planting to a depth of 10 cm (4 in.) conserves moisture and prevents most weed-seed germination.

Best Groundcovers & Vines For The Prairies

Planting Groundcovers on Slopes or Banks

Once the existing vegetation has been killed, plant the slope or bank by working from the top down. If planting on a steep slope, you can lessen erosion by digging strips of soil across the slope, while leaving alternate strips uncultivated. Alternatively, dig individual planting holes and mulch the entire slope immediately after planting. Stagger the planting holes in each row. Plant in pockets of soil well amended with organic matter, such as compost, coarse peat moss, or well-rotted manure, and two to three times the size of the pot or root ball. Leave an 8 cm (3 in.) depression around each plant so that rain and irrigation water will be "caught" for plant use rather than simply running down the slope. Once the planting is completed and watered, mulch immediately to a depth of 10 cm (4 in.) to conserve moisture, suppress weeds, and prevent erosion.

Plugs

A variety of groundcover plants are available as plugs grown in plug trays, which were developed for growing tree seedlings for reforestation. Roots grow in a "plug" of peat-based growing medium. This type of container has proven especially suitable to native plants used for vegetation restoration, bank stabilization, or large-area groundcover. Because the roots are deep in relation to the size of the plant and because the root system remains intact during transplanting, plants establish quickly with minimal maintenance.

To plant plugs, punch holes in well-prepared soil with a bar or open a slit with a spade, insert the plug, then step on the soil to firm it around the roots. Make sure the peat plug is completely covered with soil. If it is exposed, the peat may act as a wick and dry out the roots. After planting, water thoroughly to wet the soil below the depth of the plugs. Apply mulch to a depth of 10 cm (4 in.) to conserve moisture and reduce the need for weed control.

Container-grown Groundcovers

Most plants sold in garden centers are growing in containers. This is convenient for gardeners because they do not have to plant them right away as long as they are watered regularly. Depending on the type of plant, container sizes can vary from 9 cm (3.5 in.) for small perennials to 16-liter (5-gallon) pots or larger for deciduous or evergreen shrubs. Larger plants in larger containers give quicker results, but the cost per plant is greater.

To plant a container-grown plant, dig a hole about twice as wide as its root ball and slightly deeper than the level that it is planted in the container. Remove the plant from the container. If it is root bound (roots are circling the bottom of the container), cut through the sides of the root ball in three or four places deep enough to disrupt the circling roots. Place the root ball in the hole so that the top of the ball is about 2.5 cm (1 in.) below the level of the surrounding soil and backfill with topsoil until it is just covered. Pack the soil firmly and top up to the appropriate level. Water the plant thoroughly to wet the soil around the root ball and into the soil below. Add soil where it has settled and mulch to a depth of 10 cm (4 in.) around the plant to conserve moisture and limit weed growth.

Vines are most often sold as container-grown plants, with well-developed roots. Look for plants with healthy foliage and intact stems.

Plant vines as you would plant a container-grown shrub. Remove the plant from the pot and dig a hole that is a little larger than the root ball. If there are circling roots, score the root ball with a sharp knife in three or four places just deep enough to cut through the girdling roots, place the plant in the hole slightly deeper than it was planted in the pot, and backfill so soil just covers the root ball. Water well and mulch around the plant to a depth of 10 cm (4 in.) to conserve moisture and discourage weed growth.

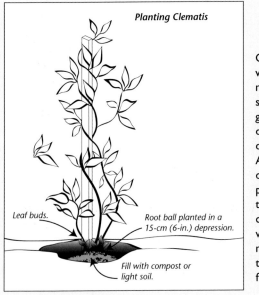

Planting Clematis

Leaf buds.

Root ball planted in a 15-cm (6-in.) depression.

Fill with compost or light soil.

Planting Clematis

Clematis are often sold as small plants with a single shoot. To survive, they need to develop a strong crown with several shoots originating from below ground. To promote this crown development, plant them in a depression about 15 cm (6 in.) deep. As the shoot grows, fill the depression with light compost. The plants will root into this compost and the buds that are covered by the compost will develop into a crown with a number of shoots. In the fall, mulch the roots of the plants to give them additional protection for the first winter.

Propagating Groundcovers and Vines

Gardeners may want to propagate their own groundcovers and vines for a variety of reasons: to save money on the large number of plants required for a planting; to grow a plant species or cultivar that is not readily available; or because they enjoy the challenge of growing plants from seeds or cuttings. If the methods used are appropriate to the plant, many groundcovers and vines are quite easy to propagate.

SEED

Plants that come true from seed can be grown from seeds obtained from commercial sources or collected in your garden or that of a friend. In nature, plants have evolved a number of mechanisms to ensure that seeds germinate when they have the best chance for survival. For instance, seeds that mature in the fall usually need to go through a cold period before they germinate, a process called stratification. This is done by putting layers of seeds between layers of moist sand or peat moss in a plastic bag or other container. They are then held at fridge temperature (about 2°C or 36°F) for two to four months.

Horticulturists have devoted years of work to understanding the requirements for the germination of seeds of various species. Information on germinating specific plant seeds can be found in seed catalogues and books on propagation.

Seeds need moisture, warmth, and, in some cases, light to germinate. These conditions can be produced indoors in a greenhouse or under growlights or outdoors in protected beds or cold frames under conditions that imitate the natural germination requirements. Seeds of woodland plants require partial shade and a covering of decomposing leaves during germination, while those of native prairie grassland plants germinate best in the sun with a light covering of mulch. Seeds that germinate following fire usually benefit from heat and open soil.

SUCKERS, DIVISIONS, AND LAYERS

The nature of vines and groundcover plants means that many can be easily propagated by suckers, divisions, or layers. Their natural means of vegetative increase works to your advantage in the garden.

Plants like pearly everlasting (*Anaphalis margaritacea*), shrubs like rugosa roses (*Rosa rugosa* hybrids), and vines like Virginia creeper (*Parthenocissus quinquefolia*) produce sucker shoots away from the original crown. These can be separated and planted in a new location. The best time of year for successfully transplanting bare-root sucker shoots is in early spring when plants are dormant. When separating sucker shoots, dig down to get pieces that have some lateral roots. Transplant the shoots into a prepared site and water regularly until they are established.

Some plants develop from a crown that increases in diameter over time and can be multiplied by digging and dividing the crown once it has stooled out. Examples of plants that are easily propagated by division are lady's mantle (*Alchemilla mollis*), ribbon grass (*Phalaris arundinacea* 'Picta'), and solitary clematis hybrids (*Clematis integrifolia* hybrids). These can be divided in early spring or in mid-summer after they have bloomed.

Other plants spread by layering. Mountain avens (*Dryas octapetala*),

Transplanting Sucker Shoot

Sever and transplant the piece with roots.

Dividing Perennials

Spade

creeping juniper (*Juniperus horizontalis*), or bearberry (*Arctostaphylos uva-ursi*) all share this characteristic, which gives them excellent soil-holding ability and allows you to increase the number of plants. In addition to plants that increase naturally in this way, many other plants can be induced to produce roots by pinning stems to the ground, wounding the underside of the stems, and covering them with soil.

Best Groundcovers & Vines For The Prairies

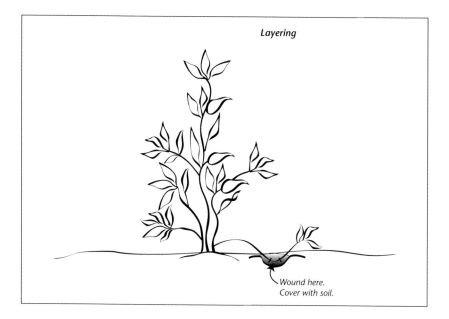

Layering

*Wound here.
Cover with soil.*

HARDWOOD AND SOFTWOOD CUTTINGS

Some plant species root and develop new shoots from stem pieces. A few woody species root from wood that has hardened and gone through a dormant period; however, hardwood cuttings are seldom used to propagate plants used as groundcovers on the prairies. Many more species can be rooted from the current year's growth while it is still soft in the summer. For successful rooting, it is important to protect the cuttings from drying out until they are able to root and draw water. In addition, cuttings require sunlight on their leaves and air in the zone where rooting is taking place. The ideal situation, and the one used by commercial propagators, is a greenhouse with an intermittent mist system, although many plants will root under conditions that can be provided by gardeners. A key to success is planting the cuttings in a rooting medium that provides excellent drainage, such as sharp sand, vermiculite, or perlite. Place the cuttings in a sunny window or outdoors in a location where they are protected from the wind, such as in a cold frame or shielded by polyethylene or burlap wind barriers.

Timing is crucial when starting plants from softwood cuttings. The best shoots for rooting are taken from the new growth before flowering. They should be mature enough to "snap" when bent over. Cuttings rooted in early summer have a better chance of developing roots that are mature enough to survive the winter.

Take cuttings from plants that are healthy and in good condition. Cut the stems with a very sharp knife and remove leaves from the bottom portion of the cutting that will be inserted into the medium. Dip the stems in a commercial rooting hormone (number 1 for most perennials and number 2 for most woody plants), plant the cuttings 5 to 8 cm (2 to 3 in.) deep in the medium, mist them, and place them in bright light. To maintain high humidity, cover the container with a plastic bag or a clear plastic cover. Periodic misting will be necessary to keep the cuttings from wilting. After a few days, the frequency of misting can be gradually decreased. Once the cuttings begin to grow roots, they can be carefully removed from the rooting medium and planted in soil-less mix in a pot. The pot should be appropriate to the size of the plant. If the pot is too big, the plant will be too wet; if it's too small, the plant will dry out quickly.

Once rooted cuttings have been established in pots, they can be grown in the pot or hardened off for planting in the garden. To harden off plants, gradually introduce them to sunlight and wind. A cold frame is ideal for this purpose.

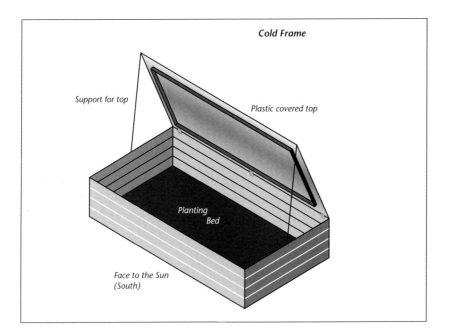

Cold Frame

Support for top

Plastic covered top

Planting Bed

Face to the Sun (South)

Maintaining Groundcovers and Vines

Groundcovers and vines are a diverse group of plants that require a variety of maintenance techniques to keep them healthy and performing their function in the landscape. All plants respond to good gardening practices that promote plant health, such as supplying adequate water and nutrients and controlling problems caused by environmental stresses (cold, heat, and drought), weeds, insects, and diseases.

MULCHING

If plants are placed in soil that has been amended with organic matter to provide good drainage and promote good aeration, water retention, and nutrient-holding capacity, they will benefit from mulching the soil surface to conserve moisture, modify soil temperature during periods of extreme weather, and control germination of weed seeds. A variety of organic materials can effectively modify soils to make them more favorable for healthy plant growth. Mulch materials that are available free of charge to most gardeners, such as grass clippings and fallen leaves, break down and add nutrients and organic matter to the soil over time. A light covering of coarse peat moss can be used to cover grass clippings and make them more attractive. Other effective materials are wood chips, post peelings, bark chips, or flax shives (left over from the processing of flax straw). These materials moderate soil temperature, which is especially important in winter when establishing new plantings in exposed locations.

PRUNING

Woody Groundcovers
Woody plants may need periodic pruning to promote health, encourage dense growth, and control spreading. Prune back the tips of branches to encourage side branches to grow into an effective groundcover that shades the ground and competes with weeds. The best time to prune deciduous shrubs is in early spring when the plants are dormant. For evergreen shrubs, such as creeping juniper, the best time is in late June, just as new growth is becoming woody.

Perennial Groundcovers
Perennial groundcovers may require deadheading during the growing season and the removal of dead foliage in spring to keep them in prime condition. A few perennials, such as peonies and lilies, benefit from top growth being removed in the fall just before freeze-up. This helps to control diseases such as botrytis (gray mold) that overwinter on dying foliage. Apply a fresh layer of mulch in late fall to compensate for losing the snow-holding benefits of top growth. Perennials that have evergreen foliage should not be cut back severely (e.g., some *Dianthus* spp., *Dryas* spp., and *Penstemon* spp.). These should be trimmed to shape the plants and can be deadheaded after blooming.

Pruning Clematis

Clematis require special pruning. They are usually divided into three groups, depending on growth and blooming habit.

Those in Group A flower on wood produced the previous year that has survived the winter. They should only be pruned to remove dead or damaged stems and to shape or control the size of the plant. Examples of Group A clematis are *Clematis alpina* cultivars and *C. macropetala* hybrids.

Group B plants produce flowers on the previous season's growth in the early part of the season and on the current season's growth in late summer and fall. Most Group B hybrids are too tender for the wood to survive in the prairie climate, so are of limited value in prairie gardens unless they can be laid down and covered with mulch to protect them from cold injury. Only a few hardy varieties, such as *Clematis tangutica* 'Bill MacKenzie', are found in this group. Prune them back hard every second or third year to renew the vines.

Plants in Group C flower on the current season's growth. They begin to bloom in July and continue blooming until September. Prune them back to near ground level in early spring. In warmer climates, these vines start to grow from near the top if left unpruned, but since flowers are only produced near the top, early spring pruning is usually recommended even in these areas. Hybrids of *Clematis viticella* and *C. integrifolia* fall into this group.

Taller perennial grasses often provide attractive seed heads to give color and structure to the garden in winter. Cool-season grasses grow and mature early in the season so cutting back spent growth in summer, once they have died back, makes them neater until they begin to grow again in the fall. Some grasses should not be allowed to self-seed; for example, seedlings of variegated brome grass will not be variegated and can quickly overrun the garden. To avoid this and keep the foliage in good condition, cut back or mow these cultivars after plants bloom in early summer.

Vines

Vines such as Virginia creeper only require pruning to control growth, while clematis have specific pruning requirements depending on type. Most vines, for example, honeysuckles, grape vines, or Virginia creeper, grow more densely if stems are pruned back in the early growth stages.

FERTILIZING

Most garden soils, or soils amended with composted manure or rich compost, have enough nutrients to get plants started. The addition of phosphate in the form of bonemeal to the planting hole may encourage new root growth. Heavier soils with a high-clay content hold generous amounts of nutrients and seldom need more than periodic additions of compost and organic mulch. Sandy soils hold nutrients poorly and may benefit from the addition of a slow-release fertilizer each spring. A soil test is a worthwhile guide to the available nutrients in the soil. Do not overfertilize. It can cause lush, weak growth that is prone to disease. In extreme instances, too much fertilizer can cause the soil to become saline—a difficult problem to correct.

Best Groundcovers & Vines For The Prairies

PEST AND DISEASE CONTROL

The best defense against common insect and disease problems is to maintain plants in healthy condition. Before you plant, ensure there is good drainage and the soil has been improved where necessary to provide adequate nutrients and water-holding capacity. Choose plants that are suited to the growing environment of your garden and are adapted to your climatic area.

Weeds

It is important to remove perennial weeds, including their roots, before planting groundcovers, as they will be difficult to control once the plants have started to grow. Areas that are infested with difficult perennial weeds like quack grass and Canada thistle can be cleared of weeds by careful use of glyphosate (Roundup™). Follow label instructions and all regulations and exercise caution to avoid killing desirable plants. When planting, be sure to space plants closely enough to give complete cover in a short period of time. Plants will grow to shade the soil, giving them a competitive edge over any weeds. Hand weeding will be required periodically. Remember—it is easier to remove weeds when they are small. In areas where it is difficult to weed, use plants that are allelopathic (restrict the growth of other plants), such as blue fescue ornamental grass, or use a combination of plants that provide a dense and competitive cover. Mulching the soil surface between the groundcover plants to a depth of 10 cm (4 in.) provides the most effective weed control as it discourages the germination of weed seeds.

Insects

The first step in avoiding insect problems is to select plants that are relatively free of pest problems and are well adapted to the growing environment. Use integrated pest-management techniques that are the least harmful to people and the surrounding environment. For

N, P, K: The Fertilizer Numbers Game

The numbers in a fertilizer formula indicate the percentages of three major nutrients: nitrogen (N), phosphorous (P), and potassium (K). Thus, a fertilizer with the formula 10-52-10 is 10 percent nitrogen, 52 percent phosphorous, and 10 percent potassium. A balance of nutrients is needed for healthy growth. Nitrogen stimulates vegetative growth, phosphorous is important to energy reactions in the plant and stimulates flower and root development, and potassium helps the plant resist environmental stress and disease. In addition, most fertilizers contain a number of micronutrients, such as magnesium (Mg), a vital component of chlorophyll, iron (Fe), which is essential for the production of chlorophyll, and molybdenum (Mo), an important catalyst in reactions to build proteins.

example, blister beetles that may appear on clematis are large and usually present only in small numbers. Pick and destroy them by hand, but use gloves as these beetles produce allergic blisters in some people. Small insects like leafhoppers and aphids can be discouraged and their numbers reduced significantly with a blast of water from the hose whenever they appear. Use cultivars that are resistant to insect infestations.

Encouraging natural predators like ladybug beetles often keeps aphids in check. To promote a natural balance in your garden that will result in insect pest control, restrain the urge to spray toxic chemicals at the first sign of an insect. Tolerate minor insect damage and seek less harmful alternatives wherever possible.

Disease

Think of your disease-control program as a "plant health" program. Select plants that are resistant to disease and well adapted to the conditions you can provide, and give them adequate soil fertility and moisture. Prune to remove damaged and diseased plant parts and to encourage healthy growth. Remove dead flowers and leaves during the growing season and before growth starts in the spring. Be sure to clean and disinfect your tools regularly, especially if you are experiencing a disease problem.

[4]

Groundcovers and Vines
for Prairie Gardens

Plant at a Glance is a quick and easy reference that gives gardeners a starting point for plant selection. It briefly defines the type of plant, its size, spacing, cultural needs (light and soil conditions), distinguishing features, landscape use, and propagation methods. We also provide the pronunciation of the Latin names. Latin pronunciations vary from continent to continent. In most cases we have provided the pronunciations most often used in prairie Canada. Here's an explanation of the terms used.

Type

broad-leafed evergreen shrub: broad-leafed (non-coniferous) shrub that is evergreen

coniferous evergreen shrub: evergreen shrub in the conifer family (Coniferae) characterized by needle-like leaves and seed borne in cones

deciduous shrub: a shrub that drops its leaves each fall

evergreen perennial: non-woody plant with stems and foliage that remain green throughout the winter

evergreen shrub: a shrub such as *Mahonia repens*, with foliage that remains green and alive throughout the winter

evergreen sub-shrub: evergreen plant of small size, with persistent woody stems and evergreen foliage

herbaceous perennial: non-woody plant that dies to ground level each winter

ornamental grass: non-lawn grasses that have long, narrow leaves with parallel veins; grass-like plants such as *Carex* are included in this category

semi-evergreen perennial: a plant that may be evergreen or deciduous, depending on environmental conditions

semi-evergreen shrub: a shrub that may be evergreen or deciduous, depending on environmental conditions

vine: a plant with slender stems that twine or clasp a support; can be woody (having woody stems that live for several years, adding growth each year) or herbaceous (having stems that die down each season and grow up again from the crowns each spring)

Climbing Mechanism (for Vines)

twining (twisting) around the stems of supporting trees or shrubs; honeysuckle climbs by twining
sending out tendrils (slender, threadlike extensions) that curl around branches or other supports; Virginia creeper is an example of this
sending out tendrils with adhesive discs on the end that stick to surfaces and can cling to a wall without support; Englemann's ivy climbs this way
sending out leaf petioles (stalks) that twine around objects and provide support to the vines; many clematis climb by twining leaf petioles

Height and Spread

These measurements indicate how tall and wide a plant will be once mature. They are given first in metric, followed by the imperial measurement.

Spacing

The recommended spacing between plants used as groundcovers.

Light

full sun: more than 6 hours of sunlight per day
partial shade: less than 6 hours of sunlight per day
shade: less than 2 hours of sunlight per day

Soil

This indicates the plant's moisture, drainage, and fertility requirements.
adaptable: plant will grow in most soils
evenly moist: not allowed to dry out
lean: soil is low in organic matter and nutrients
loam: a soil that has equal proportions of sand, silt, and clay particles. It has a high capacity to hold water and nutrients
rich in organic matter: soil contains generous amounts of peat moss, compost, well-rotted manure, or other sources of organic matter
well drained: water does not accumulate; includes most sandy soils

Distinguishing Features

This provides a brief description of flowers, foliage, and other outstanding physical characteristics of the plant.

Groundcovers
accent plant: focal point to which attention is immediately drawn
back lane plantings
breaking up large expanses of lawn
delineating space and defining property lines
directing foot traffic: pavement plantings, cutting corners, barrier plantings
edging: used to surround or front a bed or border
lawn replacement: groundcover replaces an area of lawn not being used as lawn
mass plantings: used en masse
mixed border: border that includes perennials, shrubs, vines, bulbs, and ornamental grasses—grasses or grass-like plants other than lemongrass used in landscaping
naturalizing: plants with a capacity to multiply rapidly through self-seeding, stolons, or rhizomes
over walls: cascading down walls
perennial border: border of perennials
prairie restoration: planting of native plants intended to restore a site to native vegetation
reclamation: revegetation of a disturbed site
rock garden: contains alpine plants of low stature
screening: screening spring-bulb foliage or hiding unsightly objects
shady understory
slopes or banks
small, inaccessible, or inhospitable areas: small—not large enough for either lawn or border; inaccessible—difficult to get to, such as a far corner or a bank; inhospitable—wet and boggy or hot and dry, not suitable for a lawn or border
transition plantings
unifying shrub beds: lower, finer-textured groundcover is woven through a shrub border, visually uniting it
waterside plantings: by a pond or stream or in a bog garden

Vines
fences or walls: to break up the expanse of a structure
trellises: open latticework structures used to train climbing plants; they may be against a wall, part of a fence or arbor, or a free-standing structure
arbors: structures that create a shady recess
accent: to draw attention to a focal point
summer screening: to hide structures, compost piles, undesirable views

Propagation

See Chapter Three, pages 32–36, for a detailed explanation of propagation terms.

Groundcovers

Achillea
a-*kil*-lee-a
Yarrow

The genus *Achillea* was named for the Greek warrior Achilles, who is said to have used yarrow to heal the wounds of his soldiers. It has been found to be haemostatic, that is, it slows blood flow from wounds. English common names such as "soldiers' woundward" and "carpenters' grass" attest to this usage.

Yarrow was also used to cure the common cold, and it is now known that several species contain derivatives of salicylic acid similar to compounds found in aspirin. Other traditional uses included treating burns, stopping diarrhea (in domestic rabbits), and as a substitute for hops in ale to increase its alcoholic content.

How to Grow
Yarrows are exceptionally drought tolerant once established and do well in full sun in almost any well-drained soil. Plants form a dense ground-cover through self-seeding and an ever-extending fibrous root system. Yarrows do not benefit from fertilizer. Especially avoid nitrogen as it causes them to become tall and lanky. Deadhead to prolong bloom and prevent self-seeding as the seedlings will not be identical to the cultivars from which they came. Yarrows are easily propagated by seed or spring division.

Achillea millefolium
a-*kil*-lee-a mil-le-*foe*-lee-um
Common yarrow

Plant at a Glance
Type: herbaceous perennial
Height/spread: 60 to 100 cm (24 to 40 in.) / 60 cm (24 in.)
Spacing: 45 to 60 cm (18 to 24 in.)
Light: full sun
Soil: well drained
Distinguishing features: flat-topped flower clusters; pungent, gray-green, lacy foliage
Landscape use: perennial or mixed border; small, inaccessible, or inhospi-table areas; slopes and banks; delineating space and defining property lines; breaking up large expanses of lawn; transition plantings; back lane plant-ings; screening
Propagation: seed; division

Achillea millefolium 'Terracotta' ('Terracotta' common yarrow) (Sara Williams)

If you gave up on yarrows years ago because of their wanderlust, floppy stems, dull colors, or determined self-seeding, try again. The newer cultivars are generally much more erect and clump forming and have flowers of greater color intensity. As well, it's a genus that attracts butterflies and provides egg-laying sites for ladybugs. Native to Europe and western Asia, they have been cultivated for centuries for their medicinal properties and have become naturalized in many parts of the world.

Common yarrow bears large, flat-topped clusters, or corymbs, of flowers throughout much of the summer. The flowers, held above finely divided foliage, range in color from pastel pinks to salmon, yellow, orange and red, to purple. The species name *millefolium* means "thousands of leaves" and refers to the lacy, but pungent, olive green foliage.

Cultivars

- 'Cerise Queen' is an older cultivar, with cherry red flowers, growing from 40 to 60 cm (16 to 24 in.) tall. It can be more invasive and floppy than other cultivars.
- 'Colorado' is a mixture, used primarily for drying, growing 45 to 60 cm (18 to 24 in.) tall.
- 'Fire King' bears rose-red flowers and reaches 40 to 60 cm (16 to 24 in.) in height.
- 'Galaxy' hybrids (*Achillea taygetes* x *A. millefolium*) have larger flowers, more intense colors, and stronger stems than many other yarrows. There are several cultivars within this series, including 'Apple Blossom', with peach to light pink flowers, growing to 90 cm (36 in.); 'Heidi', with cherry pink flowers, 45 to 60 cm (18 to 24 in.) tall; and 'Paprika', with red flowers that have a golden eye, 45 to 70 cm (18 to 28 in.) in height.
- 'Summer Pastels', an All-America Selection winner, has flowers of several different shades. It is 45 to 60 cm (18 to 24 in.) in height.
- 'Terracotta' has salmon pink to rusty orange flowers, like terra-cotta pots, and grows 75 to 90 cm (30 to 36 in.) tall.

Achillea ptarmica
a-*kil*-lee-a *tar*-mah-ca
Sneezewort, sneezeweed

Plant at a Glance
Type: herbaceous perennial
Height/spread: 30 to 45 cm (12 to 18 in.) / 45 to 60 cm (18 to 24 in.)
Spacing: 30 cm (12 in.)
Light: full sun
Soil: well drained
Distinguishing features: tiny, white, button-like flowers
Landscape use: perennial border; small, inaccessible, or inhospitable areas; breaking up large expanses of lawn
Propagation: seed; division

Achillea ptarmica 'The Pearl' ('The Pearl' sneezewort) (Sara Williams)

Native from Europe to Siberia and widely naturalized elsewhere, both the common and botanical names of sneezewort allude to the use of its dried and powdered leaves as snuff since classical times. The species name, *ptarmica*, is derived from the Greek word *ptarmos*, meaning "sneezing."

The white, daisy-like flowers are small, only 2.5 cm (1 in.) in diameter, but numerous, and form 8 to 15 cm (3 to 6 in.) corymbs in July and August. The dark green leaves are linear to lance-shaped and finely toothed.

Cultivars
- 'Ballerina' is an improved selection, shorter and more compact than 'The Pearl'.
- 'The Pearl' ('Boule de Neige') has double, snow-white flowers and an airy, delicate appearance. It grows to 60 cm (24 in.).
- 'Perry's White' is less sturdy and more open and grows 40 cm (16 in.) tall.

Achillea tomentosa
a-*kil*-lee-a toe-men-*toe*-sa
Woolly yarrow

Plant at a Glance
Type: herbaceous perennial
Height/spread: 15 to 30 cm (6 to 12 in.) / 20 cm (8 in.)
Spacing: 20 cm (8 in.)
Light: full sun
Soil: well drained
Distinguishing features: yellow flowers; woolly, silver foliage
Landscape use: perennial border; rock garden; over walls; small, inaccessible, or inhospitable areas; pavement plantings; accentuating focal points
Propagation: seed; division

Extremely drought tolerant, woolly yarrow goes well beyond being merely a groundcover. It is also ideal in a rock garden, at the front of a border, and as a pavement planting.

Native to Europe and western Asia, both the common and botanical name (*tomentosa* means "hairy") refer to the fine hairs, or trichomes, on the foliage. These hairs increase the plant's drought tolerance by deflecting wind over the leaf surface at the same time as they shade it. The common name, yarrow, can be traced back to the Anglo-Saxon *gearwe* and to the Middle English *yarowe*, probably an early name for this plant.

Woolly yarrow foliage is gray-green, aromatic, and finely cut. The tiny, bright yellow flowers are formed in 5 to 10 cm (2 to 4 in.) corymbs in late spring to early summer. The fibrous root system soon forms a dense, impenetrable carpet. 'Aurea' is yellow and 20 cm (8 in.) tall.

Divide every three or four years to prevent overcrowding, which is sometimes indicated by dieback in the center of the plant.

Aegopodium podograria 'Variegatum'
ee-go-*poh*-dee-um poe-da-*grar*-ee-a
Goutweed, bishop's goutweed

Plant at a Glance
Type: herbaceous perennial
Height/spread: 30 to 38 cm (12 to 15 in.) / 1 m (3.3 ft.)
Spacing: 30 cm (12 in.)
Light: full sun to partial shade
Soil: evenly moist
Distinguishing features: attractive green and creamy white variegated foliage
Landscape use: slopes and banks; transition plantings; back lane plantings; shady understory

Aegopodium podograria 'Variegatum'
(variegated goutweed) (Sara Williams)

Propagation: division

Goutweed is the first plant that novice gardeners are taught to hate by their more-experienced mentors. Why? Because it does its job so effectively. It is the grand dame of all groundcovers. When we first see it, we are instantly enamored by a plant that has such attractive variegated foliage and seems to do so well with so little effort on our part. Then we plant it in the wrong place. It should come with a surgeon general's warning: "Plant only where its rampant growth can be restricted." Never place it in a border or rock garden.

The plant's common name stems from the old belief that it could cure gout, a condition to which bishops, with their rich diet and supposed lack of exercise, were particularly prone. The genus name is derived from the Greek words *aix*, "goat," and *podion*, "little foot," said to describe the bi-ternately (twice divided into three segments) compound leaves. The specific epithet *podagraria* means "a remedy for gout," from the Greek *podagra*, meaning "gout in the foot." 'Variegatum' refers again to the foliage.

The creamy white and green foliage, held on fleshy stalks, has the fragrance of a carrot, to which goutweed is related. The white flowers form in compound umbels above the foliage and resemble Queen Anne's lace. Even the creeping rhizomes are aromatic—and they are so very good at what they do.

Groundcovers with a Bad Reputation

Mention goutweed or ribbon grass at a gathering of gardeners and the response is generally less than positive. "Weed" is the least offensive of the terms heard. These two plants have many "weedy" characteristics. They are pretty, but wildly aggressive and often grow out of control. You can't blame a plant for doing a good job, but it behooves you to consider its placement very carefully.

Barriers, such as edging, are seldom effective in the long run. These plants can sometimes be quite literally "contained" by being planted in large pots sunk into beds or borders, but more often than not, they eventually escape and cause us grief. Alternatively, they become overcrowded in their constrained quarters and die. The best policy is to plant them where they are free to do what they do. In rural settings where space is plentiful, this could be on the edge of the bush as a transition zone between manicured and non-maintained areas. In urban areas, treat them poorly and use them in a back lane.

Best Groundcovers & Vines For The Prairies

Use goutweed as a groundcover on a woodland edge where it can act as a transition planting, between a building and a sidewalk where its rampant growth can be controlled, or to brighten dense shade as an understory beneath large, canopy trees, especially on a hill or slope where lawns would be difficult to establish and downright dangerous to maintain.

How to Grow

Goutweed will grow in sun or light shade in almost any soil, as long as it has even moisture. During the heat of summer, the foliage may suffer from sun scorch and turn brown and shabby if not irrigated. Mow and water for fresh new foliage. On occasion, the variegated foliage reverts to green; remove these portions.

Ajuga reptans
a-*ju*-gah *rep*-tanz
Bugleweed, carpet bugle

Plant at a Glance
Type: herbaceous perennial
Height/spread: 8 to 10 cm (3 to 4 in.) / 30 cm (12 in.)
Spacing: 30 cm (12 in.)
Light: partial shade
Soil: well drained; rich in organic matter
Distinguishing features: blue-purple flowers; bronzy foliage
Landscape use: rock garden; edging; lawn replacement; small, inaccessible, or inhospitable areas; unifying shrub beds; accentuating focal points; shady understory
Propagation: division

Today, bugleweed is planted extensively as a groundcover and used in rock and shade gardens, in borders, and as edging—rather tame uses that belie its more exciting

Ajuga reptans 'Chocolate Chip' ('Chocolate Chip' bugleweed) (Sara Williams)

past. Native to the woodlands of central Europe and Asia Minor, it was once applied to wounds to stop bleeding. The leaves are considered mildly narcotic and the plant was also said to cure hangovers. More domestically, it was used as a black dye for wool.

A member of the mint family, bugleweed is characterized by square stems and opposite leaves. The botanical name is from the Latin prefix *a*, meaning "no," and *zugon*, meaning "yoke," indicating that the lobes of the calyx are not divided as are many of the mints. The specific epithet *reptans* means "creeping" and refers to its low, spreading form.

The flowers and foliage are both attractive, giving it value over a long season. Blue to blue-violet, two-lipped flowers in terminal spikes are produced in late spring on short stems. The glossy foliage ranges from bronzy green to browny purple. The oval leaves arise from compact rosettes that quickly form a dense groundcover through underground stolons.

How to Grow

Plant *Ajuga* in well-drained organic soil in light to medium shade. It does well in full sun if irrigated through the heat of summer. If it lacks water, it is vulnerable to leaf scald. In cold, wet soils with poor drainage, crown rot may occur in late winter or early spring. Divide every few years to avoid overcrowding. Cultivars do not come true from seed and should be deadheaded (or mowed in large areas) to prevent the appearance of inferior seedlings. Bugleweed cultivars are easily propagated by division in early spring.

Cultivars

- 'Alba' bears cream flowers; its green foliage turns purple in winter.
- 'Bronze Beauty' has intense, almost metallic, purple-bronze foliage and soft blue-purple flowers.
- 'Burgundy Glow' has variegated tri-colour foliage of pink, cream, and green. It is considered less hardy in zone 2.
- 'Catlin's Giant' displays larger, bronze-green foliage and blue flowers.

Other Species and Hybrids

- *Ajuga pyramidalis* (pi-ra-mi-*dah*-lis) 'Metallica Crispa', pyramidal bugleweed, has triangular flower spikes. It is less hardy and doesn't spread.
- *Ajuga* x *tenorii* (ten-*or*-ee-i) 'Chocolate Chip' has dark purple foliage and blue flowers. It is one of the best and most vigorous bugleweed cultivars and highly recommended.

Alchemilla mollis
al-ke-*mil*-la *mol*-lis
Common lady's mantle

Plant at a Glance
Type: herbaceous perennial

Height/spread: 30 cm (12 in.) / 60 cm (24 in.)
Spacing: 45 cm (18 in.)
Light: full sun to partial shade
Soil: well drained; rich in organic matter
Distinguishing features: frothy yellow flowers; pubescent, soft green foliage
Landscape use: perennial or mixed border; accent plant; mass plantings; unifying shrub beds; breaking up large expanses of lawn; accentuating focal points
Propagation: seed; division

Alchemilla is from an Arabic name that derives from the same root as alchemy—the blooms change from silvery green to gold—while *mollis* means "soft" or "soft and hairy" and describes the leaves. Native to Europe, common lady's mantle is a herbaceous member of the rose family, noted for its felted, round leaves that are scalloped and toothed on the edges.

Alchemilla mollis (lady's mantle) (Sara Williams)

The foliage is particularly beautiful on mornings when the sun shines on captured dew drops. Lady's mantle produces clusters of chartreuse green flowers in early summer that provide a striking frothy display, despite their lack of petals. It is attractive as an accent on the edge of a border or mass planted as a groundcover in a partly shaded location.

How to Grow

Lady's mantle grows best in partial shade in moist but well-drained soil that is rich in organic matter. It grows in full sun if given even moisture. Plants propagate easily from seed or from divisions made and planted in early spring.

Other Species and Hybrids

- *Alchemilla alpina* (al-*pie*-na), alpine lady's mantle, is a compact plant growing 10 cm (4 in.) high that has dark green, palmately compound leaves, with a silver edge.
- *Alchemilla erythropoda* (er-ith-ro-*po*-da), dwarf lady's mantle, bears bluish green, felted, palmate foliage and is of similar stature to *A. alpina*.

Anaphalis margaritacea
a-*nah*-fa-lis mar-ga-ri-*tah*-kee-a
Pearly everlasting

Plant at a Glance
Type: herbaceous perennial
Height/spread: 30 to 80 cm (12 to 32 in.) / 60 cm (24 in.)
Spacing: 45 cm (18 in.)
Light: full sun to partial shade
Soil: moist; well drained; rich in organic matter
Distinguishing features: small, white flower heads; silver foliage
Landscape use: rock garden; small, inaccessible, or inhospitable areas
Propagation: division

Anaphalis margaritacea is a native member of the sunflower family. The genus name, *Anaphalis*, is an ancient Greek word. The species name, *margaritacea*, means "pearl-bearing," and like the common name refers to the tightly packed flower heads that resemble pearls. The flower heads are arranged in dense clusters atop leafy stems. The narrow, linear leaves are densely hairy on the underside and somewhat hairy on the top, giving them a silvery appearance. It spreads aggressively by underground rhizomes and can be used as a silver-leaved groundcover in partial shade.

As the common name implies, the flowers can be collected and dried for winter bouquets.

How to Grow
Pearly everlasting naturally grows at woodland edges. It prefers moist, organically rich soil, but is quite drought tolerant. It grows best in sun or partial shade and spreads aggressively under favorable conditions. It is easy to propagate by transplanting divisions in early spring.

Andropogon gerardii
an-droe-*poe*-gon jer-*ar*-dee-i
Big bluestem

Plant at a Glance
Type: ornamental grass
Height/spread: 1.5 to 2.1 m (5 to 7 ft.) / 60 cm (24 in.)
Spacing: 45 cm (18 in.)
Light: full sun to partial shade
Soil: evenly moist; well drained
Distinguishing features: bluish or reddish foliage; reddish fall color
Landscape use: accent plant; prairie restoration; slopes and banks; screening

Best Groundcovers & Vines For The Prairies

Propagation: seed; division

Big bluestem waves in the breezes of the tall-grass prairie. The bluish green foliage is topped by stems of a similar color (hence, the common name), with flower heads that resemble a bird's foot. As the flowers open in late summer, the red or yellow anthers color the tall-grass prairie pink to orange. The flowers expand into fluffy plumes as the seed ripens. The name *Andropogon* is derived from the Greek words meaning "man's beard" and refers to the bearded seed heads. The attractive strap-shaped, bluish green leaves appear once the soil warms in early summer. Planted in a large stand, it forms an impressive backdrop; it can also be used in small groups with other grasses and prairie wildflowers or as

Andropogon gerardii (big bluestem) (Sara Williams)

a specimen plant. Because of its deep roots, it is very effective for bank stabilization.

How to Grow

Big bluestem, a warm-season grass, is a deep-rooted plant that naturally grows in full sun. In the garden, it thrives on moist, fertile soil and tolerates partial shade. It is drought tolerant once established. Be prepared to dig a deep sod to divide the deeply rooted clumps. Mow or burn the plants in spring to remove the previous season's growth and renew them. Propagate by seed, plugs, or clump division in early spring.

Anemone
a-*nem*-oh-nee
Windflower

Native to open, sunny woods and meadows in North America, Europe, and Asia, both the common and botanical names reflect this plant's habitat. *Anemone* is from the Greek word *anemos*, meaning "wind." All are dainty of flower and foliage, but vary in their fecundity.

How to Grow

Windflowers are adapted to most soils in sun or shade, but prefer those that are well drained, amended with organic matter, and evenly moist. They are most easily propagated by division.

Anemone canadensis
a-*nem*-oh-nee can-a-*den*-sis
Canada anemone

Plant at a Glance
Type: herbaceous perennial
Height/spread: 30 to 40 cm (12 to 16 in.) / 45 cm (18 in.)
Spacing: 30 cm (12 in.)
Light: full sun to full shade
Soil: evenly moist; well drained; rich in organic matter
Distinguishing features: pure white flowers; delicate blue-green foliage
Landscape use: naturalizing; shady understory
Propagation: seed; division

Dainty of flower and foliage, the Canada anemone is more aggressive than it looks and is ideal for naturalizing in a shade or woodland garden. As the species name *canadensis* suggests, it is native to much of North America, including aspen and poplar forests and the moist grasslands of the Canadian prairies.

The small, up-facing, solitary flowers appear in summer. Bright white, with distinct yellow stamens, each flower consists of four to five sepals. The foliage is typical of anemones, palmately divided, generally with five lobes, light green, and covered in fine hairs. Although the taproot is bulb-like, the plant spreads steadily through rhizomes.

Other Species and Hybrids
- *Anemone multifida* (mul-*tif*-i-dah), the cutleaf anemone, is native to North America, spring blooming, and very similar to *A. canadensis*.

Anemone sylvestris
a-*nem*-oh-nee sil-*ves*-tris
Snowdrop anemone, windflower

Plant at a Glance
Type: herbaceous perennial
Height/spread: 30 to 50 cm (12 to 20 in.) / 30 to 38 cm (12 to 15 in.)
Spacing: 45 cm (18 in.)
Light: full sun to partial shade
Soil: average to moist; well drained; rich in organic matter
Distinguishing features: pure white flowers; blue-green, palmately lobed foliage
Landscape use: naturalizing; small, inaccessible, or inhospitable areas; breaking up large expanses of lawn; back lane plantings; accentuating focal points; shady understory
Propagation: division

Gardeners are seldom neutral when it comes to the snowdrop anemone, or windflower. As a friend once said, "With friends like these, who needs anemones?" On the one hand, we welcome the pure white flowers in spring. They look especially pleasing under a birch, echoing the white bark. We revel at how very adept they are at naturalizing through stolons and self-seeding. On the other hand, their very success is their downfall in the eyes of some. They naturalize all too well. The solution is simple: plant them where they can "do their thing." Never blame a plant for a job well done.

Blooming in May, the fragrant, white flowers are 4 to 5 cm (1.5 to 2 in.) across and consist of five sepals. They are held well above the attractive dark blue-green foliage, which is palmately divided into three to five distinct lobes. The specific epithet, *sylvestris,* means "of the woods."

Anemone sylvestris 'Flore plano' (double snowdrop anemone) (Sara Williams)

The double-flowering form 'Flore Pleno' is somewhat shorter, with flowers resembling those of a cushion mum. As equally rugged as the species, it is adaptable to sun or partial shade and very drought tolerant once established.

Antennaria rosea
An-ten-*ah*-ree-a *row*-zay-ah
Pink pussytoes

Plant at a Glance
Type: herbaceous perennial
Height/spread: 15 cm (6 in.) / 40 cm (16 in.)
Spacing: 20 cm (8 in.)
Light: full sun
Soil: well drained
Distinguishing features: pink flower heads; tiny, silver, ground-hugging foliage
Landscape use: perennial border; rock garden; edging; lawn replacement;

small, inaccessible, or inhospitable areas; unifying shrub beds; pavement planting; accentuating focal points
Propagation: division

Antennaria rosea forms silvery mats of tiny, oblong, densely hairy leaves. Various species of *Antennaria* grow on gravelly soils in sunny locations throughout the prairie region, but this species is more common in the southwest. The genus *Antennaria* derives its name from the resemblance of the pappus of its flowers to insect antennae. The species name, *rosea,* refers to the pink flower heads that emerge in dense clusters and resemble the pads of a cat's foot (hence, the common name) atop leafless stems in early summer. Pussytoes are suitable for planting among stepping stones, as a low groundcover, at the front of a border, as edging, or in a rock garden.

How to Grow
Pussytoes need very well drained soil and a sunny location to thrive. These plants are extremely drought tolerant. Propagation is easy by transplanting divisions in the spring.

Other Species and Hybrids
- *Antennaria parvifolia* (par-vee-*fol*-ee-a), small-leaved pussytoes, forms a very dense mat of low foliage. It bears creamy white flowers in June.
- *Antennaria plantaginifolia* (pla-ta-gee-nee-*fol*-ee-a), plantain-leaved pussytoes, has larger leaves, flower stems up to 50 cm (20 in.) tall, and creamy white flowers.

Arabis alpina
(syn. *A. caucasica, A. alpina* subsp. *caucasica*)
air-a-bis al-*pie*-na
Rock cress, mountain rock cress

Plant at a Glance
Type: herbaceous perennial
Height/spread: 15 to 20 cm (6 to 8 in.) / 30 to 60 cm (12 to 24 in.)
Spacing: 30 cm (12 in.)
Light: full sun to partial shade
Soil: well drained
Distinguishing features: pink or white flowers; gray rosettes of foliage
Landscape use: perennial border; rock garden; edging; lawn replacement; small, inaccessible, or inhospitable areas; pavement planting; accentuating focal points
Propagation: seed

Best Groundcovers & Vines For The Prairies

Given full sun and well-drained soil, rock cress is an easy plant to grow. It is useful not only as a groundcover but also in the rock garden, the front of a border, or as edging. *Arabis* is the Greek word for Arabia, to which some species are native. There is

Arabis alpina (alpine rockcress) (Sara Williams)

some confusion in the nomenclature of the species and several synonyms may appear in catalogues and on plant tags. The specific epithet *alpina* refers to the alpine meadows that form much of its native habitat from the Alps, the Mediterranean region, and the Caucasus Mountains into Turkey and Iran.

Its small, pink or white flowers are fragrant and bloom in early spring. They consist of four petals, each only 1.5 cm (0.5 in.) long, in loose racemes. The gray-green leaves, in rosettes, are oval to oblong, coarsely toothed, and covered in soft hairs. Spreading by rhizomes, the plants eventually form loose mats.

How to Grow

Fertilize rock cress very little, if at all. Shear lightly after flowering to maintain a more compact form and divide every three to four years in early spring if plants appear overcrowded. Some dieback may occur in zone 2 during severe winters lacking snow cover. Rock cress is easily grown from seed.

Cultivars
- 'Flore Plena' bears double, white flowers and is longer flowering than most other rock cresses. It is usually sterile or produces little seed.
- 'Rosabella' has rose flowers that fade as they age and light green foliage.
- 'Rosea' produces soft pink to dark pink flowers.
- 'Snowball' is a compact, mounding variety, growing 10 to 15 cm (4 to 6 in.) tall, with pure white flowers.
- 'Snow Cap' is compact, reaching 15 cm (6 in.), and bears larger, pure white flowers.
- 'Snow Peak' has single, white flowers on compact, 10 cm (4 in.) plants.
- 'Variegata' is less hardy and shorter lived; the variegated foliage often reverts to green. It has white flowers.

Aralia nudicaulis
a-*rah*-lee-a nu-di-*cawl*-us
Wild sarsaparilla

Plant at a Glance
Type: herbaceous perennial
Height/spread: 40 cm (16 in.) / 50 cm (18 in.)
Spacing: 40 cm (16 in.)
Light: shade
Soil: well drained; rich in organic matter
Distinguishing features: large, compound leaves
Landscape use: shady understory
Propagation: seed; division

The derivation of the name *Aralia* is obscure. Wild sarsaparilla produces exotic-looking pinnately compound leaves on long, naked stalks, giving rise to the species name *nudicaulis*, meaning "naked stalk." Each leaf is formed from three to five broadly lance-shaped leaflets, which are coarse in texture and 8 to 13 cm (3 to 5 in.) long. Small, greenish flowers are borne in umbels, with three umbels normally arising on a flowering stem. The flowers are followed by black berries. Leaves and flowers arise from thick rhizomes that grow on rich soils under the tree canopy. The rhizomes of wild sarsaparilla were collected by Native Americans to treat various medical conditions.

How to Grow
Wild sarsaparilla is a common understory plant of woodlands throughout the prairie region and grows best in dappled shade on well-drained soil, rich in organic matter. It can be propagated by transplanting rhizome pieces or by sowing fresh seed in early spring.

Arctostaphylos uva-ursi (bearberry) (Sara Williams)

Arctostaphylos uva-ursi
ark-teh-*sta*-ful-us oo-va-*ur*-see
Bearberry

Plant at a Glance
Type: broad-leafed evergreen shrub
Height/spread: 10 cm (4 in.) / 60 cm (24 in.)
Spacing: 45 cm (18 in.)
Light: full sun to partial shade
Soil: well drained; lean to average
Distinguishing features: dense, evergreen foliage; red berries
Landscape use: slopes or banks; lawn replacement; small, inaccessible, or inhospitable areas; accentuating focal points; shady understory; rock garden
Propagation: layering

The name *Arctostaphylos* combines the Greek words for "bear" and "grape," while *uva-ursi* repeats this in Latin. The species has a circumpolar distribution in the northern hemisphere and is usually found on well-drained soils in sunny or partially shaded situations. The dense cover of evergreen foliage is very beautiful as a groundcover. Leathery, dark evergreen, oval leaves, 1.5 to 2.5 cm (0.5 to 1 in.) long, alternate on trailing, woody stems and turn bronze to burgundy in the fall on most plants. Pale pink, urn-shaped flowers appear in terminal clusters in early summer, followed by bright red berries. The berries are mealy but edible, while other parts of the plant have been used medicinally by Aboriginal peoples in Canada. 'Vancouver Jade' is a vigorous cultivar from the University of British Columbia Botanical Garden.

Use bearberry at the front of a mixed border, to accentuate a focal point, as a lawn alternative under evergreen trees, or to stabilize a sandy bank.

How to Grow
Bearberry grows best on lean, sandy soils. A plant will cover a large area over time, but to establish it as a groundcover, space plants about 30 cm (12 in.) apart. Although usually thought to be acid-loving, bearberry tolerates lime-based soils and is also salt tolerant. Because it is difficult to transplant, it is best to use container-grown plants. Propagate in early spring by removing and transplanting branches that have layered and developed roots.

Aronia melanocarpa
ah-*row*-nee-a meh-len-oh-*kar*-pa
Black chokeberry

Plant at a Glance
Type: deciduous shrub

Height/spread: 1 to 2 m (3.3 to 6.5 ft.) / 1 m (3.3 ft.) and suckering
Spacing: 0.6 to 1 m (2 to 3.3 ft.)
Light: full sun
Soil: evenly moist; lean to average
Distinguishing features: white flowers; black fruit; red fall color; suckering habit
Landscape use: waterside plantings; mass plantings; delineating space and defining property lines
Propagation: seed; suckers; softwood cuttings

Aronia melanocarpa (aronia) (Sara Williams)

The genus name *Aronia* is derived from *aria*, a species of mountain ash, which emphasizes its relationship to the *Sorbus* genus; *melanocarpa* refers to its black fruit. Black chokeberry is native to Eastern Canada and the United States and is often found growing in wet areas, spreading vigorously from underground rhizomes. Its oval leaves are dark green, shiny, and toothed on the margin. White flowers are borne in terminal clusters that give rise to black berries similar to those of mountain ash. Black chokeberry adapts to various growing conditions, but prefers wet, acidic soil. The University of British Columbia Botanical Garden cultivar 'Autumn Magic' is compact, up to 1.5 m (5 ft.) in height, has excellent red fall color, and is worthy of trial in favorable growing areas on the prairies.

Plant black chokeberry en masse in wet locations or at the edge of woodland or natural areas.

How to Grow
Although black chokeberry naturally grows in swamps, it tolerates dry and relatively poor soils. Plant bare-root plants in spring or container-grown plants throughout the growing season. Propagate black chokeberry by transplanting sucker shoots, by sowing seed in fall or stratified seed in the spring, or by softwood cuttings.

Arrhenatherum bulbosum 'Variegatum'

are-hen-a-*ther*-um bul-*bo*-sum
Variegated tuber oat grass

Plant at a Glance

Type: ornamental grass
Height/spread: 40 cm (16 in.) / 40 cm (16 in.)
Spacing: 30 cm (12 in.)
Light: full sun to partial shade
Soil: well drained; average
Distinguishing features: variegated foliage
Landscape use: edging; small, inaccessible, or inhospitable areas; breaking up large expanses of lawn; back lane plantings; shady understory
Propagation: division

A cool-season grass, tuber oat grass begins to grow early in the spring and develops into neat, low clumps of narrow, green and white variegated foliage. The seed heads are oat-like panicles, 30 to 45 cm (12 to 18 in.) tall. *Arrhenatherum* is from a Greek word meaning "male awn" and refers to the awned male florets. The species name *bulbosum* refers to the bulb-like tubers that form near the soil surface. Tuber oat grass is effective in the garden with spring-blooming bulbs and perennials or combines well with hostas, pulmonarias, and ferns in a partially shaded garden.

Arrhenatherum bulbosum 'Variegatum' (variegated tuber oat grass) (Hugh Skinner)

How to Grow

Variegated tuber oat grass grows well in normal garden soil in full sun to partial shade. Foliage persists throughout the summer, but can be improved by cutting back in July to encourage renewed growth. Propagate by transplanting tubers in the spring.

Cool-season Grasses

Cool-season grasses generally originate in temperate areas and initiate growth in early spring. They are short to medium in stature and usually reach their ultimate height prior to the onset of summer heat. They may go dormant during the hot summer or become shabby if they are not irrigated. Mow or cut them back if this occurs, and wait for regrowth in early fall.

Examples: variegated tuber oat grass (*Arrhenatherum*), feather reed grass (*Calamagrostis*), blue lyme grass (*Elymus*, syn. *Leymus*), blue fescue (*Festuca*), ribbon grass (*Phalaris*)

Warm-season Grasses

Warm-season grasses are generally taller than cool-season grasses and have showier flower and seed heads. Because these grasses originate in warmer climate zones, they are later to initiate growth in the spring, waiting for the warmer temperatures of their natural habitats, generally over 25°C (77°F). They tend to be drought and heat tolerant and perform well during hot weather. Remove old foliage in early spring.

Examples: bluestem (*Andropogon*), switch grass (*Panicum*)

Artemisia ludoviciana
ar-te-*meez*-ee-a lew-doe-vik-ee-*aye*-na
Artemisia, wormwood, ghost plant, silver sage

Plant at a Glance
Type: herbaceous perennial
Height/spread: 60 to 90 cm (24 to 36 in.) / 60 to 90 cm (24 to 36 in.)
Spacing: 45 cm (18 in.)
Light: full sun
Soil: well drained; lean
Distinguishing features: attractive silver-gray foliage
Landscape use: naturalizing; small, inaccessible, or inhospitable areas; slopes and banks; transition plantings; back lane plantings
Propagation: division

For drought tolerance in a hot, dry, sunny location, artemisia is hard to beat. In larger rural landscapes, it's ideal as a transition planting between the intensively maintained areas of a yard and the bush, bunch grass, or native prairie beyond.

Native to the dry grasslands of North America from British Columbia to Mexico, the genus honors the Greek goddess of chastity, Artemis. The species name means "of Louisiana," a reference to the whole of the Louisiana Purchase surveyed by the Louis and Clark expedition in 1804. Native peoples have long used this plant for cleansing and purification.

Upright and somewhat bushy, artemisia's long, lance-shaped leaves are an attractive silver-gray, while the stems are woolly and nearly white. The late-summer flowers, formed in tight clusters along the stem, are considered insignificant and are sometimes removed by fussy gardeners with lots of time on their hands. Artemisia spreads by creeping rhizomes.

How to Grow
Grow this one lean and mean. If overwatered, overfertilized, or planted in the shade, it soon loses its upright appearance. Shear lightly if it becomes floppy. Propagate through division in late spring, after the soil has warmed, to mid-summer.

Cultivars
- 'Silver Frost' has finely cut foliage and reaches 45 to 60 cm (18 to 24 in.) in height.
- 'Silver King' has lanceolate leaves and silver-white flowers. This vigorous cultivar grows 75 to 90 cm (30 to 36 in.) tall.
- 'Valerie Finnis' is more compact, has wider leaves, and is less invasive than 'Silver King'. It grows 45 to 60 cm (18 to 24 in.) tall.

Other Species and Hybrids
- *Artemisia lactiflora* (lak-ti-*flor*-ah) 'Silver Queen' has intensely silver, lanceolate foliage, with jagged margins. It is shorter than 'Silver King'.
- *Artemisia stelleriana* (stel-la-ree-*ah*-na) 'Silver Brocade' (syn. 'Boughton Silver') is low and compact, with scalloped foliage, and is a perfect perennial version of the annual dusty miller. It seems to come true from seed. More fastidious gardeners remove the nondescript yellow flowers. It grows 30 cm (12 in.) tall and 60 cm (24 in.) wide and is an excellent plant for edging, rock gardens, or lawn replacement.

Asarum canadense
a-*sah*-rum kan-a-*den*-say
Canadian ginger, wild ginger

Plant at a Glance
Type: herbaceous perennial
Height/spread: 10 to 15 cm (4 to 6 in.) / 30 cm (12 in.)
Spacing: 30 cm (12 in.)
Light: shade
Soil: evenly moist; well drained; rich in organic matter
Distinguishing features: light green, kidney-shaped foliage
Landscape use: lawn replacement; small, inaccessible, or inhospitable areas; accentuating focal points; shady understory
Propagation: division

Although its foliage is not as shiny and attractive as that of European ginger (*Asarum europaeum*), Canadian ginger is far ahead in durability. It's a groundcover you can count on to gradually cover even a heavily shaded area.

The plant's common name is derived from the ginger-like smell of its roots and its native range in the woodlands of a large area of northeastern North America, from New Brunswick to Manitoba and south to South Carolina. *Asarum* is the classical Greek name for this plant, while *canadense* reflects that part of its range is in Canada.

The rhizomes, close to the soil surface and easily collected, have a long history of folk use in treating heart palpitations, as a contraceptive, masking the smell of bad meat, and as a substitute for ginger. They contain aristolochic acid, which acts as an anti-microbial. Since the foliage can cause dermatitis, sensitive individuals should exercise care when handling it.

Canadian ginger forms a steadily increasing low, dense mound of light green, pubescent foliage. The paired leaves are kidney to heart shaped and 8 to 13 cm (3 to 5 in.) in diameter. Small, reddish brown, bell-shaped flowers are produced in spring. Sometimes called "little brown jugs" because of their resemblance to the pottery jugs that once held home brew, they are mostly at ground level and difficult to see unless you are on your belly. The root system is composed of creeping rhizomes.

How to Grow
Plant Canadian ginger in a shaded location in well-drained, evenly moist soil amended with organic matter. Propagate through division in early spring.

Asarum canadense (Canadian ginger, wild ginger) (Sara Williams)

Best Groundcovers & Vines For The Prairies

Astilbe simplicifolia 'Sprite'
a-*stil*-bee sim-plea-see-*fol*-e-ah
Dwarf astilbe

Plant at a Glance
Type: herbaceous perennial
Height/spread: 30 to 45 cm (12 to 18 in.) / 30 cm (12 in.)
Spacing: 30 cm (12 in.)
Light: shade
Soil: evenly moist; rich in organic matter
Distinguishing features: miniature, plume-like, pink panicles; bronze-green foliage
Landscape use: screening spring-bulb foliage; accentuating focal points; shady understory
Propagation: division

Selected as the 1994 Perennial Plant of the Year, 'Sprite' is one of the few astilbes that can really be counted on throughout the prairie region. Although it lacks the stature of its taller brethren, it will be in your garden for the long haul, its stolons forming a dense, slowly increasing mat.

One of the *Astilbe simplicifolia* hybrids developed by mostly German and British plant breeders, this plant's foliage and flowers are a far cry from the origins of its botanical name. *Astilbe* is derived from the Greek preface *a*, meaning "no," and *stilbe*, meaning "brightness," alluding to the dull foliage and insignificant flowers of some species.

'Sprite' is an excellent groundcover, with good foliage (British garden designer Gertrude Jekyll is shouting approval from above), prolific flowers, and an ability to suppress weeds as it slowly forms dense, compact clumps. The plume-like panicles are composed of many small, shell pink flowers that sit on stiff stems above the foliage and bloom in late summer. The shiny, bronze-green foliage is pinnately compound, with an almost lacy appearance.

How to Grow
This astilbe is considerably tougher than it looks. Although it performs better in a shaded situation in evenly moist organic soil, 'Sprite' is much more drought tolerant than most other astilbes. While forming an ever-increasing mat, it seldom dies out in the centre. 'Sprite' is generally late to emerge in the spring, so don't lose hope and plant something else on top of it. Like other cultivars, it is propagated by division in spring.

Other Species and Hybrids
- *Astilbe chinensis* 'Pumila' (chin-*en*-sis pew-*mill*-ah) has dark green, pinnately compound leaves and stiff panicles of puffy, mauve to pink flowers in late summer. It grows 30 to 38 cm (12 to 15 in.) tall and 38 cm

(15 in.) wide and has a stoloniferous root system that soon forms dense mats. More drought tolerant than most astilbes, it's ideal as a groundcover or for edging.

Aurinia saxatilis (syn. *Alyssum saxatile*)
aw-*rin*-ee-a saks-ah-*til*-is
Perennial alyssum, basket-of-gold, madwort

Plant at a Glance
Type: herbaceous perennial
Height/spread: 22 to 30 cm (9 to 12 in.) / 30 cm (12 in.)
Spacing: 30 cm (12 in.)
Light: full sun
Soil: well drained
Distinguishing features: tiny, yellow flowers; gray foliage
Landscape use: rock garden; over walls; lawn replacement; small, inaccessible, or inhospitable areas; pavement plantings; accentuating focal points
Propagation: seed

Perennial alyssum is a gardener's dream. It is easy to grow from seed, long-lived, and low maintenance, and it has a bloom period of six weeks, from late spring through early summer. An alpine plant native to Europe, the genus name, *Aurinia*, is the Latin word for "golden," an apt reference to the flowers. The specific epithet *saxatilis* means "growing among rocks," its natural habitat.

Despite a change in botanical nomenclature that may confuse those still looking for *Alyssum saxatile* in garden centers, perennial alyssum remains a mainstay of the spring garden, forming a loose mat of pubescent, gray-green leaves. The tiny, golden yellow, cruciform flowers have four petals and are produced in dense panicles that almost hide the foliage. Although the crown is somewhat woody, the roots are fibrous.

Aurinia saxatilis (perennial alyssum) (Sara Williams)

How to Grow
Plant perennial alyssum in full sun in

Best Groundcovers & Vines For The Prairies

well-drained soil. Shear lightly after flowering to maintain compactness. Drought tolerant once established, they tend to sprawl if overwatered, overfertilized, or grown in shade. Propagate by seed. It's easy!

Cultivars
- 'Ball of Gold' is smaller and more rounded, but also less hardy and robust than the species.
- 'Citrinum', compact and soft yellow, reaches 25 cm (10 in.) in height, but is less hardy and robust than the species.
- 'Compactum', canary yellow, grows to 25 cm (10 in.), with a neat, compact habit.

Bergenia cordifolia
ber-*gen*-ee-a kor-di-*foe*-lee-a
Heart-leaved bergenia, pigsqueak

Plant at a Glance
Type: evergreen perennial
Height/spread: 30 to 45 cm (12 to 18 in.) / 30 cm (12 in.)
Spacing: 30 cm (12 in.)
Light: full sun to shade
Soil: average
Distinguishing features: pink flowers; evergreen, leathery foliage
Landscape use: perennial border; rock garden; edging; waterside plantings; mass plantings; naturalizing; small, inaccessible, or inhospitable areas; unifying shrub beds; delineating space and defining property lines; breaking up large expanses of lawn; transition plantings; back lane plantings; shady understory
Propagation: seed; division

Bergenia cordifolia (bergenia) (Hugh Skinner)

In 1976, the famous British garden writer Graham Stuart Thomas described bergenia as "a godsend to those dry windy gardens where hostas do not thrive." At the turn of the last century, Gertrude Jekyll, who appreciated the value of good foliage and helped reinvent the modern perennial border, planted it so widely that it became known as one of her "signature plants." The species is as tough on the Canadian prairies as it is in England, so we should heed the opinions of these two fine British gardeners and make wider use of it.

Named after Karl A. von Bergen (1704–1766), a professor of botany at Frankfurt University, both the common name and the species name *cordifolia* refer to the handsome heart-shaped leaves, with undulating margins. Another, but less frequently used, common name, pigsqueak, is from the sound made by rubbing the leaf between thumb and finger.

Bergenia is native to the Altai Mountains, Mongolia, and Siberia. It is hardy, vigorous, practically indestructible, long-lived, and adapted to a wide range of habitats and uses. The tiny, waxy, pink flowers grow in dense spikes on thick stems, just above the foliage, blooming in spring. The large, glossy leaves are leathery, thick, and evergreen, turning a gorgeous red-purple in late fall. The root system is almost like a broomstick, slowly forming clumps but non-invasive and easily divided.

How to Grow

Of easy culture, bergenia thrive in almost any soil, from sand to clay, in sun or shade. Once established, they are extraordinarily drought tolerant, yet do equally well as waterside plantings. Bergenia can be propagated by seed, but divisions made during the growing season are easier and quicker.

Cultivars

None of the cultivars are as tough and robust as the species, so for mass plantings ensure you obtain *Bergenia cordifolia*. In sheltered locations, the following cultivars may be worth trying.
- 'Baby Doll' has pink flowers and grows 25 to 30 cm (10 to 12 in.) tall.
- 'Bressingham Ruby' bears rose-red flowers and has attractive ruby colored fall foliage. It grows 30 to 35 cm (12 to 14 in.) tall.
- 'Bressingham White' is a white-flowered cultivar that reaches 30 to 40 cm (12 to 16 in.) in height.

Bouteloua gracilis
bou-te-*loo*-ah gra-*sill*-is
Blue grama grass

Plant at a Glance
Type: ornamental grass
Height/spread: 30 cm (12 in.) / 30 cm (12 in.)
Spacing: 20 cm (8 in.)
Light: full sun
Soil: dry; well drained
Distinguishing features: fine, green foliage; comb-shaped seed heads

Landscape use: perennial or mixed border; edging; prairie restoration; small, inaccessible, or inhospitable areas; slopes and banks
Propagation: seed; division

The genus *Bouteloua* was named in honor of Spanish botanist Claudius Boutelou; *gracilis* means "graceful" or "slender." Noted for its curious comb-shaped seed heads, blue grama grass is a native of the short-grass prairie and a suitable companion for prairie wildflowers. Plants have fine, green leaves, 3 mm (0.12 in.) wide and 2 to 15 cm (0.8 to 6 in.) long, which are often curled at the edges and tapered to the tip.

Bromus inermis 'Skinner's Golden' ('Skinner's Golden' brome grass) (Hugh Skinner)

Blue grama spreads slowly from short, scaly rhizomes and remains as a dense clump. It is suitable for stabilizing banks, planting in a well-drained, sunny border, or as a substitute for lawn grass on sandy soils.

How to Grow
Blue grama grass is very drought tolerant, preferring dry, well-drained soil. It can be grown from seed, sown once the soil has warmed in the spring. If sown indoors in the winter, it may benefit from moist cold stratification [see p. 33] prior to spring seeding. Divide plants in early spring before growth is initiated or plant plugs.

Bromus inermis 'Skinner's Golden'
bro-mus in-*er*-mus
'Skinner's Golden' brome grass

Plant at a Glance
Type: ornamental grass
Height/spread: 60 cm (24 in.) / 60 cm (24 in.)
Spacing: 45 cm (18 in.)
Light: full sun
Soil: moist; well drained
Distinguishing features: golden foliage
Landscape use: small, inaccessible, or inhospitable areas; slopes and banks; transition plantings; back lane plantings; screening
Propagation: division

'Skinner's Golden' brome grass is an aggressive, spreading grass that it is very effective for holding soil on banks. The genus name *Bromus* is from the Greek word for "food" and it was originally applied to oats. The attractive golden-striped foliage starts growing early in spring and develops into a thick groundcover. Plant 'Skinner's Golden' brome grass only where it has room to spread without interfering with more-refined plantings.

How to Grow
'Skinner's Golden' brome grass thrives in a sunny location in moist, well-drained soils. The plants should be mowed in mid-summer to renew their golden foliage and prevent seeds from being dispersed (seedlings will have green leaves). This grass is easily propagated by transplanting rhizome pieces in early spring or mid-summer. Make sure the pieces are from variegated plants.

Brunnera macrophylla
bru-*ner*-ah mak-ro-*fil*-la
Alpine forget-me-not

Plant at a Glance
Type: herbaceous perennial
Height/spread: 50 cm (20 in.) / 50 cm (20 in.)
Spacing: 40 cm (16 in.)
Light: partial shade to shade
Soil: moist; rich in organic matter
Distinguishing features: azure blue flowers; attractive foliage, especially the variegated forms
Landscape uses: perennial border; edging; accent plant; shady understory
Propagation: seed; division (variegated cultivars)

Brunnera macrophylla 'Variegata' (variegated alpine Forget-me-not) (Hugh Skinner)

The genus *Brunnera* derives its name from nineteenth-century Swiss botanist S. Brunner, while the species name, *macrophylla,* refers to its large leaves. The handsome but bristly, oval foliage emerges in the spring, followed by sprays of delicate, azure blue flowers, 3 to 5 mm (0.12 to 0.2 in.) across. The species is native to the Caucasus Mountains and to Siberia. A number of cultivars have been selected for variegated or speckled foliage.

Alpine forget-me-not makes an attractive feature plant at the edge of the perennial border or it can be planted in masses under trees as an effective groundcover.

How to Grow
Alpine forget-me-not grows best in rich, moist soil in partial shade. It can be propagated by seed or by division in spring or mid-summer. Variegated cultivars should be propagated by division and may require removal of sections that revert to green.

Cultivars
- 'Hadspen Cream' has attractive cream-bordered leaves.
- 'Langtrees' features unique silvery speckled leaves.
- 'Variegata' has beautiful foliage, with a wide band of white along its leaf edges.

Calamagrostis x *acutiflora* 'Karl Foerster' (syn. *C.* x *acutiflora* 'Stricta')
kal-ah-mah-*gros*-tis ah-cute-tah-*fol*-ee-ah
'Karl Foerster' feather reed grass

Plant at a Glance
Type: ornamental grass
Height/spread: 1.5 to 2 m (5 to 6.5 ft.) / 90 cm (36 in.)
Spacing: 90 cm (36 in.)
Light: full sun to partial shade
Soil: average
Distinguishing features: light purple flower plumes; tall, upright grass
Landscape use: accent plant; delineating space and defining property lines; breaking up large expanses of lawn
Propagation: division

'Karl Foerster' is one of the most popular ornamental grasses on the prairies, and deservedly so. It's tall, handsome, well mannered, and long-lived, and it has four-season landscape value. As a groundcover, it needs a setting in scale with its size, which is up to 2 m (6.5 ft.) when in bloom. As garden writer Rick Darke noted, it provides "motion to the garden," shifting gracefully "with even a barely perceptible breeze." It also serves as an admirable accent plant, with its tall, stiff foliage topped by narrow plumes of flowers that emerge green, turn pink-purple through the growing season, and then an attractive beige over the winter.

The genus name is formed by two Greek words, *kalamos*, meaning "reed," and *agrostis*, a type of grass. The specific epithet describes the flower head—*acuti*, meaning "sharply pointed," and *flora*, "flower."

Who was Karl Foerster?

Born in Berlin, Germany, on 3 September 1874, Karl Foerster was one of five children of Wilhelm Foerster, a well-known astronomer and director of the Royal Observatory in Berlin, and painter Ina Foerster. Karl studied as a garden apprentice from 1889 to 1891 in Schwerin and from 1892 to 1903 at the Wildpark bei Potsdam Gardening Academy. He also worked under plant-breeder and landscape-architect Ludwig Winter in Bordighera on the Italian Riviera. It was there that his lifelong interests in photography and perennial plants began.

Foerster restored his parents' nursery, retaining only those plants with the most beauty, resilience, and durability. After moving the nursery to Potsdam, he developed an accompanying show garden. He published his first catalogue in 1907, wrote his first major article in 1909, and gave his first public lecture in 1910. Together with landscape architects Hermann Mattern and Herta Hammerbacher, he transformed his hometown of Bornim into a mecca for gardeners.

His horticultural career was devoted to plant breeding, writing, lecturing, and garden design. Foerster worked for decades under difficult political circumstances, struggling through two totalitarian regimes. During the Nazi era, he took the risk of employing many Jewish friends in his nursery and resisted the Nazi demand to propagate and sell only "pure" native German plants. After the war, the nursery was taken over and managed by the Soviet military administration and was the only perennial supplier for East Germany. Creativity was not encouraged.

In addition to his lectures, writing, and plant breeding, Foerster also designed show gardens in Bern, Switzerland, and Riga, Latvia, as well as demonstration gardens in Bavaria, Hannover, and Hamburg. In 1950, he received an honorary doctorate from Humboldt University in East Berlin.

Karl Foerster died on 27 November 1970 at the age of ninety-six in his home in Bornim. His global living legacy includes grasses such as 'Karl Foerster' feather reed grass, delphiniums, 'Goldstrum' rudbeckia, 'Rosyveil' baby's breath, and 'Golden Plume' heliopsis, as well as many other perennial plants.

How to Grow

Given full sun to partial shade and average soil and moisture conditions, 'Karl Foerster' soon forms large vertical clumps. Divide in early spring.

Calamagrostis x *acutiflora* 'Karl Foerster' ('Karl Foerster' feather reed grass) (Sara Williams)

Best Groundcovers & Vines For The Prairies

Campanula
kam-*pan*-ew-la
Bellflower

Bellflowers compose a large genus, many of which are useful as groundcovers.

Campanula is the Latin word for "little bell," a reference to the size and form of the flowers. The plants themselves are quite variable in height, ranging from 10 to 90 cm (4 to 36 in.).

How to Grow
Of easy culture, bellflowers do well in sun or shade in well-drained soil and benefit from division every few years. Propagate the species by seed or division during the growing season and the cultivars by division.

Campanula cochlearifolia (syn. *C. pusilla*)
kam-*pan*-ew-la coch-leer-ee-*fo*-lee-ah
Dwarf bellflower, fairy thimble

Plant at a Glance
Type: herbaceous perennial
Height/spread: 10 cm (4 in.) / 15 to 20 cm (6 to 8 in.)
Spacing: 20 cm (8 in.)
Light: full sun to shade
Soil: well drained
Distinguishing features: blue, bell-like flowers; tiny, tough tufts of foliage
Landscape use: rock garden; edging; lawn replacement; small, inaccessible, or inhospitable areas; pavement planting; unifying shrub beds; accentuating focal points
Propagation: seed; division

Everything about this groundcover is dainty and diminutive, yet its tiny flowers and foliage readily occupy the space made available to them, filling in around paving stones in a path or creeping

Campanula cochlearifolia (dwarf bellflower, fairy thimble) (Sara Williams)

into soil-filled rock crevices. And it's a lot tougher than it looks!

A true alpine, native to the mountains of Europe, *cochlearifolia* is Latin for "little spoon," alluding to the leaf shape. This rugged, mat-forming groundcover is on a scale suited to smaller areas of a garden. Its small, nodding, bell-shaped flowers, in blue or white, bloom in mid-summer on wiry stems. The foliage forms tufted rosettes above creeping rhizomes.

Cultivars

Although the species is widely grown and dependable on the prairies, some of the cultivars might do better in a more-protected microclimate.
- 'Alba' is white and probably as vigorous as the species, but not as hardy.
- 'Elizabeth Oliver' has double, blue flowers.
- 'Miranda' has pale, icy blue flowers.

Campanula glomerata
kam-*pan*-ew-la glom-er-*a*-ta
Clustered bellflower, Danesblood bellflower

Plant at a Glance
Type: herbaceous perennial
Height/spread: 30 to 60 cm (12 to 24 in.) / 45 cm (18 in.)
Spacing: 45 cm (18 in.)
Light: full sun
Soil: average
Distinguishing features: vivid purple flowers
Landscape use: small, inaccessible, or inhospitable areas; delineating space and defining property lines; breaking up large expanses of lawn; transition plantings; back lane plantings; directing foot traffic
Propagation: seed; division

Long-lived, vigorous, and dependable, the clustered bellflower quickly achieves presence, color, and mass as a mid-height groundcover. Both the botanical and common names refer to the fact that the flowers are formed in clusters atop their stems. Native from Britain through Europe and Siberia, it has been a denizen of prairie gardens for almost a century.

The violet-purple flowers form in dense clusters along the stem and in terminal heads in mid to late summer. The dark green leaves along the stem are ovate to lanceolate and 8 to 10 cm (3 to 4 in.) long; the basal leaves are more heart shaped. The roots can be invasive, making it more appropriate as a groundcover than in a manicured perennial border. For the perennial border, select the smaller version, *Campanula glomerata* var. *acaulis*, the dwarf clustered bellflower, which grows 15 to 25 cm (6 to 10 in.) tall, is almost stemless, and has violet-blue or white flowers. Adapted to a range of soils, the clustered bellflower does best in full sun. Divide every three or four years, and shear after flowering for a tidier appearance.

Cultivars
- 'Superba' reaches 50 to 75 cm (20 to 30 in.) and has more intense purple-violet flowers than those of the species.
- 'Superba Alba' is similar to 'Superba' but has white flowers.

Campanula persicifolia
kam-*pan*-ew-la per-si-ki-*fo*-lee-a
Peach-leaved bellflower

Plant at a Glance
Type: herbaceous perennial
Height/spread: 60 to 90 cm (24 to 36 in.) / 30 to 45 cm (12 to 18 in.)
Spacing: 45 cm (18 in.)
Light: full sun to partial shade
Soil: average
Distinguishing features: pure blue or white flowers; deep green foliage
Landscape use: perennial border; small, inaccessible, or inhospitable areas; delineating space and defining property lines; breaking up large expanses of lawn; shady understory
Propagation: seed; division

Nothing lightens and brightens a shaded area more than the intermingled duo of blue and white peach-leaved bellflowers. The well-respected British gardener and writer Graham Rice appraised this bellflower as "one of the finest of all perennials." Found in the Balkan Peninsula through Turkey and into Russia, it is long lasting and durable across the prairies.

As both the common and botanical names suggest, the foliage is similar to that of a peach, forming basal rosettes of lance-shaped, deep green leaves. The blue or white flowers, in loose, terminal racemes, are held on slender, erect stems well above the foliage and bloom in mid-summer. Branched, creeping rhizomes ensure its steady spread.

Peach-leaved bellflowers are easy to grow, doing well in sun or light shade in a range of soils with moderate moisture. Divide every few years.

Cultivars
- 'Alba', with white flowers, is the most robust and reliable cultivar.
- 'Alba Flore-pleno' has double, white flowers.
- 'Chettle Charm' has white flowers, edged in blue.
- 'Moerheimii' features semi-double, white flowers.
- 'Telham Beauty' bears 10 cm (4 in.), pale blue flowers on 90 cm (36 in.) stems.

Caragana arborescens 'Pendula'

kare-rah-*gah*-nah are-bore-*res*-sens
Weeping caragana

Plant at a Glance
Type: deciduous shrub
Height/spread: 90 cm (36 in.) / 90 cm (36 in.)
Spacing: 90 cm (36 in.)
Light: full sun to shade
Soil: well drained
Distinguishing features: twisted, gnarled, weeping form once mature
Landscape use: rock garden; slopes and banks; delineating space and defining property lines; breaking up large expanses of lawn; screening
Propagation: softwood or hardwood cuttings

Weeping caragana is almost always sold budded or grafted onto a standard, giving it an odd umbrella-like appearance. But it is best grown on its own roots, left to tumble down a hot, dry, inhospitable slope or a shady corner.

'Pendula' has pinnately compound leaves, with small leaflets similar to the caraganas of prairie shelterbelts. It also has the same green stems, spines, and yellow, pea-like flowers in June. The long pods that develop can be heard "popping" during the hot days of August. 'Pendula' differs from the species in its branch structure, which at maturity is heavy, weeping, and given to a dramatic twisted and gnarled appearance.

Native to Siberia and Mongolia, *Caragana arborescens* was once used for rope. The genus is from the Mongolian common name, *karaghan*, while *arborescens* means "treelike" or "woody" and refers to the species. *Pendula*, of course, means "weeping" and describes its form. 'Walker' ('Lorbergii' x 'Pendula'), 1.2 m (4 ft.) tall and 1 m (3.3 ft.) wide, has a similar trailing form to 'Pendula', but with finely divided foliage that is similar to an asparagus fern.

Caragana arborescens 'Walker' ('Walker' weeping caragana) on own roots in a rock garden. (Sara Williams)

How to Grow
Place 'Pendula' in full sun to full shade in well-drained soil. It is very drought tolerant once established. Propagate by taking softwood or hardwood cuttings.

Best Groundcovers & Vines For The Prairies

Other Species and Hybrids

- *Caragana pygmaea* (pig-*mee*-ah), pygmy caragana, is native to northwest China and Siberia and makes an excellent barrier planting. Its gray-green foliage is fine textured, each pinnately compound leaf consisting of four small leaflets. Pygmy caragana, 75 cm (30 in.) in both height and spread, has attractive flowers but also bears a profusion of spines. Its cultural demands (or lack thereof) are identical to other caragana species. Place it in an open, sunny situation where it is less susceptible to spider mites and its form can be appreciated. It is useful as a low barrier hedge or planted en masse.

Carex
kah-reks
Sedge

Carex is a very large genus of grass-like perennials. Most species grow in wet areas but some, like sun-loving sedge, grow on dry ground. Sedge stems are three-sided and solid, with leaves arising in threes. The flowers are always unisexual and plants may be monoecious or dioecious. *Carex* is the classical Latin name for the genus. It is derived from the Greek word *kairo*, "to cut," which describes the sharp leaf margins of some of the species.

How to Grow

Sedges have varying cultural requirements. Native to the moist meadows of North America, including parts of Manitoba, palm sedge is ideal for consistently moist areas in full sun to partial shade in soil that is well amended with organic matter. However, it is also quite drought tolerant in clay soil. Sun-loving sedge prefers a well-drained, sunny location but tolerates some shade. Propagate sedges by division in spring or mid-summer.

Carex muskingumensis
kah-reks mus-kin-gum-*en*-sis
Palm sedge

Plant at a Glance
Type: ornamental grass
Height/spread: 60 cm (24 in.) / 30 cm (12 in.)
Spacing: 30 cm (12 in.)
Light: full sun to partial shade
Soil: evenly moist; rich in organic matter
Distinguishing features: narrow, arching, light green foliage
Landscape use: edging; waterside plantings; accentuating focal points
Propagation: division

Typical of sedges, the stems of palm sedge are three-sided, with narrow, arching, green leaves growing at right angles to them. Small spikes of beige flowers are produced in early to mid summer. The plants spread slowly by creeping rhizomes.

The specific epithet, *muskingumensis*, comes from the Muskingum River that begins in Ohio and flows into Pennsylvania, a part of this plant's natural range. The common name is from the resemblance of its foliage to that of a palm.

Carex muskingumensis (palm sedge) (Sara Williams)

Carex pennsylvanica
kah-reks pen-sil-*van*-ih-ka
Sun-loving sedge

Plant at a Glance
Type: ornamental grass
Height/spread: 10 to 40 cm (4 to 16 in.) / 30 cm (12 in.)
Spacing: 15 cm (6 in.)
Light: full sun
Soil: well drained
Distinguishing features: grassy foliage
Landscape use: lawn replacement; small, inaccessible, or inhospitable areas; slopes and banks
Propagation: division

Sun-loving sedge is a native, grass-like plant that spreads by stolons to form a dense mat of foliage on coarse, dry soils. Staminate flowers are produced on a short, terminal spike, with pistillate flowers in one to four short spikes below the staminate spike on the stem. The species is quite variable. Selected forms serve well as a non-mowed lawn alternative, particularly on slopes.

When is Grass not Grass? When It's a Sedge

Sedges are plants that on first impression look like grasses. However, close examination reveals key differences between these two related plant families.

- The stems of grass are usually hollow, while those of sedge are usually solid.
- The leaves of grass usually arise in pairs, while those of sedge arise in threes.
- The leaf sheaths of grass are split, while those of sedge are not.
- Most sedges grow in wet soils but there are exceptions, like sun-loving sedge, that thrive in dry soils. They are generally difficult to grow from seed and are propagated by division.

Cerastium tomentosum
ser-*as*-ti-um to-men-*to*-sum
Snow-in-summer

Plant at a Glance
Type: herbaceous perennial
Height/spread: 15 to 30 cm (6 to 12 in.) / 45 cm (18 in.)
Spacing: 45 cm (18 in.)
Light: full sun
Soil: well drained
Distinguishing features: pure white flowers; low, woolly, silver foliage
Landscape use: perennial or mixed border; rock garden; lawn replacement; small, inaccessible, or inhospitable areas; slopes and banks; unifying shrub beds; back lane plantings; pavement plantings; accentuating focal points; over walls
Propagation: seed; division; cuttings

As gardeners, we often have unspoken contempt for the easy or familiar. Snow-in-summer is one such easy and commonly available perennial groundcover. But why should we dismiss it because of these virtues? It fills a variety of niches in our landscape, grows readily from seed, and has attractive flowers and foliage.

Cerastium tomentosum and *Thymus serpyllum* (Lesley Reynolds)

The characteristic giving rise to the genus name is not immediately apparent. *Cerastium* is from the Greek word *keros*, meaning "horn," and refers to the shape of the seed capsules. The reason for the specific epithet is more obvious. The Latin word *tomentosum* means "woolly" or "covered in soft hairs," which describes the silver hairs on its leaves and stems. Although native to Italy and Sicily, this old-fashioned heritage plant was available to prairie gardeners prior to World War I.

The tiny, white flowers, each of which has five notched petals, are carried on 20 to 30 cm (10 to 14 in.) stems and bloom for four to six weeks in late spring to early summer. The equally small leaves are silver and oblong, about 2.5 cm (1 in.) long, and are held on freely branching, prostrate stems. Snow-in-summer soon forms thick mats, spreading by creeping roots.

How to Grow
Plant snow-in-summer in full sun in well-drained soil. It is very drought tolerant once established. Easy to grow from seed, it can also be propagated by cuttings or division in spring.

Chelone obliqua
chel-*oh*-nee o-*blee*-kwa
Pink turtlehead

Plant at a Glance
Type: herbaceous perennial
Height/spread: 60 to 75 (24 to 30 in.) / 60 to 90 cm (24 to 36 in.)
Spacing: 45 cm (18 in.)
Light: full sun to partial shade
Soil: evenly moist; rich in organic matter
Distinguishing features: pink flowers that look like a turtle's head
Landscape use: waterside plantings; small, inaccessible, or inhospitable areas; accentuating focal points; shady understory
Propagation: seed; division

Pink turtlehead is not commonly seen in prairie gardens and seldom used as a groundcover—but it should be. It's

Chelone obliqua (pink turtlehead)
(Sara Williams)

hardy, long-lived, long blooming, and easy to maintain and it adapts to full sun or partial shade.

One has only to look at the flower to understand the derivation of both the common name and the genus. *Chelone* is the Greek word for "tortoise," and it does indeed resemble a turtle. The species name, *obliqua*, means "lopsided," a possible reference to the irregular, two-lipped flowers.

Although native to eastern North America, pink turtlehead has found a niche in prairie landscapes in woodland gardens, beside streams and ponds, and in bog gardens. As long as the site is reasonably moist, it feels at home. The fibrous root system is rhizomatous. Like hostas, turtleheads are late to emerge from the soil in spring, but soon form dense, upright clumps. The glossy, rose-pink flowers are two-lipped and about 2 cm (1 in.) long; they bloom in summer for about six weeks. There is also a white-flowered form called 'Alba'. The attractive dark green leaves are simple, opposite, and toothed.

How to Grow
Plant pink turtlehead in evenly moist soil in sun or shade. Pinch young shoots in spring for denser growth. Turtleheads can be grown from seed or division.

Other Species and Hybrids
- *Chelone glabra* (*gla*-bra), white turtlehead, grows 60 to 90 cm (24 to 36 in.) tall.
- *Chelone lyonii* (lie-*on*-ee-ee), also known as pink turtlehead, is adapted to average garden conditions. It is similar to *C. obliqua* but has coarsely toothed foliage.

Chrysanthemum zawadskii, subsp. *zawadskii* 'Clara Curtis' (syn. *Chrysanthemum* x *rubellum*)
kris-*an*-them-um zah-*wad*-ski-i
'Clara Curtis' chrysanthemum

Plant at a Glance
Type: herbaceous perennial
Height/spread: 60 to 75 cm (24 to 30 in) / 60 to 90 cm (24 to 36 in.)
Spacing: 60 cm (24 in.)
Light: full sun
Soil: average; well drained
Distinguishing features: single, pink, daisy-like flowers
Landscape use: perennial and mixed borders; small, inaccessible, or inhospitable areas; delineating space and defining property lines; breaking up large expanses of lawn
Propagation: division

Dendranthema zawadskii
(Clara Curtis chrysanthemum)
(Sara Williams)

'Clara Curtis' is one of the few chrysanthemums that are truly hardy on the prairies, but she remains sadly underused and should be much more widely available. Although its namesake remains a mystery, the plant seems to be a hybrid of *Chrysanthemum zawadskii* and *C. yezoense*, which was found in the public gardens of Llandudno, Wales, in 1929. It was introduced by Perry's Nursery in 1937. The species from which 'Clara Curtis' was hybridized are native to large areas of Europe and Asia.

It should be noted that the botanical name of the genus has recently changed. What for years was a *Chrysanthemum* became a *Dendranthema*, from the Greek words *dendron*, meaning "tree," and *antheon,* "a flower," alluding to the woody flower stems. It has now reverted to *Chrysanthemum.*

'Clara Curtis' forms a clump of branched stems, woody at the base, as the new genus name suggests. The single, pink, daisy-like flowers are about 5 to 8 cm (2 to 3 in.) in diameter, with a raised yellow center, and are formed in terminal heads in late summer to fall, when they bloom for six weeks or more. The foliage is much divided and deeply lobed. The fibrous root system forms runners rather than remaining in a tight clump, giving it an advantage as a groundcover.

How to Grow
'Clara Curtis' is an undemanding perennial, requiring only full sun and average, well-drained soil. Pinch for denser growth in early summer if the spirit moves you. Divide it when you require more plants or when it becomes less vigorous due to overcrowding.

Convallaria majalis
kon-va-*lah*-ree-a mah-*jah*-lis
Lily-of-the-valley

Plant at a Glance
Type: herbaceous perennial
Height/spread: 15 cm (6 in.) / 30 cm (12 in.) to indefinite
Spacing: 20 cm (8 in.)
Light: partial shade to full shade
Soil: moist; rich in organic matter
Distinguishing features: fragrant, bell-shaped flowers; strap-shaped leaves

Best Groundcovers & Vines For The Prairies

Landscape use: lawn replacement; small, inaccessible, or inhospitable areas; breaking up large expanses of lawn; back lane plantings; accentuating focal points; shady understory
Propagation: division

Convallaria majalis (lily-of-the-valley) (Sara Williams)

As its common name suggests, lily-of-the-valley is a member of the lily family. The genus name *Convallaria* means "of the valley," while the species name, *majalis*, "of May," refers to the plant's spring-bloom time. The dark green, strap-shaped leaves are 10 to 20 cm (4 to 8 in.) long and 2.5 to 8 cm (1 to 3 in.) wide. Plants spread by thin underground rhizomes that form a dense, turf-like groundcover in favorable conditions. From each pair of leaves, a stem arises, holding a raceme of several fragrant, white, bell-shaped flowers, about 7.5 mm (0.3 in.) across. The cultivar 'Rosea' bears light pink blooms. Flowers are followed by three-celled, red berries with a few seeds.

Lily-of-the-valley is an ideal groundcover for shady spots beside buildings or under trees.

How to Grow

Lily-of-the-valley prefers moist, organically rich soil and grows best in partial shade to full shade. It is easily propagated by transplanting "pips" (rhizome pieces with a bud) in early spring. In favorable locations, it thrives with very little attention once established.

Cornus canadensis
kor-nus can-a-*den*-sis
Bunchberry, dwarf dogwood

Plant at a Glance
Type: evergreen perennial
Height/spread: 15 cm (6 in.) / 20 cm (8 in.)
Spacing: 15 cm (6 in.)
Light: partial shade to shade
Soil: moist; rich in organic matter
Distinguishing features: white floral bracts; evergreen foliage; red berries
Landscape use: shady understory
Propagation: division

Bunchberry is a common understory plant of the Canadian boreal forest. *Cornus*, from the Latin for "horn," refers to the hard wood of woody species in the genus, while the species name, *canadensis*, refers to part of its native range. The compound leaves of bunchberry rise about 15 cm (6 in.) from an underground woody, creeping rootstock. Flowering stems have six elliptical leaflets, while non-flowering stems have four. Clusters of tiny, greenish flowers are surrounded by four to six showy white bracts that appear as a single showy flower. These develop into clusters of red berries that have been used as an emergency food source and medicine by Aboriginal peoples of Canada. The foliage turns reddish in the fall and persists over winter until new foliage emerges in the spring. Bunchberry forms an attractive groundcover over large areas in moist, shaded situations that are similar to its favored native habitat.

How to Grow
Bunchberry grows well with other low-growing, woodland groundcovers. Some garden writers believe it requires acid soil, but on the prairies, it grows on lime-based, well-drained soils, rich in organic matter and supplied with adequate moisture. Bunchberry is difficult to germinate, so propagation is best accomplished by transplanting rhizomes or pieces of sod that include rhizomes in early spring.

Coronilla varia
ko-ro-*nil*-la *var*-ee-ah
Crown vetch

Plant at a Glance
Type: herbaceous perennial
Height/spread: 30 to 60 cm (12 to 24 in.) / 90 cm (36 in.)
Spacing: 30 to 60 cm (12 to 24 in.)
Light: full sun to shade
Soil: well drained
Distinguishing features: pale pink flower clusters; delicate foliage
Landscape use: small, inaccessible, or inhospitable areas; slopes and banks; back lane plantings
Propagation: seed; division; cuttings

Crown vetch is an aggressive legume that is effective when mixed with grasses for soil stabilization on well-drained slopes. The genus name *Coronilla* is Latin for "little crown" and refers to the radial form of the flower cluster. The species name *varia* refers to the varied colors of the flowers on a single plant, from near white to deep pink. The pinnately compound leaves are formed from eleven to twenty-five oval or oblong leaflets, each 1.5 to 2 cm (0.5 to 0.8 in.) long. The pea-like flowers appear from late June until frost.

Best Groundcovers & Vines For The Prairies

Coronilla varia (crown vetch) (Hugh Skinner)

Crown vetch spreads aggressively by underground rhizomes and is useful for erosion control on steep rocky or sandy slopes. However, this rampant growth habit makes it unsuitable for more-refined garden situations, such as perennial borders, where it can become a difficult weed.

How to Grow
Crown vetch thrives on well-drained soils in full sun but also tolerates shade. It can be propagated from seed, by cuttings, or by root divisions in spring. Soak seed overnight in water before sowing.

Cotoneaster horizontalis 'Perpusillus'
cuh-toe-nee-*ass*-ter hor-ri-zon-*tahl*-lis
Ground cotoneaster

Plant at a Glance
Type: deciduous shrub
Height/spread: 15 cm (6 in.) / 90 cm (36 in.)
Spacing: 50 cm (20 in.)
Light: full sun to partial shade
Soil: well drained
Distinguishing features: small, dark green leaves; red berries
Landscape use: rock garden; over walls; small, inaccessible, or inhospitable areas; slopes or banks; accentuating focal points
Propagation: layering; softwood cuttings

Ground cotoneaster is a low-growing shrub, with small, round to oval leaves that are leathery and may be semi-evergreen. *Cotoneaster* is Latin for "resembling quince," while *horizontalis* refers to the plant's habit of spreading along the

Cotoneaster adpressus (creeping cotoneaster)
(Sara Williams)

ground, often rooting where branches touch the soil. 'Perpusillus' means "exceptionally small." The branches of this plant grow in an interesting herringbone pattern. If used as a groundcover, plants should be set about 50 cm (20 in.) apart to achieve cover within a reasonable time. Ground cotoneaster can be an exceptionally beautiful groundcover on a slope or planted where it can cascade over a wall.

How to Grow
Plant ground cotoneaster in full sun to partial shade in well-drained soil. It has a sparse root system and is best transplanted as a container-grown plant. Encourage dense growth by pruning back the ends of branches in the first two or three years after planting. The species is difficult to grow from seed, but softwood cuttings will root quite readily in early summer. It may also be propagated by layering.

Other Species and Hybrids
- *Cotoneaster adpressus* (ad-*pres*-us), creeping cotoneaster, has dull green leaves that are pubescent on the underside when young. It grows to 30 cm (24 in.) tall.
- *Cotoneaster adpressus* var. *praecox* (*prie*-koks), Nan Shan cotoneaster, is a taller form, from 50 to 80 cm (20 to 32 in.) tall, which is occasionally available from prairie nurseries. This variety is winter hardy only in the most favorable locations on the prairies.

Cytisus decumbens
sy-*tis*-iss day-*kum*-benz
Prostrate broom

Plant at a Glance
Type: deciduous shrub
Height/spread: 10 cm (4 in.) / 50 cm (20 in.)
Spacing: 30 cm (12 in.)
Light: full sun
Soil: well drained; lean
Distinguishing features: abundant yellow, pea-like flowers; tiny, dark green leaves on green stems

Landscape use: mixed border; rock garden; slopes and banks; delineating space and defining property lines
Propagation: softwood cuttings

Cytisus is an ancient Greek name for a type of clover; *decumbens* refers to the plant's habit of lying on the ground with its stem tips ascending. Prostrate broom increases in height only as its grayish green stems grow over top of one another. Tiny, oval, simple leaves are sessile along the branches and have fine, silky hairs on the underside. Small, yellow, pea-like flowers cover the plant in a spectacular show in late spring. It is a useful groundcover on well-drained sunny slopes and in rock garden plantings.

How to Grow
Prostrate broom needs very good drainage. Because it is difficult to transplant, it is best to purchase container-grown plants or propagate it by softwood cuttings.

Other Species and Hybrids
- *Cytisus purpurea* var. *procumbens* (purr-purr-*ree*-ah var. pro-*kum*-benz), dwarf purple broom, is an arching plant that has compound leaves with three leaflets. The slender, green stems form a dense clump up to 30 cm (12 in.) wide. One to three purple, pea-like flowers, 2 cm (0.8 in.) long, are produced in spring at each leaf axil of the previous year's wood. Plants can be managed for maximum bloom by pruning stems back immediately after blooming. Excellent drainage is necessary for these plants to thrive.

Cytisus decumbens (golden broom) (Hugh Skinner)

Dianthus gratianopolitanus
die-*anth*-us grah-tee-ah-no-po-li-*tah*-nus
Cheddar pinks

Plant at a Glance
Type: evergreen perennial
Height/spread: 15 cm (6 in.) / 30 cm (12 in.)
Spacing: 20 cm (8 in.)
Light: full sun
Soil: well drained
Distinguishing features: fragrant, pink flowers; bluish grassy foliage
Landscape use: mixed or perennial border; rock garden; lawn replacement; small, inaccessible, or inhospitable areas; unifying shrub beds; pavement planting
Propagation: seed; cultivars by cuttings or divisions

With its Greek name meaning "Jove's flower," the genus *Dianthus* holds an exalted position in the plant kingdom. The species name *gratianopolitanus* indicates its origin near Grenoble, France, while the common name arises from another part of its native range, the Cheddar Gorge in Somersetshire in southwest England, also known for its cheese. The evergreen, grass-like foliage is glaucous bluish green and forms a dense, matted clump topped with fragrant, medium rose-pink flowers about 2.5 cm (1 in.) in diameter. The cultivar 'Tiny Rubies' is smaller in all aspects than the species and bears numerous double flowers, 1 cm (0.4 in.) across, for most of the summer. Cheddar pinks are an effective drought-tolerant groundcover for the front of a border or in a rock garden.

Dianthus gratianopolitanus 'Tiny Rubies'
('Tiny Rubies' Cheddar pinks) (Sara Williams)

How to Grow
Dianthus grow best in full sun in well-drained soils that are high in lime (not a problem in most prairie gardens), but even perennial types may die out periodically. The chances of survival are increased by covering the bed with evergreen boughs in late fall to hold snow. Fungal and bacterial wilts and mosaic viruses can cause the

demise of *Dianthus* plants. Careful sanitation of propagation tools and control of sucking insects such as aphids and thrips help to keep plants healthy.

Dianthus species are easy to grow from seed, but the more desirable cultivars are propagated by dividing plants in early spring or by rooting cuttings in the summer.

Other Species and Hybrids
- *Dianthus deltoides* (del-*toi*-deez), maiden pinks, have pink or red flowers above dense mats of dark green foliage. These species usually survive in prairie gardens but may succumb to winter conditions some years. Maiden pinks are easy to grow from seed and will self-seed in the garden.
- *Dianthus plumarius* (ploo-*mah*-ree-us), cottage pinks, have gray-green foliage and flower stems from 30 to 50 cm (12 to 20 in.) tall. The clove-scented flowers vary in color from white to deep pink, usually with a darker eye. Cottage pinks grow easily from seed, but double-flowered cultivars are propagated by cuttings.

Diervilla lonicera
dee-er-*vil*-la lon-*niss*-ur-uh
Diervilla, dwarf bush honeysuckle

Plant at a Glance
Type: deciduous shrub
Height/spread: 1.2 m (4 ft.) / 1.2 m (4 ft.)
Spacing: 1.2 m (4 ft.)
Light: full sun to shade
Soil: average
Distinguishing features: glossy foliage
Landscape use: mass plantings, slopes and banks; delineating space and defining property lines; breaking up large expanses of lawn; transition plantings; barrier plantings; screening; shady understory
Propagation: suckers

Diervilla lonicera (diervilla, dwarf bush honeysuckle) (Sara Williams)

Although native to the boreal forest on the eastern edge of the prairies, diervilla has only recently become generally available in prairie garden centers. A little over a meter (about 4 ft.) in height, with an equal spread, its suckering habit makes it ideal as a groundcover for mass plantings, on slopes, and as an understory.

The plant is named after Dr. N. Dierville, a French surgeon and plant collector who introduced it to Europe in 1700. The specific epithet, *lonicera*, indicates its close relationship to honeysuckle. The new spring foliage is a metallic bronze-green that becomes glossy green by mid-summer and turns reddish in the fall. The opposite leaves are oval and finely toothed. In mid-summer, small, tubular, two-lipped, yellow flowers are produced in axillary and terminal clusters.

How to Grow
Diervilla grows in sun or shade in almost any soil, gradually increasing in diameter through suckering. Once established, it is fairly drought tolerant and even grows in dry shade. To propagate, remove and replant the suckers in spring.

Dracocephalum grandiflorum
dra-ko-*sef*-a-lum gran-di-*flo*-rum
Bigflower dragonhead

Plant at a Glance
Type: herbaceous perennial
Height/spread: 30 cm (12 in.) / 30 cm (12 in.)
Spacing: 20 to 30 cm (8 to 12 in.)
Light: full sun to partial shade
Soil: moist; well drained
Distinguishing features: showy two-lipped, blue flowers atop square stems
Landscape use: perennial border; rock garden; edging; mass planting; small, inaccessible, or inhospitable areas; slopes and banks
Propagation: seed; division

The genus name of these Siberian members of the mint family is Greek for "dragon's head." Like the common name, this refers to the two-lipped flowers. The opposite, oval leaves are medium green, conspicuously veined, and notched on square stems. The 5 cm (2 in.) long, blue flowers are borne on short spikes in June and early July. The flowers are striking in color and very showy in a mass planting.

How to Grow
For best results, plant dragonhead at the front of a border, in sun or partial shade. It prefers well-drained soil, supplied with copious moisture. Propagate dragonhead from seeds or by division in the spring.

Other Species and Hybrids
- *Dracocephalum ruyschianum* (riesh-ee-*ah*-num), Russian dragonhead, grows to 60 cm (24 in.) high and has narrow, linear leaves and spikes of bright azure blue flowers in late summer.
- *Dracocephalum sibericum* (si-*beer*-i-cum) 'Souvenir d'Andre Chaudron' (syn. 'Blue Beauty') (syn. *Nepeta siberica* 'Souvenir d'Andre Chaudron') grows to 80 cm (32 in.) and is graced with medium blue flowers for most of the summer.

Dryas octopetala
dri-as ok-to-*pet*-a-la
Mountain avens

Plant at a Glance
Type: evergreen sub-shrub
Height/spread: 10 cm (4 in.) / 60 cm (24 in.)
Spacing: 30 cm (12 in.)
Light: full sun
Soil: well drained
Distinguishing features: creamy white flowers; dark green, evergreen foliage
Landscape use: rock garden; lawn replacement; small, inaccessible, or inhospitable areas; slopes and banks
Propagation: seed; division; layering; cuttings

Mountain avens is a member of the rose family and has a circumpolar distribution at high altitudes. *Dryas* is from a Greek word meaning "wood nymph," while the specific name, *octopetala*, refers to the eight petals of the white flowers that rise singly on stems above the dense mats of foliage. The dark evergreen leaves are about 1 cm (0.4 in.) long and look like miniature oak leaves. Roots grow where the creeping, woody stems touch the ground and provide excellent bank stabilization. It can also be planted on a slope in a sunny rock garden.

How to Grow
Grow mountain avens in sunny, well-drained situations. It can be propagated from seed, but more often is grown by transplanting divisions or layers in early spring or from cuttings in summer. Stems will root where partially covered by sandy soil.

Other Species and Hybrids
- *Dryas drummondii* (dru-*mond*-ee-ee), Drummond avens, has nodding, yellow flowers that remain closed. It is native to the Rocky Mountains, where it forms large, green mats on gravel scree.

- *Dryas* x *suendermannii* (soon-der-*mahn*-ee-ee), Suendermann avens, is intermediate in flower characteristics and form between the preceding two species. Its flowers open yellow and fade to white; it is also native to the Rocky Mountains.

Elymus arenarius (syn. *Leymus arenarius*)
ee-*li*-mus a-ray-*nahr*-ee-us
Blue lyme grass

Plant at a Glance
Type: ornamental grass
Height/spread: 2 m (6.5 ft.) / 3 m (10 ft.)
Spacing: 2 m (6.5 ft.)
Light: full sun to partial shade
Soil: well drained
Distinguishing features: wide, glaucous blue foliage; tall seed heads
Landscape use: accent plant; mass plantings; slopes and banks; transition plantings
Propagation: division

Blue lyme grass is native to the sand dunes of coastal Europe and its job description is to hold them in place. The genus name is from *elymos*, the Greek word for "millet," while *arenarius* means "growing in sandy places." Given space and left to its own devices, blue lyme grass soon grows into a massive but somewhat irregular clump. The flat leaves are a glaucous blue, 2.5 to 5 cm (1 to 2 in.) wide and 90 to 120 cm (36 to 48 in.) long. The beige flower spikes are tall, narrow, and often reach 2 m (6.5 ft.) or more. This plant can be an absolute attention grabber. The rhizomatous root system spreads through suckering.

Despite its aggressive nature, blue lyme grass was a favorite of Gertrude Jekyll, the famous English garden designer, although her gardeners must have hated it. Placed in a herbaceous border, it only brings grief. The location of this plant is critical, so remember

Elymus arenarius (blue lyme grass) (Sara Williams)

Best Groundcovers & Vines For The Prairies

its origins. Use it as a groundcover to control erosion or as an ever-expanding accent in difficult situations, such as a hot, dry slope or bank.

How to Grow
A warm-season grass, it is extremely drought tolerant and is not slowed by our hot, dry prairie summers. Grow in full sun to light shade on well-drained soils. Propagate through division.

Erigeron speciosus
e-*ri*-ge-ron spee-see-*o*-sus
Oregon fleabane

Plant at a Glance
Type: herbaceous perennial
Height/spread: 50 to 60 cm (20 to 24 in.) / 30 to 60 cm (12 to 24 in.)
Spacing: 45 cm (18 in.)
Light: full sun to partial shade
Soil: well drained; average
Distinguishing features: pastel, daisy-like flowers, with yellow centers
Landscape use: perennial or mixed border; rock garden; small, inaccessible, or inhospitable areas; delineating space and defining property lines; breaking up large expanses of lawn
Propagation: division

Erigeron speciosus is native to the foothills region of southwest Alberta but is seldom found in gardens or garden centers. However, it has been used extensively in breeding and about a half-dozen selections and hybrids of fleabane are readily available.

The genus name is from the Greek words *geron*, "old man," and *eri,* meaning "early," and describes the fluffy, white seed heads. The species name, *speciosus*, means "showy," a reference to the flowers. The entire plant, when crushed, has long been used as an insect repellent, thus, the common name.

Fleabane has a bushy, branched habit

Erigeron speciosus (Oregon fleabane) (Sara Williams)

and daisy-like flowers, 4 cm (1.5 in.) in diameter, in mid-summer. The flowers are pink, mauve, blue, or purple, with yellow centers. Although some lance-shaped leaves are found alternately on the stems, most are basal in neat clumps.

How to Grow
Plant fleabane in full sun to light shade in average, well-drained soil. In overly rich soil, the stems become weak and floppy. Shear plants after they have finished blooming, and divide every three or four years. Except where noted, most cultivars are propagated by division in spring.

Cultivars
- 'Azure Beauty' and 'Azure Fairy' are seed-propagated. Both have semi-double, lavender-blue flowers and are 60 to 75 cm (24 to 30 in.) tall.
- 'Double Beauty' has double, light blue flowers and is 45 cm (18 in.).
- 'Pink Jewel', although variable from seed, is more compact, with single, bright lavender-pink flowers.
- 'Prosperity' has single, mauve-blue flowers and grows to 45 cm (18 in.).
- 'Quakeress' has pink flowers.

Euonymus nanus var. *turkestanicus*
yew-*on*-im-us *nan*-nus tur-kes-*tahn*-i-kus
Dwarf Turkestan burning bush

Plant at a Glance
Type: semi-evergreen or deciduous shrub
Height/spread: 1.5 m (5 ft.) / 1.5 m (5 ft.)
Spacing: 1.5 m (5 ft.)
Light: shade
Soil: moist; well drained
Distinguishing features: pink-red seed pods; red fall foliage
Landscape use: slopes and banks; delineating space and defining property lines; breaking up large expanses of lawn; directing foot traffic; barrier plantings; shady understory
Propagation: suckers; softwood cuttings

The dwarf Turkestan burning bush is grown primarily for its attractive multiple-season foliage and bright two-tone seed capsules. The small, narrow leaves emerge blue-green in the spring, lose a bit of their blue through the summer, and turn a brilliant red in the fall. Although the small flowers are green and inconspicuous, they are followed by pink seed capsules that split open to expose bright orange-red seeds.

Upright but some-what sprawling and informal of habit, burning bush is characterized by thin stems, green bark, and an amazing ability to spread by layering (stems that root as they come into contact with the soil). The root system is shallow and fibrous.

Euonymus nanus var. *Turkestanicus* (dwarf burning bush) (Brian Baldwin)

Native from the Caucasus Mountains to western China, *Euonymus* derives its name from Latin words meaning "of good name." In this case, the phrase is applied ironically as this plant is poisonous to some animals.

How to Grow

Burning bush performs best in light shade in moist, well-drained soil, but it can be grown in sun and is much more drought tolerant than generally believed. It is most easily propagated by suckers, but does grow from softwood cuttings.

Other Species and Hybrids

- *Euonymus nanus*, dwarf narrow-leafed burning bush, is a beautiful low, evergreen groundcover for shade. It is only 20 to 30 cm (8 to 12 in.) tall, but otherwise it is similar to *E. nanus* var. *turkestanicus*, with the same attractive foliage and seed pods. It creeps along the ground and can be mowed to form a lovely evergreen groundcover under trees.

Eupatorium maculatum (syn. *E. purpureum*, *E. purpureum* subsp. *maculatum*)

yew-pa-*tor*-ee-um mak-yew-*lah*-tum
Joe Pye weed, boneset

Plant at a Glance

Type: herbaceous perennial
Height/spread: 2 m (6.5 ft.) / 1 m (3.3 ft.)
Spacing: 1 m (3.3 ft.)
Light: full sun to partial shade
Soil: moist; rich in organic matter
Distinguishing features: architectural plant, with soft pink flowers
Landscape use: waterside plantings; naturalizing; delineating space and

Why Joe Pye?

Eupatorium maculatum is native to both eastern North America and Europe, and its nomenclature also reflects stories from both sides of the Atlantic. The genus was named to honor King Eupator (136–63 BC) who lived near the Black Sea and used the plant as an antidote for poison. The European species has long been associated with folk medicine. The specific epithet, *maculatum*, is the Latin word for "spotted" and describes the purple spots of the stem.

The common name, Joe Pye weed, honors an Indian living near the Massachusetts Bay Company in the late 1600s. He is said to have cured early colonists of typhoid fever using a tea brewed with the leaves of this plant. The other common name, boneset, also commemorates its use in traditional medicine for healing.

defining property lines; breaking up large expanses of lawn; directing foot traffic; screening

Propagation:
seed; division; cuttings

Groundcovers cover ground, but they don't have to be short. At over 2 m (6.5 ft.), Joe Pye weed is an architectural plant that is useful for naturalizing in large, moist areas in more-extensive landscapes. As the well-known British gardener Graham Rice wrote, "For so substantial a plant to have such a quiet presence in the autumn garden is something of a blessing." Given sufficient space and adequate moisture, Joe Pye weed spreads quickly by rhizomes to form large, erect clumps of tall plants, bearing soft, puffy, pink flowers from late July through September. The flat-topped corymbs are 15 to 20 cm (6 to 8 in.) in diameter and composed of many small, tubular florets. The simple, dark green, lance-shaped leaves are 8 to 15 cm (3 to 6 in.) long and produced in whorls of four to five.

How to Grow
Plant Joe Pye weed in full sun or light shade in moist soil. It is propagated most easily through division in spring.

Eupatorium maculatum (Joe Pye weed) (Sara Williams)

Best Groundcovers & Vines For The Prairies

Cultivars
- 'Atropurpureum' has wine red flowers, purple leaf veins, and solid purple-red stems.
- 'Gateway' is more compact, at 1.2 to 1.5 m (4 to 5 ft.) in height, and has wine-red stems.

Other Species and Hybrids
- *Eupatorium purpureum*, native to eastern and central North America, is slightly less hardy than *E. maculatum*.

Euphorbia cyparissias
yew-*for*-bee-uh si-par-*iss*-i-as
Cypress spurge

Plant at a Glance
Type: semi-evergreen perennial
Height/spread: 25 cm (10 in.) / 50 cm (20 in.)
Spacing: 30 cm (12 in.)
Light: full sun to shade
Soil: well drained; lean
Distinguishing features: chartreuse spring bracts; attractive needle-like foliage
Landscape use: naturalizing; small, inaccessible, or inhospitable areas; slopes and banks; back lane plantings
Propagation: division; cuttings

The chief value of Cypress spurge is as a groundcover in hot, dry situations on poor soils where little else will thrive, particularly on dry banks or slopes. Don't be duped by its delicate filigree appearance—it has the constitution of a Mack truck and its weed potential is enormous. It can easily get out of hand, spreading rapaciously by seed, creeping rootstocks, and underground stolons, so it behooves the gardener to select its location with care.

The genus is named after Euphorbus, a first-century physician in ancient Mauritania, North Africa, who appreciated its medicinal value. It was once used as a cosmetic in Ukraine—because the latex of many species is toxic, it causes skin irritations and when applied to the cheeks, it acts like rouge, causing a rosy glow. Both Cypress and *cyparissias* refer to its foliage, which is thought to resemble a cypress tree. The common name, spurge, is from the Latin word *expurgare*, meaning "to cleanse" or "to purge," another reference to its ancient medicinal use.

Like other *Euphorbia*, the so-called "flowers" are actually highly colored bracts similar to those of a poinsettia. Yellow, with a noticeable red tinge, they appear from late spring to mid-summer. The real flowers are an inconspicuous greenish yellow color, with neither sepals nor petals. The foliage has a milky sap and is generally considered poisonous. The small, needle-like leaves, a delicate, fresh green in color, are formed in whorls along the stem.

How to Grow
Native to areas of sandy soil on the Alps Mountains of Europe, Cypress spurge is equally at home in sun or shade and in moist or dry situations. Propagate by division at any time during the growing season.

Festuca glauca
(syn. *F. ovina* var. *glauca, F. cinerea* var. *glauca*)
fes-*tu*-kah *gla*-kah
Blue fescue

Plant at a Glance
Type: ornamental grass
Height/spread: 10 to 20 cm (4 to 8 in.) / 30 cm (12 in.)
Spacing: 25 cm (10 in.)
Light: full sun to partial shade
Soil: well drained
Distinguishing features: neat tufts of narrow, blue foliage
Landscape use: perennial or mixed border; rock garden; edging; small, inaccessible, or inhospitable areas; breaking up large expanses of lawn; pavement planting; accentuating focal points
Propagation: division

Many cultivars of blue fescue are relatively short-lived, making them ineffective as groundcovers, but 'Skinner's Blue' seems to have the required durability. It forms a neat, tufted, dense clump of fine-textured, blue grass, 15 to 20 cm (6 to 8 in.) in height. Attractive panicles of golden flowers complement the glaucous foliage in June. Extremely hardy, it is the preferred selection in the prairie provinces.

Festuca is native to Eurasia; the name derives from the Latin word for "grass stalk."

Festuca glauca (blue fescue) (Sara Williams)

Best Groundcovers & Vines For The Prairies

Like other blue fescues, 'Skinner's Blue' is well behaved, staying within its clumps and never invasive. Yet one seldom finds weeds in the bare soil between the clumps. Most fescues release an exudate from their roots containing allelopathic compounds that inhibit the germination of seeds within their root space. From the fescue's point of view, it means reduced competition from other plants for space, sunlight, nutrients, and moisture. From the gardener's, it means little or no weeding.

In the search for alternative methods of weed control, there is ongoing research into the allelopathic properties of other plants such as thyme (*Thymus* spp.), snow-in-summer (*Cerastium tomentosum*), lily-of-the-valley (*Convallaria majalis*), artemisia (*Artemisia* spp.), and barren strawberry (*Waldsteinia ternata*).

The word *glauca* refers to the waxy bloom, or coating, responsible for its blue color.

How to Grow

Very drought tolerant once established, blue fescue requires only well-drained soil in full sun or light shade. Propagate through division in spring.

Filipendula ulmaria 'Flora Plena'
fil-i-*pen*-dew-la ul-*mare*-e-ah
European meadowsweet

Plant at a Glance
Type: herbaceous perennial
Height/spread: 90 to 120 cm (36 to 48 in.) / 60 to 90 cm (24 to 36 in.)
Spacing: 60 cm (24 in.)
Light: full sun to partial shade
Soil: evenly moist; rich in organic matter
Distinguishing features: architectural plant, with puffy, pink or white flower heads
Landscape use: perennial or mixed border; waterside plantings; accent plant; delineating space and defining property lines; breaking up large expanses of lawn; screening; shady understory
Propagation: division

Meadowsweet is grown as much for its foliage as its flower appeal. The handsome dark green or variegated leaves are pinnately compound and deeply cut and soon form large clumps, 90 to 120 cm (36 to 48 in.) tall. Creamy white or pink florets emerge in large, puffy, terminal panicles atop tall, thin stems in early summer. Although the crown is woody and close to the soil surface, it spreads by creeping rhizomes.

Filipendula is from the Latin words *filum*, meaning "thread," and *pendulus*, "hanging," a description of the thread-like roots that connect the root tubers. The specific epithet, *ulmaria*, indicates that the leaflets look like those of an elm tree.

Meadowsweet has long been used in traditional medicine to treat fevers, coughs, and colds, and with good reason. It contains salicylate, from which salicylic acid was first made in 1835. It is also a source of fragrant oil, and the roots were once used for tanning and as a yellow dye.

Its native habitat, moist meadows from Europe into Siberia, recommends its landscape use: bog gardens, edging streams and ponds, and on the edge of woodland gardens.

How to Grow

You can grow meadowsweet in full sun to light shade as long as the soil is well amended with organic matter and kept evenly moist. Long-lived and easy to maintain, meadowsweet may become floppy and flowerless if given too much shade. In the heat of summer, the leaves may scorch and appear tatty if moisture is lacking. Shear and wait for re-growth. Cultivars do not come true from seed and it is best to deadhead them to prevent inferior seedlings. Remove any shoots on variegated cultivars that revert to green. Propagate through division in spring.

Cultivars
- 'Aurea' has white flowers and aromatic, golden yellow foliage; it does better in light shade.
- 'Variegata' grows 60 to 90 cm (24 to 36 in.) tall and its green leaves have blotches of creamy yellow in their centers.

Other Species and Hybrids
- *Filpendula palmata* 'Nana' (pahl-*mah*-ta), dwarf Siberian meadowsweet, grows to 40 cm (16 in.) in height and spreads to 50 cm (20 in.). Panicles of tiny, pink flowers resembling those of *Spiraea* (as *Filipendula* was once classified) grace the plant for most of the summer. The dark green leaves are pinnately compound, with a terminal palmate leaflet, hence, the species name.

Fragaria virginiana
fra-*gare*-ee-a vir-gin-ee-*an*-ah
Wild strawberry

Plant at a Glance
Type: semi-evergreen perennial
Height/spread: 30 cm (12 in.) / indefinite spread
Spacing: 30 cm (12 in.)
Light: full sun to partial shade

Soil: average; well drained; rich in organic matter

Distinguishing features: white flowers; sweet, red fruit

Landscape use: naturalizing; lawn replacement; small, inaccessible, or inhospitable areas; slopes and banks; unifying shrub beds; back lane plantings; accentuating focal points

Propagation: separating plantlets produced by stolons

Fragaria 'Pink Panda' ('Pink Panda' strawberry potentilla) (Sara Williams)

Common throughout the prairies and parklands and long used medicinally by Native peoples, the genus name is from the Latin word *fraga,* meaning "sweet smelling" or "fragrant," which aptly describes the aroma of the fruit, while *virginiana* means "of Virginia," part of its native range.

The white, five-petaled flowers bloom throughout the summer, but more profusely in spring through early summer; they are followed by small, red, cone-shaped fruit. The leaves, typical of strawberries, are compound and divided into three leaflets, each serrated and 2.5 to 10 cm (1 to 4 in.) long. The foliage generally turns red in fall, adding to its landscape value.

How to Grow
Although garden strawberries need careful and constant coddling in terms of soil, water, and weeds, the native strawberry is nothing if not resilient. Once established, it is fairly drought tolerant and flourishes in average to occasionally dry soil, in full sun to light shade. It quickly forms a solid cover through plantlets produced by stolons. The bonus? Small but exceedingly sweet, edible berries. If it looks tatty in the spring, simply mow it.

Other Species and Hybrids
- 'Pink Panda' (*Fragaria* x *ananassa* x *Potentilla palustris*), also called the strawberry potentilla, is a large, pink-flowered strawberry. It was raised by Dr. Jack Ellis in 1966 by crossing a garden strawberry with the wild marsh cinquefoil, native to North America; it was introduced by Blooms of Bressingham Nursery in England in 1989. The plants are 10 to 15 cm (4 to 6 in.) in height and produce dark pink flowers sporadically throughout the growing season. It was the first and is still considered the most vigorous of the ornamental strawberries, spreading rapidly by stolons. It performs best in sun or light shade in evenly moist soil that is well amended with organic matter.

Galium odoratum (syn. *Asperula odorata*)

gay-lee-um o-do-*ra*-tum

Sweet woodruff, bedstraw

Plant at a Glance

Type: herbaceous perennial

Height/spread: 20 to 30 cm (8 to 12 in.) / indefinite spread

Spacing: 30 cm (12 in.)

Light: partial to full shade

Soil: evenly moist; rich in organic matter

Distinguishing features: delicate, green foliage

Landscape use: accentuating focal points; screening spring-bulb foliage; shady understory

Propagation: division

Galium odoratum (sweet woodruff) (Sara Williams)

Sweet woodruff has tiny, fragrant, four-petaled flowers that are pure white and form in loosely branching cymes in late spring. The delicate foliage is an attractive green, in whorls of six to eight sessile, linear leaves, each about 2.5 cm (1 in.) long. The overall appearance is of erect but delicate foliage. Stems are four-sided and fragrant when dried.

Spreading by slender underground rhizomes, sweet woodruff acts as a delicate filler in combination with taller plants such as Solomon's seal and the smaller, non-aggressive ferns. Don't expect it to effectively cover large areas on its own—begin on a small scale and, if it works, gradually add more plants.

How to Grow

Sweet woodruff requires a protected prairie microclimate, with shade and even moisture. Leave dead foliage over winter to give it added protection and shear or mow in early spring to allow new growth to develop. Propagate by division in spring.

A plant cloaked in folk use and folklore, sweet woodruff, or bedstraw, is native to Great Britain and Europe and has been a mainstay of herb gardens for centuries. Its history is well embedded in its nomenclature. It's called bedstraw because it was long used in mattresses in both Europe and North America and is said to have insect-repelling characteristics. Some even believe it was the straw used in the stable where Christ was born.

The leaves have been used medicinally and as flavoring for wine and liqueurs since the Middle Ages; their vanilla-like scent is due to the compound coumarin. In England in the 1600s, the crushed leaves were applied to wounds.

The genus is derived from the Greek word *gala*, meaning "milk." One of the species was once used to curdle milk in cheese making. The specific epithet, *odoratum*, "sweet-smelling," is appropriate for a plant that is also used in potpourri and perfumes.

Genista lydia
jen-*niss*-tah *lid*-dee-ah
Lydia broom

Plant at a Glance
Type: deciduous shrub
Height/spread: 30 cm (12 in.) / 60 cm (24 in.)
Spacing: 45 cm (18 in.)
Light: full sun
Soil: well drained
Distinguishing features: spectacular yellow flowers; green stems, with very small leaves
Landscape use: mixed border; rock garden; accent plant; delineating space and defining property lines; breaking up large expanses of lawn; accentuating focal points
Propagation: softwood cuttings

Genista is the ancient Latin name for the genus; the species name refers to the city of Lydia in Turkey, within its native range. The plant's interesting appearance is due to the thin, green stems that develop into a circular stack of branches. The leaves are very much reduced and are about 1 cm (0.4 in.) long by 2 mm (0.08 in.) wide. *Genista lydia* is very beautiful when covered in yellow flowers in June.

Plant Lydia broom to provide a spectacular accent in a rock garden or to draw attention to a graceful birdbath, garden statuary, or other focal point.

How to Grow
Genista lydia requires full sun and excellent drainage and should be planted in a protected location in prairie gardens. It is difficult to transplant so it is best planted from container stock. Propagation is usually by softwood cuttings in early summer.

Genista lydia (Lydia broom) (Hugh Skinner)

Other Species and Hybrids

• *Genista sagittalis* (sa-gee-*tal*-ez), arrow broom, is a low-growing groundcover that has winged, green stems and small, simple leaves. Six to eight flowers are produced in June at the end of upright stems. It makes an attractive groundcover in well-drained, sunny locations. It is not widely available but deserves wider trial on the prairies.

Gentiana acaulis
gen-tee-*ah*-na a-*kaw*-lis
Stemless gentian

Plant at a Glance
Type: herbaceous perennial
Height/spread: 15 cm (6 in.) / 15 cm (6 in.)
Spacing: 15 cm (6 in.)
Light: full sun to partial shade
Soil: moist; well drained
Distinguishing features: true blue flowers
Landscape use: perennial border; edging; rock garden; lawn replacement; small, inaccessible, or inhospitable areas; accentuating focal points; shady understory
Propagation: seed; division

Stemless gentian is most notable for its beautiful display of 8 cm (3 in.), funnel-shaped, true blue flowers that cover the plant in May and early June and may repeat in the fall. The 5 cm (2 in.) rosettes of lance-shaped, green leaves grow into a dense mat. *Gentiana* is named for Gentius, a king of Illyria, an ancient country east and north of the Adriatic Sea; *acaulis* means "stemless" or "apparently stemless." In fact, the stems are below ground, arising from underground rhizomes, and the plants spread slowly as the diameter of the clump increases with new stems. Stemless gentians are sure to attract attention if planted at the front of a border or in a rock garden.

How to Grow
Some gentian species require acidic soil that is rich in organic matter, but the species included here are tolerant of our limestone-based soils, provided

Best Groundcovers & Vines For The Prairies

they are given moist soils and good drainage. Gentians grow best in partial shade, but tolerate full sun. Although they have a reputation for being difficult to grow, gentians can be propagated by sowing fresh seed or division in early spring.

Other Species and Hybrids
- *Gentiana paradoxa* (pear-ah-*dox*-ah) produces medium to dark blue, trumpet-shaped flowers on 25 cm (10 in.) stems in the fall. It prefers sunny, well-drained locations in normal garden soil.
- *Gentiana septemfida* (sep-*tem*-fi-da), everyman's gentian, and its prostrate subspecies, *G. septemfida lagodechiana* (lag-oh-dek-ee-*an*-ah) are summer blooming and easier to grow than the stemless gentian. They have deep blue, trumpet-shaped flowers that are spotted on the inside. Stems with lance-shaped, smooth, dark green leaves spread along the ground. They are attractive plants at the front of a flower border or as a groundcover in a woodland planting.

Gentiana acaulis (stemless gentian) (Hugh Skinner)

Geranium x *cantabrigiense*
ge-*ra*-nee-um can-tah-bree-*gen*-see
Perennial geranium, cranesbill

Plant at a Glance
Type: herbaceous perennial
Height/spread: 20 cm (8 in.) / 40 cm (16 in.)
Spacing: 30 cm (12 in.)
Light: full sun to partial shade
Soil: well drained; average
Distinguishing features: repeat blooming, with showy white or pink flowers; fragrant, shiny green foliage

Landscape use: mixed or perennial border; edging; small, inaccessible, or inhospitable areas; slopes and banks; delineating space and defining property lines; breaking up large expanses of lawn; back lane plantings; directing foot traffic; accentuating focal points; screening spring-bulb foliage; shady understory

Propagation: division

Geranium x *cantabrigiense 'Biokova'* ('Bikova' perennial geranium) (Hugh Skinner)

These geraniums are hardy relatives of the commonly grown bedding plant or houseplant that has been transferred to the genus *Pelargonium*. The genus *Geranium* gets its name from the Greek word for "crane" and refers to the long "beak" on its seed pod. The hybrid species *Geranium* x *cantabrigiense* is relatively new and is a hybrid of *G. dalmaticum* (Dalmatian cranesbill) and *G. macrorrhizum* (bigroot perennial geranium). It is more vigorous and spreading than *G. dalmaticum* and lower growing than *G. macrorrhizum*. The round leaves are light, shiny green, intensely fragrant, and lobed into seven segments. The sterile flowers are 2.5 cm (1 in.) in diameter and are held well above the attractive foliage, which turns red in the fall.

Cultivars
- 'Biokova' has white flowers, with pink centers and stamens. It is similar in stature to 'Cambridge'.
- 'Cambridge' grows to 20 cm (8 in.) in height and spreads to 40 cm (16 in.). It bears bright pink flowers repeatedly through the summer.

How to Grow
Perennial geraniums thrive in average, well-drained soils in full sun to partial shade, but bloom less in deep shade. They are easily propagated by transplanting divisions in early spring or mid-summer. *Geranium* x *cantabrigiense* is sterile so does not produce seed (an advantage over some species that self-seed and become weedy).

Other Species and Hybrids

- *Geranium* x 'Johnson's Blue' is a sterile hybrid (*G. himalayense* x *G. pratense*). A vigorous and hardy plant, it is about 50 cm (20 in.) tall, with a somewhat sprawling habit. It has lobed leaves, divided into seven segments, and large, blue flowers that are prolific throughout the summer.
- *Geranium macrorrhizum* (mak-ro-*rye*-zum), bigroot perennial geranium, is an excellent groundcover for dry, shaded gardens. It grows from thick rootstocks to form a dense cover of intensely fragrant, light green leaves about 30 cm (12 in.) high. The flowers are 2.5 cm (1 in.) in diameter and appear in early summer, varying in color from near white to deep magenta, depending on the cultivar. The leaves turn an attractive orange in the fall.
- *Geranium pratense* (prah-*tayn*-see) 'Plenum Violaceum', double lilac geranium, has perfectly formed small, double, violet-blue flowers and forms a dense clump about 60 cm (24 in.) high.
- *Geranium sanguineum* (sang-*gwin*-ee-um), bloody cranesbill, is native to Europe and Western Asia. It forms a mat of finely cut leaves that varies from 15 cm (6 in.) to 30 cm (12 in.) in height, depending on the cultivar, and spreads slowly by wiry rhizomes. 'Alpenglow' is low-growing, with magenta flowers, while 'Shepherd's Warning' is of similar stature but has bright rose-pink flowers. 'Cedric Morris' is taller, growing to 30 cm (12 in.), and is a prolific bloomer into late summer. *G. sanguineum* var. *striatum* (stri-*a*-tum) (syn. 'Lancastriense') has pale pink flowers, with dark red veins, over a long season and grows 10 to 15 cm (4 to 6 in.) tall.

Geum urbanum (syn. *G. urbanum* var. *sibiricum*)
jee-um ur-*bah*-num
Siberian avens, wood avens

Plant at a Glance
Type: evergreen perennial
Height/spread: 25 to 30 cm (10 to 12 in) / 25 cm (10 in.)
Spacing: 25 cm (10 in.)
Light: full sun to partial shade
Soil: well drained; average
Distinguishing features: bright orange flowers; deep green foliage
Landscape use: perennial or mixed border; rock garden; small, inaccessible, or inhospitable areas; accentuating focal points
Propagation: division

Although it is perhaps not for the faint of heart, nothing livens up the landscape like the vivid orange of Siberian avens with its contrasting bright green foliage in late spring. Native to Europe and western Asia, Siberian avens was

Geum urbanum (Siberian avens) (Sara Williams)

once worn on outer garments to ward off the devil. A medicinal staple through the Middle Ages, it contains high levels of tannins and was used as a throat gargle and to soothe eyes. Its roots were used as a substitute for cloves and to make tea.

Its common name, avens, is derived from the word *avencia,* a type of clover it was said to resemble. *Geum* is its classical Latin name, which in turn was derived from the Greek word *gaion,* meaning "of the earth." The species name, *urbanum,* "of the town or city," is perhaps a reference to its wide use and planting as a medicinal herb. It could also come from "urbane," meaning "neat or polite," a reference to the plant's neat habit.

The bright orange-red, five-petaled flowers are borne on erect stems above pinnately compound foliage in late spring to early summer. The thick rootstock is easily divisible.

How to Grow
Drought tolerant once established, Siberian avens should be planted in full sun to partial shade in well-drained soil. It can be divided in spring or mid-summer every three to four years.

Gypsophila repens
jip-*sof*-il-a *rep*-enz
Dwarf baby's breath, creeping baby's breath

Plant at a Glance
Type: herbaceous perennial
Height/spread: 15 to 20 cm (6 to 8 in.) / 30 to 45 cm (12 to 18 in.)
Spacing: 60 cm (24 in.)
Light: full sun
Soil: average; well drained
Distinguishing features: soft, misty cloud of tiny, white or pink flowers
Landscape use: rock garden; edging; over walls; small, inaccessible, or inhospitable areas; slopes and banks
Propagation: seed; softwood cuttings

Although native to the Alps and Pyrenees Mountains of Europe, baby's breath does very well on the basic soils of the Canadian prairies. The genus

Best Groundcovers & Vines For The Prairies

name is from the Greek words *gypsos*, meaning "gypsum" or "chalk," and *philos*, meaning "lover," thus, the plant is a lover of lime-based or alkaline soils. The word *repens* means "creeping" and describes its prostrate form. The common name arises from the supposed similarity of the flowers' fragrance to an infant's breath.

Dwarf baby's breath forms a soft, misty mound or mat of delicate foliage, with a myriad of tiny, pink or white flowers. The diminutive flowers, each with five petals, form loose, cloud-like panicles from early to mid summer. The equally small, linear, gray-green leaves are on wiry, branched stems. The deep root system makes it difficult to transplant once established, so give careful thought to its placement. It is ideal for cascading down a slope or bank or over rocks or walls.

How to Grow
Extremely drought tolerant, baby's breath does best in full sun in well-drained soil. It is very easy to grow from seed, but softwood cuttings are also an option.

Cultivars
- 'Alba' has single, white flowers.
- 'Rosea' is mat forming and is an excellent groundcover, with single, rose-pink flowers.
- 'Rosyveil' has semi-double, pink to white flowers in late summer. It is 45 cm (18 in.) in height and forms a mat 100 cm (40 in.) across. It does not produce seed so should be propagated by softwood cuttings. 'Rosyveil' was raised by Karl Foerster (of ornamental-grass fame) in Germany in 1933. A more protected location may be beneficial.

Gypsophila repens 'Rosyveil' ('Rosyveil' creeping baby's breath)
(Hugh Skinner)

Heliopsis helianthoides
(syn. *H. scabra, H. helianthoides* subsp. *scabra*)

hee-lee-*op*-sis heel-lee-ann-*thoy*-dees
False sunflower, rough heliopsis

Plant at a Glance
Type: herbaceous perennial
Height/spread: 90 cm (36 in.) / 60 to 90 cm (24 to 36 in.)
Spacing: 60 cm (24 in.)
Light: full sun
Soil: average; well drained
Distinguishing features: bright yellow, daisy-like flowers
Landscape use: perennial or mixed border; mass plantings; delineating space and defining property lines; breaking up large expanses of lawn; back lane plantings; directing foot traffic; screening
Propagation: division

Heliopsis helianthoides (false sunflower) (Sara Williams)

Although some avant-garde gardeners tend to categorize yellow daisies as boring, we've never tired of this one. It's bright, cheerful, dependable, and trouble free. It also serves well as an "indicator plant"; as soon as it begins to show signs of wilt (from which it springs back instantly), it's time to water the whole area.

Heliopsis is the Greek word for "resembling the sun," while *helianthoides* means "resembling a sunflower." Perhaps it's a bit of overkill in terms of sun, but one gets the point that it looks like a sunflower but on a slightly smaller scale. The older species name, *scabra,* means "rough," and describes the hairy leaf surface.

Although native to eastern North America, including Ontario and Quebec, false sunflowers do extremely well on the prairies and can be counted on to remain perennial for twenty years or longer. The yellow, single or double, daisy-like flowers, 5 to 8 cm (2 to 3 in.) across, bloom from July through August. The dark green, lance-shaped leaves are simple, opposite, and toothed. Both the stems and leaves have a sandpaper-like texture, thus, the common name, rough heliopsis. The root system is strong and fibrous. This plant is excellent as a distinctive tall groundcover, for mass planting, or in a border.

How to Grow
Long-lived and requiring no support despite their height, false sunflowers need only full sun, moderate moisture, and average, well-drained soil. Divide in spring every four years.

Cultivars
- 'Golden Plume' is a 1949 Karl Foerster introduction. It is 1.2 to 1.5 m (4 to 5 ft.) in height, with large, double, golden flowers and golden foliage.
- 'Loraine Sunshine' is 90 cm (36 in.), with creamy white and green variegated foliage; seedlings seem to come true.
- 'Summer Sun' has single to semi-double, bright yellow flowers and is an old standby. It is 60 to 90 cm (24 to 36 in.).

Hemerocallis fulva
heh-mer-o-*kal*-is *full*-vah
Orange or tawny daylily

Plant at a Glance
Type: herbaceous perennial
Height/spread: 120 cm (48 in.) / 90 cm (36 in.)
Spacing: 90 cm (36 in.)
Light: full sun to partial shade
Soil: average to moist; well drained
Distinguishing features: orange flowers; grassy foliage
Landscape use: perennial or mixed border; mass plantings; naturalizing; small, inaccessible, or inhospitable areas; slopes and banks; delineating space and defining property lines; breaking up large expanses of lawn; transition plantings; back lane plantings; directing foot traffic; screening
Propagation: division

Long used as a food crop in its native China, the daylily is without doubt one of the most popular perennials in North America, where bistros and gourmet restaurants use its buds, flowers, roots, and leaves in their cuisine. It had been introduced to Europe by the mid-1500s, where it was quickly naturalized.

Its common name stems from its resemblance to a lily, qualified by the fact that individual flowers bloom for only a day. The botanical name is similar. The Greek word *hemera* means "day," while *kallos* is "beauty."

Hemerocallis fulva, introduced from Japan in 1576, is probably the best

Hemerocallis fulva (tawny daylily) (Sara Williams)

groundcover among the daylilies and is now found naturalized in many parts of Europe and North America. The strap-like, green foliage forms a loose, arching mound that is topped by long stems bearing orange flowers in mid-summer. It is unusual for a daylily in that it spreads by rhizomes and is capable of filling in a large area fairly quickly. It's also more shade tolerant than many other daylilies.

How to Grow
Although they perform best in full sun in deep, fertile, well-drained soil with even moisture, daylilies are fairly adaptable and grow well in ditches. They are long-lived and require division when they become overcrowded and begin to flower less freely.

Cultivars
• 'Kwanso' (syn. 'Flore Pleno') is double flowered but as vigorous as the species.

Other Species and Hybrids
• 'Bertie Ferris' is an early flowering dwarf cultivar, with persimmon orange flowers.
• 'Happy Returns' is very floriferous, light yellow, fragrant, and a repeat bloomer. It is 45 cm (18 in.).
• *Hemerocallis lilioasphodelus* (lil-*ee*-o-ass-fo-*del*-us) (syn. *H. flava*), the lemon daylily, is about 90 cm (36 in.) in height and one of the first to bloom, producing light yellow, fragrant flowers. A true heritage plant, it arrived with the early European settlers and is still seen in older gardens. It flowers well into the evening, making it ideal as a mass planting in a night garden. It has been extensively used in breeding programs to obtain early and longer blooming cultivars.
• 'Hyperion' is a lemon yellow, repeat-flowering cultivar that grows to 1 m (3.3 ft.).
• 'Pardon Me' is a bright red, repeat-flowering cultivar that grows to 45 cm (18 in.).
• 'Stella d' Oro' (1975) is a popular and long-blooming golden yellow cultivar. It combines low height with an extended bloom period, flowering early to mid season. It is used extensively as a groundcover.

Best Groundcovers & Vines For The Prairies

Hepatica nobilis
he-*pa*-ti-ka *no*-bi-lis
Hepatica, European liverleaf

Plant at a Glance
Type: evergreen perennial
Height/spread: 10 cm (4 in.) / 20 cm (8 in.)
Spacing: 15 cm (6 in.)
Light: partial to full shade
Soil: moist; rich in organic matter
Distinguishing features: early blue, pink, purple, or white flowers: shiny, three-lobed foliage
Landscape use: shady understory
Propagation: seed; division

Hepatica nobilis is a lovely little woodland plant noted for its white, blue, pink, or purplish flowers that arise from below ground on slender stems in early spring, even before the trees leaf out. *Hepatica* describes the resemblance of its three-lobed leaves to the liver; *nobilis* means "noble" or "renowned." The shiny, three-lobed, dark green leaves persist over winter. If allowed to grow undisturbed for several years, plants spread by rhizomes to develop into a large mat of handsome foliage, with spectacular effect when in bloom. Hepaticas are among the most shade-tolerant groundcover perennials.

How to Grow
Hepatica thrives in shady, woodland conditions similar to its native habitat, preferring moist, organically rich, lime-based soil that has a near-neutral pH. Propagate hepatica by division after the plant has flowered. Seed should be sown immediately after it is ripe.

Hepatica transsylvanica (liverleaf) foliage

Other Species and Hybrids
- *Hepatica transsylvanica* (trahns-sil-*vah*-ni-ka) has blue flowers and lobed leaves that are pale green, with scalloped edges. Cultivars with pink and white flowers are available.

Heuchera Morden hybrids
hew-ker-ah
Coral bells, alumroot

Plant at a Glance

Type: semi-evergreen perennial
Height/spread: 50 to 60 cm (20 to 24 in.) / 30 to 45 cm (12 to 18 in.)
Spacing: 30 cm (12 in.)
Light: full sun to partial shade
Soil: average; well drained
Distinguishing features: tiny, pink flowers; attractive rosettes of scalloped foliage
Landscape use: perennial or mixed border; rock garden; edging; mass plantings; small, inaccessible, or inhospitable areas; breaking up large expanses of lawn; accentuating focal points
Propagation: division

Heuchera 'Brandon' ('Brandon Pink' coral bells)
(Hugh Skinner)

In terms of their use as a groundcover on the prairies, it's crucial to distinguish between the older Manitoba hybrids and the newer coral bells with their purple or green-and-white variegated foliage (developed in Britain, Europe, and the United States) that now constitute most of the coral bells found in prairie garden centers. If you want a dependable, hardy, long-lived plant that needs no fuss or coddling, stick to the Morden (or Brandon) hybrids. Dr. Henry Marshall, working first at Brandon and later at Morden, used *Heuchera richardsonii*, a plant with dull, greenish white flowers that is native to the Canadian prairies, to impart hardiness, drought tolerance, and disease resistance, and *H. sanguinea*, a tender native of the southwestern United States, with blood red flowers, to impart beauty to these Manitoba cultivars.

The genus was named to honor Johann Heinrich von Heucher (1677–1747), a professor of medicine at Wittenberg, Germany. The common name, alumroot, refers to the high concentration of tannin in the roots, a compound once used to stop bleeding.

Myriad dainty, pink to red bells on slender, wiry stems are held well above a basal rosette of foliage. The dark green, semi-evergreen leaves are rounded to heart shaped, with scalloped margins. As Henry Marshall noted, "Heuchera foliage is frequently evergreen, resembling a geranium leaf in outline and texture." The woody crown slowly increases to large clumps without ever becoming invasive.

How to Grow
Coral bells thrive in full sun to light shade (but expect fewer flowers in shade) in average, well-drained soil. Deadhead to prolong flowering. They are exceptionally drought tolerant once established. Propagate coral bells by dividing the plants in spring.

Cultivars
The original crosses for these plants were made at Brandon, followed by selection at Morden. These cultivars do not come true from seed, but are easily divided.

- 'Brandon Pink' produces deep coral pink flowers in July. It has dense, nearly evergreen, faintly mottled foliage and reaches 60 cm (24 in.) in height. It won a 1965 Western Canadian Society for Horticulture (WCSH) Merit Award.
- 'Brandon Glow' is slightly shorter than 'Brandon Pink', reaching only 45 cm (18 in.) in height. It has darker pink flowers, more-open panicles, and distinct white-mottled foliage.
- 'Northern Fire' has dark red flowers that last for six weeks from June to early July. It boasts attractive foliage all summer long and grows to 60 cm (24 in.) tall. It won a WCSH Merit Award in 1983.
- 'Ruby Mist' has evergreen, dark green foliage and upright stems, with ruby red flowers. It is similar but superior to 'Northern Fire', being shorter, only 45 cm (18 in.) tall, not as floppy, and with a longer bloom period.

Hosta
hos-ta
Hosta

Plant at a Glance
Type: herbaceous perennial
Height/spread: 13 to 90 cm (5 to 36 in.) / 30 to 90 cm (12 to 36 in.) or greater
Spacing: 45 cm (18 in.)
Light: partial sun to full shade
Soil: moist; well drained; rich in organic matter
Distinguishing features: foliage, foliage, foliage!

Landscape use: perennial or mixed border; naturalizing; lawn replacement; small, inaccessible, or inhospitable areas; delineating space and defining property lines; breaking up large expanses of lawn; accentuating focal points; shady understory
Propagation: division; rossizing

Trying to select a favorite hosta among the many suitable as groundcovers is like trying to select a puppy. They're all cute. Hostas vary in size, color, and texture, but usually share the common characteristic of a rhizomatous root system. Shoots arise from thick underground rhizomes, some of which travel horizontally at a fairly fast rate, producing new plantlets and making them very effective groundcovers.

The genus was named to honor the Austrian botanist Nicholas Tomas Host (1761–1834). Hostas are native to China, Japan, and Korea.

Although long-lived (twenty-five years or more), hostas may take four to six years to reach maturity, by which time they attain their characteristic color, variegation, leaf texture, and size. So the baby you purchase in its small pot may not yet resemble the picture on the plant tag or the one in a book. It's a matter of having patience or paying more for a larger plant and the accompanying instant gratification.

Hostas are primarily foliage plants, with leaves in shades of green, blue, gold, and various types of variegation. Leaf texture (puckered, ribbed, undulating, wavy, or wrinkled) and shape (heart shaped, cup-like, lance shaped, or broad) are also amazingly variable. The trumpet-shaped flowers range from white to purple and some are fragrant.

How to Grow
For best results, plant hostas in moist, well-drained soil that is well amended with organic matter. Although most do better in partial shade, cultivars and species can be extremely variable in their sun-shade tolerance. Those with yellow-gold foliage often keep their color better if given a few hours of direct sunlight but may bleach out if given too much sun. Those with greater "substance" (thicker leaves) tolerate more sun and are less susceptible to slug damage than those with thinner leaves. Blue hostas generally do better in shade and out of the wind as their coloration is caused by a bloom (a waxy coating) that gradually wears off during the summer due to the abrasive action of wind, direct sun, grit, and rain. However, because blue hostas sometimes require more heat to start growing, a location that receives partial sun in spring would be beneficial. Hostas are propagated by division or rossizing (see page 118).

Cultivars
• 'August Moon' is 64 cm (25 in.) tall and 90 cm (36 in.) wide, with pale green, slug-resistant foliage that matures to gold and pale lavender flowers.

Best Groundcovers & Vines For The Prairies

- 'Blue Boy' measures 30 cm (12 in.) tall and 50 cm (20 in.) wide; it has small, wavy, blue-green leaves and pale lavender flowers.
- 'Bold Ribbons' has olive green leaves, with irregular creamy margins,

A bed showing a variety of hosta foliage.
(Hugh Skinner)

and lush lavender flowers. It grows to 25 cm (10 in.) tall and 45 cm (18 in.) wide.
- 'Francee' is a rapid grower, reaching 60 cm (24 in.) in height and 75 cm (30 in.) in width. It has variegated, dark green leaves, with bright white margins, and lavender flowers.
- 'Ginkgo Craig' is 30 cm (12 in.) tall and 35 cm (14 in.) wide; it has dark green, white-margined leaves, with gray streaking in the center, and purple flowers.
- 'Gold Standard' has variegated leaves that are yellow, with green margins. It grows rapidly up to 60 cm (24 in.) tall and 75 cm (30 in.) wide and has lavender flowers.
- 'Golden Tiara' grows to 30 cm (12 in.) in both height and width. It has green leaves, with wide, chartreuse and white margins, and lavender flowers.
- 'Halcyon' has intensely blue, heart-shaped leaves that grow 50 cm (20 in.) tall and 60 cm (24 in.) wide and near-white flowers.
- 'Honeybells' is 70 cm (28 in.) tall and 130 cm (50 in.) wide, with glossy, medium green leaves and pale lavender flowers. A vigorous hosta, it tolerates some sun.
- *Hosta fortunei* (for-*tewn*-ee-ee) 'Aureomarginata' is 50 cm (20 in.) tall and 100 cm (40 in.) wide. It has oval- to heart-shaped green leaves, edged in cream, and violet flowers.
- *Hosta sieboldiana* (see-bold-ee-*ah*-na) 'Elegans' has heart-shaped, puckered, blue leaves, heavy in substance and slug resistant. It grows 50 cm (20 in.) tall and 100 cm (40 in.) wide and its flowers are lavender-white.
- *Hosta sieboldii* (see-*bold*-ee-ee) has white-edged, green leaves and pale mauve flowers. It grows 70 cm (28 in.) tall and 130 cm (50 in.) wide.
- *Hosta undulata* (un-dew-*la*-tah) 'Albo-marginata' has mid-green leaves, with cream margins, and violet flowers and grows up to 25 cm (10 in.) tall and 60 cm (24 in.) wide.
- 'Invincible' is 25 cm (10 in.) tall and 30 cm (12 in.) wide, with glossy, bright green leaves and white flowers. It is sun tolerant.
- 'Lancifolia' has oval- to lance-shaped, green leaves and violet flowers

This method of propagation, developed by Henry Ross, is used to encourage quicker division of *Hosta* cultivars. It is best done in spring once the plants have begun to emerge from the soil. First, remove enough soil from around the base of the crown (without disturbing the roots) to see what you're doing. Insert a small, sharp knife into the main stem just above the crown and cut down into the crown to just above the roots. On larger crowns, a second cut can be made at a 90-degree angle to the first.

The area that has been cut, or "wounded," will callous and scar, thereby stimulating the formation of a bud that will mature to a new division. Return the soil to around the crown and leave the plant undisturbed until the following spring. By then, the root systems of the new divisions will have developed enough to allow successful separation. If you're hesitant to take such drastic action on a hosta you've just paid big bucks for, try it first on one that has already had several divisions.

and grows to 40 cm (16 in.) tall and 80 cm (32 in.) wide.

- 'Lemon Lime' is 25 cm (10 in.) tall and 70 cm (28 in.) wide, with lance-shaped, yellow-green leaves and lavender flowers.
- 'Paul's Glory', a slug-resistant cultivar, has yellow, heart-shaped leaves, with blue-green margins, and lavender flowers. It grows 40 cm (16 in.) tall and 65 cm (26 in.) wide.
- 'Pearl Lake' has grayish green, cordate leaves and pale lavender flowers. It rapidly forms dense clumps that are 40 cm (16 in.) tall and 90 cm (36 in.) wide.
- 'Royal Standard' is 70 cm (28 in.) tall and 160 cm (62 in.) wide, with glossy, medium green leaves and white flowers.
- 'Sagae' has huge, thick leaves that are green, with cream margins, and pale lavender flowers. It grows 75 cm (30 in.) tall and 120 cm (48 in.) wide.
- 'Shade Fanfare' multiplies rapidly, growing 45 cm (18 in.) tall and 55 cm (22 in.) wide. The leaves are two-tone green, with white margins, and are topped by light lavender flowers.
- 'Sum and Substance' has chartreuse-gold, cordate leaves, heavy in substance, that grow up to 90 cm (36 in.) tall and 150 cm (60 in.) wide and are accompanied by white flowers.

Iberis sempervirens
i-*ber*-is sem-per-*vi*-renz
Evergreen candytuft

Plant at a Glance
Type: evergreen sub-shrub
Height/spread: 30 cm (12 in.) / 40 to 100 cm (16 to 40 in.)
Spacing: 30 cm (12 in.)
Light: full sun

Soil: well drained
Distinguishing features: white flowers; dark green, evergreen foliage
Landscape use: perennial border; edging; rock garden; small, inaccessible, or inhospitable areas
Propagation: seed; softwood or hardwood cuttings

Iberis derives its name from a number of species that originated on the Iberian Peninsula (Spain and Portugal). *Sempervirens* is Latin for "evergreen." These members of the mustard family are low sub-shrubs with narrow, 3-cm (1.25-in.) -long, evergreen leaves. The white flowers are borne in clusters that are flat at first but elongate as more flowers open. Each individual flower has four petals that open white and fade to pale pink.

Evergreen candytuft will spread to 100 cm (40 in.) in diameter from a single root if left undisturbed for several years. The plant's size can be controlled by pruning it back after it blooms in early summer. Its evergreen foliage is very attractive as an edging plant, with the added bonus of late-spring flowers.

How to Grow
Candytuft thrives in well-drained soil in a sunny location. Because of its evergreen nature, it benefits from a wind-sheltered location and a cover of evergreen branches for winter protection. Even large plants develop from a compact root system and it should not be transplanted once established. Candytuft can be grown from seed planted soon after it ripens or from softwood or hardwood cuttings.

Iberis sempervirens (candytuft) (Sara Williams)

Juniperus

jew-*nip*-per-us

Juniper

Native to Europe, Asia, and North America, junipers form a variable genus. They range from horizontal ground-huggers to trees 10 m (33 ft.) tall. Juniper foliage can be green, blue, gray, yellow, or variegated; its bark is thin and shredding. *Juniperus* comes from the classical Latin name for the European species.

Usually dioecious, the male flowers are inconspicuous yellow cones. The female flowers later form dark blue berries, which are covered in a waxy bloom. The berries mature in their second or third year and have been used to flavor gin.

The foliage can be soft or prickly. Juvenile plants generally have sharp, needle-like leaves in whorls of three, while older plants have softer, scale-like foliage on older growth and sharper leaves on newer growth. Cultivars that originated as sports (mutations) on newer growth often retain their prickly foliage for life, as do most cultivars of common juniper.

How to Grow

Junipers thrive in full sun and well-drained soil. Under deeply shaded conditions, they tend to be open and thin. However, if given sufficient indirect light, creeping junipers can be used successfully as groundcovers under large, canopy trees. Once established, most junipers are extremely drought tolerant.

Junipers may occasionally be affected by saskatoon-juniper rust, although it is never deadly and seldom disfiguring. The best approach is to prune off the galls. Spider mites are not usually a problem, but you can control them during hot, dry weather by washing them with a strong jet of cold water. Juniper cultivars are propagated by softwood or semi-hardwood cuttings.

Juniperus communis 'Depressa Aurea'

jew-*nip*-per-us kom-*yew*-nis

Common golden juniper

Plant at a Glance

Type: evergreen shrub
Height/spread: 0.6 to 0.9 m (2 to 3 ft.) / 3 m (10 ft.)
Spacing: 1 to 2 m (3.3 to 6.5 ft.)
Light: full sun
Soil: well drained
Distinguishing features: blue and gold contrasting foliage
Landscape use: mixed border; small, inaccessible, or inhospitable areas; slopes and banks; delineating space and defining property lines; breaking up large

Best Groundcovers & Vines For The Prairies

expanses of lawn; transition plantings; barrier plantings; accentuating focal points
Propagation: softwood or hardwood cuttings

'Depressa Aurea' outperforms the commonly available golden Chinese pfitzer junipers ('Pfitzeriana Aurea') in every way. It is com-

Juniperus communis 'Depressa Aurea' (common golden juniper) showing new spring growth (Sara Williams)

pletely hardy, never succumbs to winter browning, and is drought tolerant. It is especially pleasing in spring when it exhibits a striking contrast of new bright golden-yellow foliage against the mature blue-green foliage of the previous season. Hugh Knowles described it as "one of the better golden forms of any juniper regardless of species." And he's right—it's too good to lose.

Despite the fact that this is practically a perfect plant, there is a problem. It has somehow fallen through the slats of the marketplace and is seldom available in mainstream prairie garden centers. What to do? Nag! (There's nothing like grass-roots pressure, eh?)

A selection of the common juniper, 'Depressa Aurea' has a vase-shaped, arching form in which branches ascend, then dip down toward the earth (the 'Depressa' of the cultivar name). The foliage, in whorls of three, is prickly and needle-like. Its only fault is that you can't hug it.

Juniperus is the classical name for this plant; *communis* indicates that it is commonly found (except, unfortunately, in garden centers), as the species has an enormous circumpolar natural range. 'Aurea' alludes to its golden foliage.

'Effusa' is another fine *Juniperus communis* cultivar. It is an excellent low-spreading, evergreen groundcover, which was originally introduced from Holland in 1944. Bright green, it is 23 to 30 cm (9 to 12 in.) in height, with an eventual spread of 1.2 to 1.8 m (4 to 6 ft.). It is extremely soft to touch, shows no winter browning, and is drought tolerant.

Juniperus horizontalis
jew-*nip*-per-us ho-ri-zon-*tah*-lis
Creeping juniper

Plant at a Glance
Type: evergreen shrub
Height/spread: 5 to 20 cm (2 to 8 in.) / 90 cm (36 in.) or greater
Spacing: 60 cm (24 in.)
Light: full sun to partial shade

Soil: well drained
Distinguishing features: prostrate, evergreen, blue-green, gray, silver, golden variegated, or green foliage
Landscape: mixed border; rock garden; over walls; mass plantings; slopes and banks; lawn replacement; small, inaccessible, or inhospitable areas; breaking up large expanses of lawn; accentuating focal points
Propagation: layering; cuttings

Less variable than other juniper species, the name *horizontalis* says it all— creeping or prostrate. Creeping junipers form low mats or groundcovers of various colors. The leading branches root as they grow, creating an attractive pattern as they slowly extend over the soil surface.

There are numerous cultivars that range in color from green through silver to blue to golden variegated. The foliage is often plume-like and frequently turns purple in the winter. In addition to the foliage interest, female clones produce blue-black berries. Extremely versatile, creeping junipers serve as groundcovers, hold banks or slopes, cascade over walls, drape around rocks, and are used in mixed borders and rock gardens.

Cultivars

- 'Andorra' (var. 'Plumosa') was introduced by the Andorra Nurseries of Philadelphia, Pennsylvania, in 1916. 'Andorra' is flat topped, with rather dense, short, erect branches. About 45 cm (18 in.) in height, it is considered one of the best of the low, mound-forming spreading junipers. The branches radiate from the center, lending it a circular form that can reach a diameter of 2 to 3 m (6.5 to 10 ft.). Its sharp juvenile needles are blue-green in summer, becoming purple in winter.
- 'Bar Harbor', found in coastal Maine, is somewhat salt tolerant and has soft, scale-like, bluish green foliage that turns reddish purple in winter. Erect side branches lend it a deep-pile effect. It grows 20 to 30 cm (8 to 12 in.) tall and 2 m (6.5 ft.) wide.
- 'Blue Chip', introduced from Denmark, forms a prostrate, dense, circular mound, 30 cm (12 in.) tall and 2 to 3 m (6.5 to 10 ft.) wide, with bright blue foliage throughout the year.
- 'Dunvegan Blue' has a striking, exceptionally silver-blue color and sharp, needle-like foliage, with a waxy bloom. Introduced at Beaverlodge, Alberta, it forms a ground-hugging mat that can spread 2 m (6.5 ft.) in ten years.
- 'Hughes' is a low-growing, silver blue-green cultivar, with soft, scale-like foliage that retains its color all winter. It has a radial or circular branching habit, is relatively fast growing, and at maturity is 30 to 40 cm (12 to 16 in.) tall and 2.7 m (9 ft.) wide. 'Hughes' is a vigorous cultivar that is useful for massing in large areas.
- 'Prince of Wales' was selected on the Prince of Wales Ranch in High River, Alberta, in 1931 and released by the Agriculture Canada Research

Best Groundcovers & Vines For The Prairies

Station in Morden, Manitoba, in 1967. It is a dense, ground-hugging juniper that grows 15 cm (6 in.) tall and 2 to 3 m (6.5 to 10 ft.) wide. It has bright green foliage, with a waxy blue bloom, that becomes purple in winter. The foliage is soft and scale-like.

- 'Waukegan', with light steel-blue foliage, is native to the bluffs over-looking Lake Michigan and was introduced prior to 1855. It can spread 2 m (6.5 ft.) in ten years.
- 'Wiltonii' ('Blue Rug') was found on Vinal Haven Island, Maine, in 1914. Its soft, scale-like foliage is very dense and remains a glaucous blue all winter. A slow-growing cultivar, it has a rather flat appearance, with long, trailing branches and an extremely prostrate form. It grows 15 to 20 cm (6 to 8 in.) tall and 2 to 3 m (6.5 to 10 ft.) wide and is ideal for cascading over rocks and walls. 'Wiltonii' is a female selection with small, intensely silver-blue berries.

Juniperus sabina
jew-*nip*-per-us sa-*been*-a
Savin juniper

Plant at a Glance
Type: evergreen shrub
Height/spread: 0.3 to 1.5 m (1 to 5 ft.) / 2 to 3 m (6.5 to 10 ft.)
Spacing: 60 cm (24 in.)
Light: full sun
Soil: well drained
Distinguishing features: vase-shaped form; blue-green to green, evergreen foliage
Landscape use: mixed border; mass plantings; small, inaccessible, or in-hospitable areas; slopes and banks; delineating space and defining prop-erty lines; breaking up large expanses of lawn; transition plantings; barrier plantings; accentuating focal points
Propagation: cuttings

Although *Juniperus sabina* is a variable species that ranges from ground-cover to tree form, our prairie garden cultivars are generally symmetrical, distinctly vase shaped, and 0.3 to 1.5 m (1 to 5 ft.) in height. Most have soft, scale-like leaves, usually green to blue-green, with a strong and pungent oil of juniper aroma when bruised or crushed. They are useful as foundation or mass plantings and in mixed borders.

Cultivars
- 'Arcadia' is low and spreading, growing 0.6 m (2 ft.) tall and 2.5 m (8 ft.) wide, with graceful arching stems and a dense, layered form. The soft, scale-like foliage is a rich, bright green that is retained throughout

the winter. 'Arcadia' was grown from seed from the Ural Mountains.

- 'Blue Danube', an Austrian introduction, is 0.6 m (2 ft.) tall and 2.5 m (8 ft.) wide and semi-upright, with soft, scale-like, blue-green to gray-blue foliage. Low and spreading, its branches root along the ground as they grow. It may winter burn in exposed locations.
- 'Broadmoor' is a dwarf cultivar, growing to 0.3 m (1 ft.) and spreading to 2 m (6.5 ft.), with dense, bright green foliage. Hardy to zone 3, it should be placed in a protected microclimate in colder regions. 'Broadmoor' was grown from seed collected in the Ural Mountains in the 1930s.
- 'Buffalo' is a compact form of var. *tamariscifolia*, which is 0.3 m (1 ft.) tall and 2 to 3 m (6.5 to 10 ft.) wide. A female, berry-producing selection, with bright green, mostly scale-like leaves, it retains good winter color and is ideal for covering a bank or wall. Adrian Bloom, the British nurseryman, considers it "one of the best groundcovering junipers." It was grown from seed imported from a Russian government forestry station near Leningrad in 1933.
- 'Calgary Carpet' is a Monrovia Nurseries introduction and has a low, horizontal branching habit that is unique to savin junipers and soft green foliage. It grows 0.3 m (1 ft.) tall and 2 to 3 m (6.5 to 10 ft.) wide.
- 'Skandia' is extremely hardy and relatively low and compact, growing 20 to 45 cm (8 to 18 in.) tall and 2 m (6.5 ft.) wide. It is a female, berry-producing selection, with soft, scale-like, dark green leaves. It was grown from seed collected in the Ural Mountains.
- var. *tamariscifolia* (tam-a-risk-i-*fo*-lee-a), tamarix savin juniper, has been known since 1789. It forms a round, mounded shrub, 45 cm (18 in.) tall and 3 to 4 m (10 to 13 ft.) wide, and has stiff, arching branches and soft, scale-like, bright green foliage. British gardener and garden writer Christopher Lloyd considered it "absolutely weed suppressing."

Lamiastrum galeobdolon
lay-mee-*as*-trum gal-lee-*ob*-do-lon
Yellow archangel, dead nettle

Plant at a Glance
Type: herbaceous perennial
Height/spread: 30 cm (12 in.) / 30 to 45 cm (12 to 18 in.) or more
Spacing: 45 cm (18 in.)
Light: partial shade
Soil: average
Distinguishing features: yellow flowers; green and silver variegated foliage
Landscape use: lawn replacement; small, inaccessible, or inhospitable areas; slopes and banks; unifying shrub beds; delineating space and defining

Best Groundcovers & Vines For The Prairies

property lines; breaking up large expanses of lawn; accentuating focal points; screening spring-bulb foliage; shady understory
Propagation: division

Lamiastrum, together with *Lamium*, a genus to which it is closely related, make excellent groundcovers for large, shady areas. How do you tell them apart? *Lamiastrum* has yellow flowers, while those of *Lamium* are pink or white.

Lamiastrum is native from Europe into western Asia to Iran; the genus name means "resembling *Lamium*." The species and common name are closely connected. *Galeo* means "to cover with a helmet" and *dolon* is a "fly's sting"; thus, incapable of stinging, the plant is a dead nettle.

A member of the mint family, *Lamiastrum* has square stems and opposite leaves. The leaves are 2.5 to 8 cm (1 to 3 in.) long and variegated green and silver, with toothed margins. The deep yellow, hooded flowers (hence, the common name "yellow archangel") are two-lipped and found in leaf axils and in terminal whorls, forming a loose but upright spike from late spring to early summer. The roots consist of short underground stolons that root in the soil as they go.

The silver-splashed foliage and bright yellow flowers make *Lamiastrum* an excellent choice to lighten up a shaded area in a woodland garden. The attractive cultivar 'Herman's Pride' forms neat, compact mounds that grow to 20 cm (8 in.) tall. It has pointed, oval, tapered leaves that are veined with metallic silver. The variegation is more refined than that of the species.

How to Grow
Plant *Lamiastrum* in partial shade in average soil. They grow better when kept evenly moist but tolerate short periods of drought. Propagate through division in spring.

Lamiastrum galeobdolon 'Herman's Pride'
('Herman's Pride' yellow archangel) (Sara Williams)

Lamium maculatum
lay-me-um mak-yew-*la*-tum
Spotted dead nettle

Plant at a Glance
Type: herbaceous perennial
Height/spread: 20 to 30 cm (8 to 12 in.) / 30 to 45 cm (12 to 18 in.)
Spacing: 30 cm (12 in.)
Light: partial to full shade
Soil: average
Distinguishing features: white or pink flowers; variegated foliage
Landscape use: edging; lawn replacement; small, inaccessible, or inhospitable areas; unifying shrub beds; delineating space and defining property lines; breaking up large expanses of lawn; accentuating focal points; screening spring-bulb foliage; shady understory
Propagation: division

Lamium maculatum 'Beacon Silver' ('Beacon Silver' deadnettle) (Sara Williams)

"The flowers are baked with sugar as roses are, which is called sugar roset; as the distilled water of them which is used to make the heart merry, to make good colour in the face, and to refresh the vital spirits." So wrote British herbalist John Gerard of the spotted dead nettle in 1597 in his *Historie of Plants*. Native to Europe and western Asia, spotted dead nettle has been cultivated for centuries and at one time was eaten by peasants in Sweden. Did they also bake them with sugar? It's doubtful.

Lamium is the classical Latin name for these plants. Although the leaves are similar to stinging nettle, they do not sting, hence, the common name. Spotted refers to the white variegation on the foliage, as does the Latin word *maculatum*.

Cultivars recommended as groundcovers have a fibrous but stoloniferous root system that allows them to spread steadily and soon form a colony. Flowers are two-lipped and formed in whorls of white, pink, mauve, or purple. The silver and green variegated leaves are oval to heart shaped,

Best Groundcovers & Vines For The Prairies

opposite, 2.5 cm (1 in.) in diameter, and attached to square stems, indicating them as a member of the mint family.

How to Grow
Given shade and even moisture, spotted dead nettles are easy to grow. Shear or mow in mid-summer to encourage a more-compact form. Divide to obtain more plants in spring or in early summer.

Cultivars
- 'Album' has creamy white flowers and foliage blotched with silver, like the species.
- 'Aureum' has yellow leaves, with broad, white mid-ribs, and pink flowers. It needs shade and even moisture and is less robust than most cultivars.
- 'Beacon Silver' has silver leaves, with thin, green margins like 'White Nancy', but has pink flowers; it requires shade.
- 'Chequers' is a vigorous cultivar, with green, silver-splashed foliage and deep rose-pink flowers.
- 'Pink Pewter' is similar to 'White Nancy' but has clear salmon-pink flowers.
- 'Red Nancy' resembles 'White Nancy' but has deep cherry-pink flowers.
- 'Shell Pink' is compact and slower to spread than some other cultivars. Its leaves have irregular white variegation and it bears soft pink flowers.
- 'White Nancy' has white flowers and silver leaves, with thin, green margins. It is more sun tolerant than other cultivars.

Lysimachia nummularia
li-see-*mak*-ee-a num-ew-*lah*-ree-a
Creeping Jenny, moneywort

Plant at a Glance
Type: herbaceous perennial
Height/spread: 5 to 10 cm (2 to 4 in.) / 30 cm (12 in.) or more
Spacing: 45 cm (18 in.)
Light: full sun to full shade
Soil: moist; average
Distinguishing features: tiny, bright yellow flowers
Landscape use: edging; waterside plantings; naturalization; lawn replacement; small, inaccessible, or inhospitable areas; unifying shrub beds; accentuating focal points; shady understory
Propagation: division

Lysimachia nummularia (creeping Jenny) (Sara Williams)

Although prostrate in form, creeping Jenny has the vigor of a small elephant. Its soft texture and diminutive size belie an unruly, colonizing nature. It is, after all, a groundcover. And consider its botanical name. It commemorates King Lysimachos of ancient Thracia on the Black Sea, who is said to have pacified a bull using this plant. His name is derived from the Greek *lysimachos*, meaning "to end strife." Both the species name and the common name "moneywort" refer to the coin-shaped leaves; the Latin word *nummularia* means "resembling coins." Creeping Jenny has a long folk history in Europe, where it is native. Roman farmers placed its yellow flowers under the yokes of oxen to serve as an insect repellent. It has also been used as a hair dye.

Prostrate and creeping, it forms a gentle, low mound but is capable of spreading indefinitely. The golden, cup-shaped flowers, only 2.5 cm (1 in.) in diameter, are formed in late spring. The small, bright green leaves are rounded and opposite. Long, trailing stems root from the node as they go. 'Aurea' has yellow foliage but is otherwise similar to the species, although less vigorous. It does best in shade and brightens dark areas.

Think carefully about where to plant creeping Jenny. It is best used on the banks of streams or ponds (where it will actually grow into the water) or for naturalization. At the front of a border or as edging, creeping Jenny requires vigilance and a sharp spade on the part of the gardener.

How to Grow

Equally at home in sun or shade in average soil, creeping Jenny prefers even moisture. It self-propagates so well that there is little need for the gardener to do it. Simply dig up and replant the plantlets.

Other Species and Hybrids

- *Lysimachia punctata* (punk-*tah*-ta), yellow loosestrife, is as erect as creeping Jenny is prostrate. About 1 m (3.3 ft.) in height, it soon forms large clumps through creeping rhizomes and can be invasive in good soils. The oval- to lance-shaped leaves are in whorls around the stems. The yellow, star-like flowers are formed in leaf axils in late spring to early summer. Native to Asia Minor, it grows in sun or shade. This vigorous plant is useful for filling in small, inaccessible, or inhospitable areas, for delineating space and defining property lines, and for breaking up large expanses of lawn. The variegated cultivars are less useful as groundcovers.

Mahonia repens
mah-*hoe*-nee-ah *reh*-penz
Creeping Oregon grape

Plant at a Glance
Type: broad-leafed evergreen shrub
Height/spread: 30 cm (12 in.) / 30 cm (12 in.)
Spacing: 30 cm (12 in.)
Light: shade
Soil: well drained
Distinguishing features: yellow flowers; compound, holly-like, evergreen foliage; dark blue berries
Landscape use: small, inaccessible, or inhospitable areas; shady understory
Propagation: suckers

Mahonia repens has a widespread distribution from northern Mexico north to British Columbia and east to the Black Hills of South Dakota. Plants from a South Dakota provenance will grow in favored shady locations in prairie gardens. The foliage is pinnately compound, with each oval leaflet having margins with sharp teeth. Bright yellow flowers are borne in short racemes in late spring, followed by dark blue berries that are covered by a whitish bloom. Oregon grape is a highly attractive evergreen groundcover that thrives in dry, shady locations where choices are limited, such as under a tree with a shallow root system or under the eaves of a building. The fruit is used for jam in its native range.

Mahonia repens (creeping Oregon grape) (Sara Williams)

How to Grow
Creeping Oregon grape needs good drainage and prefers shade. It is easiest to start by planting container-grown plants but it can be propagated by transplanting shoots with pieces of rhizome, with the old leaves pruned off, in early spring. Leaves will re-emerge as the plants root.

Provenance is the known origin of a plant. Some plant species are native over wide areas. For example, *Mahonia repens* grows from British Columbia south to Mexico and east to South Dakota. Plants from mild climatic zones in British Columbia and states west of the Rockies are not likely to survive on the prairies. However, plants from the Black Hills of South Dakota have been subjected to much more severe conditions and over time have become adapted to those conditions and so will survive in shaded locations in prairie gardens.

Winter hardiness varies in many other plant species with wide natural distributions. Representative plants that have been subjected to conditions that are similar to our cold winters and hot, dry summers are more likely to be adapted to our climate. For the past 130 years, horticulturists have searched for plant species from provenances that best match our prairie climate.

Other groundcovers species where provenance is important are switch grass (*Panicum virgatum*) and smooth sumac (*Rhus glabra*).

Matteuccia struthiopteris
(syn. *M. struthiopteris* var. *pensylvanica*, *M. pensylvanica*)

ma-*too*-see-a strooth-ee-*op*-ter-is
Ostrich fern, American ostrich fern

Plant at a Glance

Type: herbaceous perennial
Height/spread: 1.2 m (4 ft.) / 0.9 m (3 ft.)
Spacing: 0.9 m (3 ft.)
Light: partial shade
Soil: moist; rich in organic matter
Distinguishing features: enormous, symmetrical fronds
Landscape use: small, inaccessible, or inhospitable areas; delineating space and defining property lines; directing foot traffic; accentuating focal points; screening; shady understory
Propagation: division

The ostrich fern is the largest fern in North America and very similar (if not identical) to the European species. At various times in horticultural history, the two have been lumped together as one species or split apart as two separate species.

Vase-shaped ostrich ferns form extensive colonies in the parkland and forest belts of the northern prairies. Once used medicinally by Native peoples, the fronds are edible when steamed.

The genus name honors Carlos Matteucci (1800–1868), an Italian physics professor. Both the common and species names allude to its resemblance to the plumes of an ostrich. The Greek word *struthokamelos* means "ostrich," while *pteris* means "fern."

Consider scale when placing the ostrich fern. Its height and ultimate spread should be proportional to the landscape in which it is planted.

The leaves of ferns, called fronds, are in two forms. The sterile (non-spore-bearing) fronds are called fiddleheads when young and are edible. They mature to graceful arching, pinnately compound fronds, 60 to 150 cm (24 to 60 in.) long and 20 to 40 cm (8 to

Matteuccia struthiopteris (native Ostrich fern) (Sara Williams)

16 in.) wide. The fertile fronds are semi-woody, club shaped, and 30 to 60 cm (12 to 24 in.) in height. They emerge green and mature to dark brown, releasing spores from their lower surface in spring. These plants spread by rhizomes that develop crowns that look like scaly bulbs.

How to Grow
Given organic soil, even moisture, shade, and protection from drying winds, the ostrich fern will be stunning in its size, symmetry, and freshness. Propagate by division in spring.

Microbiota decussata
mik-row-bee-*owe*-tah deck-koos-*sah*-tah
Russian cypress, Siberian cypress

Plant at a Glance
Type: coniferous evergreen shrub
Height/spread: 30 cm (12 in.) / 60 cm (24 in.)
Spacing: 60 cm (24 in.)
Light: full sun to partial shade
Soil: moist; well drained
Distinguishing features: bright green, scale-like needles
Landscape use: mixed border; edging; small, inaccessible, or inhospitable areas; delineating space and defining property lines; accentuating focal points
Propagation: softwood cuttings

Russian cypress was discovered near Vladivostock in 1921. The genus name *Microbiota* is derived from *micro*, meaning "small," and *biota*, meaning "life"; *decussata* refers to each pair of needles being at right angles to the preceding pair. This low-growing conifer has adpressed needles similar to those of cedar and gracefully nodding branch tips. The needles are bright green and may take on a bronze color in winter. The species is monoecious,

Microbiota decussata (Russian cypress) (Sara Williams)

with female plants producing cones composed of a single, naked seed surrounded by spreading scales.

How to Grow
In its native habitat, Russian cypress grows above the tree line in the sub-alpine zone in gravelly soils with excellent drainage. Although cold hardy and sun tolerant, it does best where it has afternoon shade that moderates summer heat and slows winter snow melt. Russian cypress should be planted from balled and burlapped or container-grown plants. It can also be propagated from softwood cuttings, although with some difficulty.

Molinia caerulea variegata
mo-*leen*-ee-ah sir-*oo*-lee-ah
Variegated moor grass

Plant at a Glance
Type: ornamental grass
Height/spread: 40 cm (16 in.) / 30 cm (12 in.)
Spacing: 30 cm (12 in.)
Light: full sun
Soil: moist; well drained
Distinguishing features: variegated foliage
Landscape use: mixed or perennial border; waterside plantings; mass plantings; accentuating focal points
Propagation: division

Molinia caerulea 'Variegata' (variegated moorgrass) *(Sara Williams)*

Molinia is named in honor of Chilean botanist J. Molina; *caerulea* means "dark blue" or "sky blue" and refers to the foliage color of natural forms. Variegated moor grass is a tufted perennial, with cream and green variegated leaves. The foliage clump grows to about 15 cm (6 in.) in height, with flower heads rising 30 to 40 cm (12 to 16 in.). Plants are slow to establish but easy to control in a garden bed. Use variegated moor grass as a specimen in a border or in mass plantings.

How to Grow
Plant variegated moor grass in spring in a sunny location with well-drained soil. It grows best in moist conditions but is quite drought tolerant once established. Cut back or mow in the spring to remove tufts of growth from the previous year. Plants are propagated by transplanting divisions in early spring or in mid-summer.

Monarda hybrids
mon-*nar*-dah
Monarda, wild bergamot, bee balm, Oswego tea

Plant at a Glance
Type: herbaceous perennial
Height/spread: 20 to 50 cm (8 to 20 in.) / 30 to 60 cm (12 to 24 in.)
Spacing: 30 cm (12 in.)
Light: full sun
Soil: well drained
Distinguishing features: colorful flowers; fragrant, dark green foliage

Landscape use: perennial or mixed border; rock garden; small, inaccessible, or inhospitable areas; delineating space and defining property lines; breaking up large expanses of lawn; directing foot traffic
Propagation: division; softwood cuttings

The Morden *Monarda* hybrids are the result of crosses initiated by Dr. Henry Marshall between *M. fistulosa*, native to the prairies, and *M. didyma*, native to the eastern United States and Canada. The hybrids are more-compact plants, with brighter flower colors than *M. fistulosa*, and better winter hardiness than *M. didyma* cultivars. The colorful pink to mauve or purple flowers attract bees, hummingbirds, and butterflies to the garden, giving rise to the common name "bee balm." Individual, tubular flowers are about 2.5 cm (1 in.) long and are held in tightly packed heads, usually atop stems.

Monarda has the characteristic square stems of the mint family to which it belongs. The leaves are broadly lance shaped, with toothed margins, and up to 10 cm (4 in.) in length. The top side may be either hairy or smooth, while the underside is usually hirsute. The Morden hybrids have smooth, dark green leaves that are less susceptible to mildew than *M. fistulosa*. Their strong, pleasant odor resembles the bergamot orange used to flavor Earl Grey tea, hence, the common name "wild bergamot."

The genus name honors Nicholas de Monardes, a Spanish physician and botanist, who published a book on American medicinal products in 1571. Breeding lines have been selected for a high content of the essential oils geraniol, linalool, and thymol, which are used in the pharmaceutical and cosmetics industry. Monarda has long been used by Native Americans as a medicinal plant, especially to heal the womb after childbirth and to relieve menstrual cramps or fever. The name "Oswego tea" was derived from the discovery of this use by Philadelphia botanist John Bertram on a trip to Oswego, New York.

Monarda 'Petite Delight' ('Petite Delight' beebalm) (Hugh Skinner)

How to Grow
Monarda requires very good drainage and a sunny exposure to survive. It is shallow rooted and should be mulched and planted in protected locations that hold snow in order to survive in colder parts of the prairie area. These beautiful plants are worth the effort. Propagate monarda from divisions in early

spring or softwood cuttings, or plant container-grown plants any time during the growing season. Avoid allowing plants to die out in the center by dividing and transplanting them every second year.

Cultivars
- 'Marshall's Delight' grows to 60 cm (24 in.) in height and has bright pink flowers and dark green, mildew-resistant foliage.
- 'Petite Delight' is 30 cm (12 in.) tall, with clear lavender-pink flowers.
- 'Petite Wonder' is slightly smaller than 'Petite Delight' and has clear pink flowers.

Nepeta x 'Dropmore Blue'
nee-*pee*-ta
'Dropmore Blue' catmint

Plant at a Glance
Type: herbaceous perennial
Height/spread: 40 cm (16 in.) / 50 cm (20 in.)
Spacing: 30 cm (12 in.)
Light: full sun to partial shade
Soil: well drained
Distinguishing features: grayish blue flowers
Landscape use: perennial or mixed border; edging; rock garden; small, inaccessible, or inhospitable areas; unifying shrub beds; delineating space and defining property lines; breaking up large expanses of lawn; transition plantings; back lane plantings; accentuating focal points; screening
Propagation: division; softwood cuttings

Nepeta is named for Nepete, an ancient city in west-central Italy. 'Dropmore Blue' catmint is a hybrid between *N. mussini* and *N. ukranica*, developed by Frank Skinner and introduced in his 1932 catalogue. A sprawling plant, it has attractive oval, gray-green leaves and spikes of small, tubular, lipped, blue flowers. It is also

Nepeta x 'Dropmore Blue' ('Dropmore Blue' catmint) (Sara Williams)

sterile, which means that it flowers all summer long and doesn't self-seed in a weedy fashion like some other catmints. It is a superior plant for edging and is particularly attractive grown in conjunction with roses. Gardeners in Great Britain recognize this superior plant and use it extensively.

How to Grow
'Dropmore Blue' catmint grows well in sun or partial shade in well-drained soils. It can be propagated by dividing plants in spring or by softwood cuttings.

Other Species and Hybrids
- *Nepeta* x *faasenii* (fas-*sen*-ee-i), Caucasian catmint, grows from 30 to 60 cm (12 to 24 in.) tall and has gray foliage and lavender flowers. Deadhead to encourage a second flush of bloom.

Omphalodes verna alba
umf-a-*lo*-deez *ver*-na *al*-bah
Creeping forget-me-not

Plant at a Glance
Type: herbaceous perennial
Height/spread: 20 cm (8 in.) / 40 cm (16 in.)
Spacing: 30 cm (12 in.)
Light: partial to full shade
Soil: well drained
Distinguishing features: small, white flowers; green foliage
Landscape use: small, inaccessible, or inhospitable areas; unifying shrub beds; accentuating focal points; shady understory
Propagation: division

Omphalodes verna alba (creeping forget-me-not) (Hugh Skinner)

Best Groundcovers & Vines For The Prairies

Omphalodes is derived from the Greek word meaning "navel-shaped" (as in a belly button) and describes the appearance of a scar on the seeds, *verna*, meaning "spring," refers to the bloom period, and *alba* means "white," designating flower color. Creeping forget-me-not develops a mound of medium green, hairy, oval- to lance-shaped leaves, with long petioles. As the plant matures, it develops stolons that give rise to new plantlets. The small, white, tubular, five-lobed flowers are borne on short racemes in the spring. It thrives in dry shade and provides attractive groundcover where few other plants will grow.

How to Grow
Drought-tolerant, creeping forget-me-not prefers a partially shaded or shaded location, with well-drained soil. It spreads by stolons and is easily propagated by transplanting offset plants in spring or in mid-summer.

Pachysandra terminalis
pak-i-*sand*-dra ter-min-*nal*-is
Japanese spurge

Plant at a Glance
Type: evergreen sub-shrub
Height/spread: 30 cm (12 in.) / 20 cm (8 in.)
Spacing: 30 cm (12 in.)
Light: shade
Soil: moist; rich in organic matter
Distinguishing features: glossy, dark green foliage
Landscape use: lawn replacement; small, inaccessible, or inhospitable areas; accentuating focal points; shady understory
Propagation: division

Pachysandra terminalis (Japanese spurge) (Sara Williams)

Although omnipresent and somewhat overused in milder climates, Japanese spurge is slow and difficult to establish in zones 2 and 3 of the prairies unless grown in a sheltered microclimate. The genus name is derived from the Greek *pachys*, meaning "thick," and *andros*, "male," referring to the thick stamens. The specific epithet, *terminalis*, describes the terminal flower stalks.

Originating in the moist woodlands of Japan and China, Japanese spurge is valued for its dark green, glossy, and leathery foliage. Individual leaves are alternate, simple, toothed above the middle, and usually in whorls at the end of the fleshy stems. The small, whitish flowers, lacking petals, are inconspicuous and found at the end of the stems. The root system is rhizomatous but not aggressive.

Pachysandra is best used as a groundcover for shaded foundation plantings or in other protected situations.

How to Grow
Japanese spurge requires a sheltered microclimate and adequate snow cover to do its job properly as a groundcover. Variegated forms are largely untested on the prairies and are less vigorous even in milder climates. Propagate Japanese spurge by division in early spring.

Panicum virgatum
pan-i-cum vir-*ga*-tum
Switch grass

Plant at a Glance
Type: ornamental grass
Height/spread: 0.9 to 1.5 m (3 to 5 ft.) / 1.2 m (4 ft.)
Spacing: 60 cm (24 in.)
Light: full sun
Soil: well drained
Distinguishing features: airy flower and seed heads; bluish foliage
Landscape use: perennial or mixed border; waterside plantings; mass plantings; small, inaccessible, or inhospitable areas; delineating space and defining property lines; breaking up large expanses of lawn
Propagation: seed; division

Switch grass is native to moist soils across the prairies. *Panicum* is an

Panicum virgatum (switch grass)
(Sara Williams)

ancient Latin name previously applied to another plant; *virgatum* means "twiggy" and refers to the upright stems that emerge from its creeping root-stocks. Plants are topped by airy panicles of flowers, followed by seeds. A number of selections have been made for blue foliage color, including 'Heavy Metal', 'Prairie Sky', and 'Strictum'. Others such as 'Rotstrahlbusch' have been selected for red fall color. These selections have not proven hardy in zone 2 so may not be suitable for groundcover. Selections from northern provenances may yield hardier cultivars with similar ornamental characteristics.

Switch grass is a warm-season grass that provides interest in late summer, fall, and winter if planted at the back of a border or massed as a tall groundcover.

How to Grow
Switch grass prefers a sunny location with moist, well-drained soil. Plant plugs or divide rhizomes in spring. The species can be grown from seed. Cut the plant back in spring to remove dry vegetation from the previous year.

Paronychia capitata (syn. *P. nivea*)
par-ron-*ni*-ki-a ca-pi-*ta*-ta
Whitlowwort, nailwort

Plant at a Glance
Type: herbaceous perennial
Height/spread: 15 (6 in.) / 15 cm (6 in.)
Spacing: 15 to 30 cm (6 to 12 in.

Paronychia capitata (whitlowwort) (Sara Williams)

Worts Worth Understanding

Understanding the derivation of whitlowwort's name is akin to lessons in Old English and Greek mixed with classical folk medicine. A whitlow is a sore at the quick, which is beneath a fingernail or under a horse's hoof. It can also be a swelling of the finger or thumb. Wort is an archaic term meaning "plant" or "herb." When attached to an affliction, it generally indicates that the plant is used to cure the affliction. Thus, whitlowwort is a plant traditionally used to cure sores or swellings beneath nails or hooves. The genus name, *Paronychia,* is similar, from the Greek words *para,* meaning "near" and *onyx,* meaning "nail," hence, put near the nail. Native to the Pyrenees Mountains and the Mediterranean region, whitlowwort has a long folk tradition.

Light: full sun
Soil: well drained
Distinguishing features: tiny, silver-green foliage
Landscape use: rock garden; lawn replacement; small, inaccessible, or inhospitable areas; pavement plantings; screening spring-bulb foliage
Propagation: division

The biggest problem with whitlowwort is finding it. Unfortunately, it has not yet made its way into the mainstream horticultural market from its native home in the Mediterranean region. Prairie gardeners would be well advised to ask for it at their local garden center.

Slow but persistent, whitlowwort is small and tufted. It roots as it contacts the soil, soon forming a carpet of silvery foliage. The leaves are tiny, linear, in pairs, and very pubescent. The flowers, small and gray-green, are inconspicuous, blooming in May and June but often hidden by the foliage. They are enclosed by showy silvery bracts.

There is some confusion in nomenclature. A second species, *Paronychia serpyllifolia* (syn. *P. kapela* subsp. *serpyllifolia*), native to the Pyrenees, is also described as procumbent and mat forming, with compact, silver-gray foliage.

Because of its diminutive stature, whitlowwort is an excellent companion for spring bulbs, pavement plantings, or in a rock garden. It has been used successfully as a lawn replacement for about three years in Lethbridge, Alberta, but has no tolerance for foot traffic when used in this capacity.

How to Grow
Plant in full sun in well-drained soil. It is very drought tolerant once established. Propagation is by division in spring.

Paxistima canbyi
pah-*kiss*-ti-mah *kan*-bee-eye
Cliffgreen, paxistima

Plant at a Glance
Type: broad-leafed evergreen shrub
Height/spread: 20 cm (8 in.) / 30 cm (12 in.)
Spacing: 30 cm (12 in.)
Light: full sun to partial shade
Soil: well drained
Distinguishing features: dense, evergreen foliage
Landscape use: edging; lawn replacement; small, inaccessible, or inhospitable areas; accentuating focal points; shady understory
Propagation: division; softwood cuttings

Paxistima is derived from Greek and means "thick stigma" (the part of the flower that receives the pollen). The genus *Paxistima* includes two species native to North America. The species name, *canbyi*, is for botanist William Canby. Commonly known as cliffgreen, this species has thin, four-sided stems, clothed with small, evergreen leaves that are 1 to 2 cm (0.4 to 0.8 in.) long and 0.5 cm (0.2 in.) wide, with wavy, incurved margins. Flowers are inconspicuous. The plants spread by means of distinctive orange underground rhizomes to form a dense, evergreen groundcover.

How to Grow
Cliffgreen prefers well-drained soils in partial shade or full sun. It performs best where it receives snow cover or afternoon shade and requires little or no attention once established. Plant container-grown plants and propagate by transplanting rooted divisions in spring or by taking softwood cuttings.

Paxistima canbyi (cliffgreen) (Sara Williams)

Penstemon caespitosus

pen-*stay*-mon cas-pit-*oh*-sus

Mat penstemon

Plant at a Glance

Type: evergreen sub-shrub

Height/spread: 5 cm (2 in.) / 20 cm (8 in.)

Spacing: 15 cm (6 in.)

Light: full sun

Soil: well drained

Distinguishing features: purple flowers; low, evergreen foliage

Landscape use: rock garden; small, inaccessible, or inhospitable areas; pavement plantings; accentuating focal points

Propagation: division; softwood cuttings

Penstemon caespitosus (mat penstemon) (Hugh Skinner)

Mat penstemon is a very low-growing sub-shrub, with slender stems and small, opposite, oval, evergreen leaves. The genus name, *Penstemon*, is derived from the Greek word for "five stamens" and refers to the plant's five stamens, although the fifth is sterile; *caespitosus* is Latin for "turf" and refers to its low, matted habit. The tubular, purple flowers appear in short racemes in early summer. This native of Wyoming and Colorado forms a dense, matted groundcover that lends itself to planting between stepping stones.

How to Grow

Mat penstemon requires well-drained soil and prefers full sun. It is easy to propagate by separating and transplanting rooted stems in spring or by softwood cuttings.

Other Species and Hybrids

Other penstemons suitable for groundcover in sunny prairie gardens include two taller-growing evergreen sub-shrubs that are native into Alberta. They need well-drained, moist soil and full sun to thrive and should be planted in wind-protected locations in prairie gardens. They are worth a little extra effort for their spectacular blooms.

- *Penstemon davidsonii* var. *menziesii* (day-vid-*son*-ee-ee men-*zee*-see-i) grows to about 15 cm (6 in.) in height and has lilac purple, tubular flowers and leathery, dark green, narrow, oval leaves, with toothed margins.
- *Penstemon fruticosus* (froo-ti-*ko*-sus) 'Purple Haze' is a selection from the University of British Columbia Botanical Garden. It has purple flowers and grows to 25 cm (10 in.).

Persicaria affinis (syn. *Polygonum affine*)
pur-se-*care*-ee-ah a-*fee*-nis
Himalayan fleeceflower

Plant at a Glance
Type: semi-evergreen perennial
Height/spread: 25 cm (10 in.) / 30 cm (12 in.)
Spacing: 20 cm (8 in.)
Light: full sun to partial shade
Soil: moist; well drained
Distinguishing features: colorful, two-tone flower spikes; compact, dense foliage
Landscape use: mixed or perennial border; edging; small, inaccessible, or inhospitable areas; delineating space and defining property lines; breaking up large expanses of lawn; directing foot traffic; accentuating focal points; shady understory
Propagation: division; softwood cuttings

The genus *Persicaria* belongs to the buckwheat or knotweed family, so-called because of their distinctly enlarged stem nodes. These joints are sheathed by the leafy stipules of their alternate, broadly lance-shaped, leathery leaves. The species *affinis* spreads by above-ground stolons to form a dense groundcover. The common name,

Persicaria affinis 'Dimity' ('Dimity' Himalayan fleeceflower)
(Sara Williams)

fleeceflower, refers to the tiny, pink flowers that appear in dense, nubbly spikes in mid-summer and turn red as the petals are shed. The cultivar 'Dimity' has proven adaptable to prairie garden conditions. It is attractive as edging or groundcover in mixed beds under trees.

How to Grow
Himalayan fleeceflowers thrive in sun or partial shade in moist soil. Divide every three or four years, as they become overcrowded. They can be propagated easily by transplanting divisions in spring or by softwood cuttings.

Other Species and Hybrids
- *Persicaria bistorta superba* (bis-*tor*-ta su-*per*-ba), superb European bistort, grows 60 cm (24 in.) tall. Its attractive spikes of pale pink flowers rise above medium green foliage through much of the summer. As a groundcover, this cultivar forms a dense drift under moist conditions.

Phalaris arundinacea 'Picta'
fa-*lar*-is a-run-di-*nah*-see-ah
Ribbon grass

Plant at a Glance
Type: ornamental grass
Height/spread: 60 to 120 cm (24 to 48 in.) / 90 cm (36 in.)
Spacing: 60 cm (24 in.)
Light: full sun to partial shade
Soil: moist; average

Phalaris arundinacea 'Picta' ('Picta' variegated ribbon grass) (Hugh Skinner)

Best Groundcovers & Vines For The Prairies

Distinguishing features: variegated, vertically striped, green and cream foliage
Landscape use: mass plantings; naturalization; small, inaccessible, or inhospitable areas; delineating space and defining property lines; breaking up large expanses of lawn; back lane plantings; shady understory
Propagation: division

Variegated ribbon grass is familiar to most seasoned gardeners and is often relegated to the back lane because of its aggressive tendencies in herbaceous borders. This grass is extremely variable in terms of height, ranging from 60 to 120 cm (24 to 48 in.), although it is generally 60 cm (24 in.) tall. It spreads indefinitely through invasive rhizomes, forming loose, upright clumps. The green and cream foliage is vertically variegated.

Found in moist habitats in both North America and Eurasia, *Phalaris* is the Greek name for this grass, while *arundinacea* means "reed-like." 'Picta', meaning "painted" or "brightly coloured," describes the variegated foliage.

Variegated ribbon grass is best used as a groundcover or for mass plantings. 'Feesey' is similar to 'Picta' but more compact, at 60 cm (24 in.) in both height and spread, and having more-pronounced pink and white variegation in the spring. It is not as invasive but fares worse in extreme heat.

How to Grow
Plant variegated ribbon grass in sun or shade in an area where it can be irrigated. A cool-season grass, it goes dormant and somewhat shabby in the heat of summer without sufficient water. Mow it down to 10 to 15 cm (4 to 6 in.) to remove foliage that is worse for wear and encourage new growth. Propagate through division from spring to mid-summer.

Phlox borealis
floks bore-ee-*al*-is
Arctic phlox

Plant at a Glance
Type: evergreen perennial
Height/spread: 5 to 10 cm (2 to 4 in.) / 30 cm (12 in.)
Spacing: 30 cm (12 in.)
Light: full sun to partial shade
Soil: well drained
Distinguishing features: deep pink spring flowers; evergreen foliage
Landscape use: mixed and perennial borders; rock garden; edging; lawn replacement; small, inaccessible, or inhospitable areas; pavement plantings; accentuating focal points
Propagation: division

Phlox borealis 'Rubies Choice' ('Rubies Choice' Arctic phlox)
(Hugh Skinner)

Although arctic phlox is almost pedestrian in its widespread use, we never tire of its sudden eruption into full bloom, a signal of the sure arrival of spring. Both the common and botanical names describe its northern range. *Phlox* is the Greek word for "flame," an apt description of its bright flowers; *borealis* means "northern."

Used as a groundcover, in rock gardens and pavement plantings, and as edging, arctic phlox forms a low, compact, mounded mat of bright evergreen foliage. Individual leaves are linear and only 2.5 cm (1 in.) in length. Equally small, bright pink flowers in terminal clusters are borne on short stems in early spring, practically concealing the foliage. It spreads by stolons.

How to Grow
Arctic phlox does best in well-drained soil in full sun to light shade. It may be sheared lightly after flowering. All of the cultivars are propagated through division in spring.

Other Species and Hybrids
- *Phlox carolina* (care-oh-*line*-ah) 'Bill Baker' Carolina phlox grows as a dense, spreading clump, up to 45 cm (18 in.) tall. Flowers are rose-pink over a long period in early summer. It is mildew resistant and, while not widely known, is an excellent plant worthy of greater use.
- *Phlox hoodii* (*hoo*-di-i), Hood's phlox, native to the prairies, forms prostrate tufts, with white flowers and prickly foliage.
- *Phlox subulata* (sub-u-*lah*-ta), moss phlox, is quite variable, with many cultivars in white, pink, blue, and rosy red. The prickly, evergreen foliage turns bronze-green toward autumn. Native to the woodlands of the east coast, its prostrate stems form mats up to 1 m (3.3 ft.) in diameter. 'Ellie B' is a compact miniature that has tiny, white, star-shaped flowers.

Best Groundcovers & Vines For The Prairies

- 'Rubies Choice' is a hybrid between *Phlox borealis* and *P. subulata* that combines the best characteristics of each. It has a compact, creeping habit and stems clothed with medium green, needle-like leaves. Plants are covered with deep rose-pink flowers in May and early June.

Physostegia virginiana
fy-so-*stee*-gee-a vir-jin-ee-*an*-na
Obedient plant

Plant at a Glance
Type: herbaceous perennial
Height/spread: 60 to 90 cm (24 to 36 in.) / 60 to 90 cm (24 to 36 in.)
Spacing: 45 cm (18 in.)
Light: full sun to partial shade
Soil: moist; average
Distinguishing features: pink, tubular flowers; ability to travel
Landscape use: small, inaccessible, or inhospitable areas; delineating space and defining property lines; breaking up large expanses of lawn
Propagation: division

Physostegia virginiana is called obedient plant because individual florets are on hinged stalks and remain in the position on the stem in which they are placed by flower arrangers. However, in a herbaceous border, their behavior is less than obedient, verging on downright aggressive, and gardeners have been known to call them other names. The moral of the story is to be very careful where you place them in your landscape. Put them where they can cover ground.

The genus name is derived from two Greek words, *physa*, meaning "bladder," and *stege*, "covering," and refers to the seed capsules that are covered by an inflated calyx. Virginia is part of its native range in North America, which includes Manitoba, and the area from which the first specimen was described.

Obedient plants soon form large colonies. Their erect, stiff, and four-sided stems signal their membership in the mint family. Individual leaves are opposite, lance shaped, and toothed. The two-lipped, pink, tubular flowers are formed in dense spikes in leaf axils and terminal clusters from late summer into fall, opening from the bottom to the top. Of the cultivars, only 'Bouquet Rose' (sometimes listed as 'Pink Bouquet') serves as a groundcover. It has rose-pink flowers and grows to about 80 cm (32 in.) in height. White-flowered 'Summer Snow' is less vigorous and has been known to winter kill in zone 2. 'Miss Manners', not a spreader to begin with, lacked manners and died. 'Variegata' is not a groundcover.

How to Grow
Plant in average, moist soil in full sun to partial shade. It will self-propagate or you can do it through division from spring to mid-summer.

Polygonatum multiflorum (syn. *P.* x *hybridum*)

pol-ee-go-*na*-tum mul-tee-*flor*-um
Solomon's seal

Plant at a Glance

Type: herbaceous perennial
Height/spread: 60 to 90 cm (24 to 36 in.) / 45 cm (18 in.)
Spacing: 45 cm (18 in.)
Light: shade
Soil: moist; rich in organic matter
Distinguishing features: tiny, creamy white, bell-like flowers; grassy foliage
Landscape use: waterside plantings; naturalizing; small, inaccessible, or inhospitable areas; delineating space and defining property lines; directing foot traffic; accentuating focal points; shady understory
Propagation: seed; division

Polygonatum multiflorum (Solomon's seal)
(Hugh Skinner)

Another good low-maintenance groundcover for moist, shady areas, Solomon's seal has graceful arching stems and fresh green foliage throughout the growing season. The ovate to elliptical leaves are 10 cm (4 in.) long, with parallel veins. The small, nodding, bell-shaped flowers, white with greenish tips, are suspended below leaves in clusters of four and followed by dark blue fruit. The thick, fleshy root system is made up of creeping rhizomes that spread horizontally just below the soil surface.

The common name describes the cross-section of the root that is said to resemble King Solomon's seal, a six-pointed star. The specific epithet, *multiflorum*, is Latin for "many-flowered."

How to Grow

Solomon's seal does best in evenly moist soil amended with organic matter. It is propagated most easily by division in spring. Seed can be sown into prepared garden soil in the fall and will germinate the following spring.

Other Species and Hybrids

Many species of *Polygonatum* have synonyms, which can make the nomenclature confusing.

The genus *Polygonatum* is from the Greek words *poly*, meaning "many," and *gony*, meaning "knee," a reference to the many joints in the rhizome. According to the Doctrine of Signatures (see p. 157), this was God's clue to early physicians and herbalists that it would be a plant useful in treating maladies of the joints. In fact, the roots were once widely used for this, which may not be as farfetched at it appears as the roots contain allantoin, a compound that promotes healing. Modern research indicates that root extracts of Solomon's seal help to heal cuts, lacerations, and bruises. John Gerard, the early British herbalist, whose consciousness had yet to be influenced by feminism, had this to say about it: "The root of Solomon's seale stamped while it is fresh and greene, and applied, taketh away in one night, or two at the most, any bruise, blacke or blew spots gotten by fals or womens wilfulnesse, in stumbling upon their hasty husbands fists or such like." Some references note that it is poisonous if taken internally.

- *Polygonatum commutatum* (kom-ew-*tah*-tum) (syn. *P. giganteum)*, giant Solomon's seal, is an architectural plant that can reach 1 to 2 m (3.3 to 6.5 ft.). Creamy-white flowers hang below the graceful arching stems.
- *Polygonatum falcatum* (foul-*kay*-tum), dwarf Solomon's seal, has erect stems, 10 to 15 cm (4 to 6 in.) tall, oval, pointed leaves, and flowers in the leaf axils. It makes an excellent groundcover and colonizes fairly quickly.
- *Polygonatum odoratum* var. *pluriflorum* 'Variegatum' (o-do-*rah*-tum var. plur-i-*flor*-um) (syn. *P. odoratum* 'Variegatum'), variegated Solomon's seal, has arching stems, up to 60 cm (24 in.) long, and green leaves, edged in creamy white, that turn bronze in fall. It is very slow to establish.

Potentilla
po-ten-*til*-la
Potentilla, cinquefoil

Potentilla derives its name from the Latin *potens*, meaning "powerful," which refers to its reputed medicinal properties. *Potentilla* is a diverse genus of annuals, perennials, and shrubs. As members of the rose family, they have five-petaled, disc-shaped flowers; palmately or occasionally pinnately compound leaves are arranged alternately on the stem. They are widely distributed in the northern hemisphere and a number of species are grown as garden plants.

How to Grow
Potentilla species are sun-loving plants that vary somewhat in their other cultural requirements. Silverweed is at its best in moist soil and is easily propagated by transplanting runners in spring or late summer, by seed, or by softwood cuttings.

Shrubby cinquefoil is easy to grow using container-grown or bare-root plants and adapts to most garden conditions, although it prefers well-drained soil. It is relatively easy to propagate in early summer from softwood cuttings, or stems can be layered. Pink- and orange-flowered cultivars show more intense flower color if given even moisture and afternoon shade.

Potentilla anserina (syn. *Argentina anserina*)
po-ten-*til*-la an-sa-*ree*-nah
Silverweed

Plant at a Glance
Type: herbaceous perennial
Height/spread: 15 cm (6 in.) / 30 cm (12 in.)
Spacing: 30 cm (12 in.)
Light: full sun
Soil: moist
Distinguishing features: yellow flowers; dark green foliage, with silver undersides
Landscape use: lawn replacement; small, inaccessible, or inhospitable areas; slopes and banks; transition plantings; accentuating focal points; back lane plantings
Propagation: seed; division; transplanting stolons; softwood cuttings

Potentilla anserina (silverweed) (Sara Williams)

The species name *anserina*, derived from the Latin *anserinus*, meaning "goose," probably refers to the plant's natural habitat near the water's edge. The name *Argentina* is from the Latin *argenteum*, meaning "silver," and refers to its silvery, pubescent leaves. Silverweed is a native plant that forms a dense groundcover of attractive pinnately compound, silver-backed leaves in wet areas. The leaves consist of seven to twenty-five toothed leaflets and are 8 to 60 cm (3 to 24 in.) long. The undersides are silky white and woolly. Plants spread by stolons much like strawberry plants. Disc-shaped, yellow flowers, 1 to 1.5 cm (0.4 to 0.6 in.) across, first appear in early summer and continue until fall.

Use it as a groundcover in a bog garden, along a stream, or in a damp, sunny place. Once established, it is much more drought tolerant than its native habitat would indicate.

Best Groundcovers & Vines For The Prairies

Potentilla fruticosa
(syn. *Dasiphora fruticosa* spp. *floribunda*)
po-ten-*til*-la froo-ti-*koe*-sah
Shrubby cinquefoil, potentilla

Plant at a Glance
Type: deciduous shrub
Height/spread: 30 to 120 cm (12 to 48 in.) / 60 to 120 cm (24 to 48 in.)
Spacing: 60 cm (24 in.)
Light: full sun to partial shade
Soil: well drained; average
Distinguishing features: white, yellow, orange, or pink flowers
Landscape use: mixed border; slopes and banks; delineating space and defining property lines; barrier plantings; breaking up large expanses of lawn; transition plantings; back lane plantings; accentuating focal points; screening
Propagation: layering; softwood cuttings

Potentilla fruticosa is a low-growing shrub with a circumpolar distribution. In nature, it grows in poor, calcareous soils in open ground or in bogs. It is quite shade tolerant but blooms more abundantly in sunny locations. Its five-petaled flowers, 2 to 4 cm (0.8 to 1.5 in) across, are produced singly or in small clusters along the stems. These flowers add color to the garden from early summer until fall. The pinnately compound leaves are 1 to 2 cm (0.4 to 0.8 in.) long and covered with silky hairs.

Fruticosa means "shrubby" and *floribunda* means "free flowering." *Dasiphora* is derived from the Greek *dasus*, meaning "shaggy" or "covered with hairs," and refers to the seeds. The common name cinquefoil refers to the foliage, which has five leaflets.

Many cultivars have been selected that are well adapted to prairie garden conditions. They vary in height and habit, with some being more suitable as groundcovers than others. Flower colors vary from yellow, the most common, to white, pink, and orange.

Potentilla is easy to grow and useful in many situations in the landscape. Once established, it is quite drought tolerant, which makes it an ideal groundcover for slopes and banks and for transition, back lane, and barrier plantings. The attractive flowers, produced throughout the summer, draw attention to a focal point in the yard. Plant this versatile plant to add color to mixed-shrub borders.

Cultivars
- 'Abbotswood' has pure white flowers and gray-green foliage. It grows up to 1 m (3.3 ft.) in both height and width. Flowers are produced over a long period.
- 'Coronation Triumph' is an outstanding free-flowering clone, developed

One reason for using Latin names is that the names are more stable because the language doesn't change. However, taxonomists responsible for naming plant species conduct ongoing studies to make sure that scientific names accurately reflect the relationships between plant species.

Until recently, *Potentilla* was a very broad and inclusive genus that encompassed herbaceous plants, as well as shrubby cinquefoil. However, in the 1920s and early 1930s, Dr. Per Axel Rydberg, curator of the herbarium at the New York Botanical Garden and a prominent taxonomist, proposed that *Potentilla anserina* should be accorded a new genus, *Argentina*; that *P. tridentata* should become *Sibbaldiopsis tridentate*; and that the shrubby *P. fruticosa* should become *Dasiphora fruticosa*. The wheels grind slowly but taxonomists now agree with Dr. Rydberg and these are now the officially recognized names for these species. However, since these changes are only beginning to infiltrate gardening literature and plant catalogues, we have decided to include these plants under *Potentilla* with this qualification.

by John Walker and introduced in the 1950s. It has medium green foliage, a dense habit, and prolific 2.5 cm (1 in.) flowers. Plants grow to 1.2 m (4 ft.) tall and 1 m (3.3 ft.) wide.

- 'Goldfinger' is a dense, upright shrub up to 1.2 m (4 ft.) tall. It has dark green foliage and bright yellow flowers, 4 cm (1.5 in.) in diameter.
- 'Katherine Dykes' is an upright shrub, up to 1 m (3.3 ft.) tall, with gray-green foliage and 2.5 (1 in.) flowers that are a soft lemon yellow.
- 'Mango Tango' ('Uman') is a dense, mounded plant, up to 0.8 m (2.5 ft.) tall, with a spread of up to 1 m (3.3 ft.). Its flowers are an interesting red-orange and yellow bicolor. The best flower color is produced in partial shade.
- 'McKay's White' is a creamy white sport of 'Katherine Dykes'. It grows 0.6 to 1 m (2 to 3.3 ft.) in height, with a similar spread.
- 'Orange Whisper' is a dense shrub, up to 1 m (3.3 ft.) in height and spread. Flowers are a soft apricot orange, with light green foliage. It should be planted in partial shade for the best flower color.
- 'Pink Beauty' produces double pink flowers on a dense shrub, about 60 cm (24 in.) high and 75 cm (30 in.) wide. Flowers retain their color much better in partial shade.
- 'Primrose Beauty' has gray-green foliage and soft primrose yellow flowers on a compact shrub, about 1 m (3.3 ft.) in height and spread.
- 'Snowbird' has double, white flowers on a mounded shrub, about 75 cm (30 in.) in height and spread. Its foliage is dense and dark green.
- 'Yellow Gem' is a low-growing plant, up to 38 cm (15 in.) high, with a spread to 100 cm (40 in.). It has attractive medium yellow, ruffled flowers, 3 cm (1.25 in.) in diameter, from June until frost.

Other Species and Hybrids

- *Potentilla alpestre* (al-*pez*-tree), orangespot potentilla, is a variable species with a circumpolar distribution. It grows to 25 cm (10 in.) in height and produces an abundance of 1 cm (0.4 in.), yellow flowers all summer. This species requires good drainage. It can be propagated from seed and self-seeds freely.

- *Potentilla megalantha* (meg-al-*anth*-ah), woolly cinquefoil, has densely felted leaves and yellow flowers in clusters in early summer. It grows 30 cm (12 in.) high.
- *Potentilla nepalensis* (*nep*-pa-*len*-sis), Nepal cinquefoil, is a sprawling plant, 30 cm (12 in.) tall and 50 cm (20 in.) wide, with flowers that are pink to scarlet red. It grows best in protected locations in moist soil.
- *Potentilla tridentata* (tri-den-*tat*-ah) (syn. *Sibbaldiopsis tridentata*), three-toothed cinquefoil, is a low-growing evergreen sub-shrub that is 10 to 25 cm (4 to 10 in.) high. It has dark green leaves, 1.5 to 2.5 cm (0.5 to 1 in.) long, that are topped by clusters of one to six flowers, each flower measuring about 0.5 to 1 cm (0.2 to 0.4 in.) across. Three-toothed cinquefoil is native to areas with dry, sandy soils and needs excellent drainage to survive in the garden.

Primula veris
prim-yew-la *ver*-is
Cowslip primrose

Plant at a Glance
Type: herbaceous perennial
Height/spread: 20 cm (8 in.) / 15 cm (6 in.)
Spacing: 25 cm (10 in.)
Light: partial shade
Soil: evenly moist; well drained; rich in organic matter
Distinguishing features: lovely yellow spring flowers
Landscape use: perennial and mixed borders; mass plantings; accentuating focal points; shady understory
Propagation: seed; division

We're often warned not to take the primrose path of pleasure and self-indulgence. And Shakespeare's Hamlet spoke of the "primrose path of dalliance." But when it comes to the plants themselves, why not?

Primroses have been a signal of spring for many centuries and are lovely as a groundcover, en masse, or in a shaded border, a spring garden, or a wild garden. Even the derivation of the name is sheer poetry. The genus *Primula* is from the Latin *primus*, meaning "first," and refers to their early flowers; *veris* means "of spring," their bloom period. The common name primrose is a corruption of "first rose," again a reference to their early bloom. It is with cowslip that the poetry begins to get a bit smudged. The name is from the old English *cuslype*, meaning "like slop" or, more literally, "like cow shit," as the flowers were often found in moist meadows near cow pies. Primroses have a long folk tradition of use in wine, for medicinal

Primula veris (English primrose) (Hugh Skinner)

tea, to cure jaundice, and for treating coughs in both people and cattle.

Their bright yellow, bell-shaped flowers are formed in loose, nodding, one-sided umbels on erect stems in late spring and they bloom for four weeks. They are characterized by a long, inflated calyx. The dark green foliage is in basal rosettes. Individual leaves are oval and about 15 cm (6 in.) in length. The shallow, fibrous root system is rhizomatous.

The orange to red cultivars are largely untested on the prairies and may not be readily available. Among those that may be worth trying are 'Perth Sunrise', 'Perth Sunset', and 'Sunset Shades'.

How to Grow
Cowslip primroses do well in partial shade in evenly moist, well-drained soil that is amended with organic matter. Propagate by seed or by division in spring. Primroses also self-seed but never to the point of becoming a nuisance, so transplanting seedlings is also an option.

Other Species and Hybrids
• *Primula auricula* (ow-*rik*-ew-la), the dusty miller primrose, is about 20 cm (8 in.) tall, with rosettes of thick, fleshy, gray-green leaves that are covered with a mealy white farina. The flowers of the species are yellow, but cultivars are available in many shades, including yellow, red, purple, wine, and salmon, most with a yellow or white eye, and bloom in May. The roots are long and cord-like. Rosettes are easily divided. This species tolerates much more sun than most other primroses.

Best Groundcovers & Vines For The Prairies

Prunus tenella

proo-nus teh-*nel*-ah
Russian almond

Plant at a Glance
Type: deciduous shrub
Height/spread: 0.9 to 1.5 m (3 to 5 ft.) / 0.9 to 1.5 m (3 to 5 ft.)
Spacing: 0.6 m (2 ft.)
Light: full sun
Soil: well drained
Distinguishing features: pink flowers
Landscape use: slopes and banks; transition plantings; barrier plantings; back lane plantings; screening
Propagation: seed; suckers

Prunus is the ancient name for "plum," which is also included in this genus; *tenella* means "slender" and probably refers to the plant's stems and branches. Russian almond suckers from underground rhizomes to produce numerous thin, upright stems. The shiny, dark green leaves are lance shaped and 5 to 8 cm (2 to 3 in.) long and 1 to 2.5 cm (0.4 to 1 in.) wide. Flowers emerge singly or in pairs along the stems in spring. The great profusion of rose-pink or occasionally white flowers, 2 cm (0.8 in.) across, makes a striking display. Flowers are followed by hard, densely hairy nuts, about 2 cm (0.8 in.) long, which resemble almonds.

How to Grow
Russian almond prefers a sunny location and requires well-drained soil. It can be planted bare-root in the spring or any time during the growing season as a container-grown plant. Propagate by seed sown in fall, by seed stratified and sown in spring, or by transplanting sucker shoots in early spring.

Other Species and Hybrids
- *Prunus pumila* (*pew*-mi-la), dwarf sandcherry, grows naturally on the dry, sandy slopes of the southeastern Canadian prairies.

Prunus tenella (Russian almond) (Sara Williams)

It is a low, suckering shrub, up to 30 cm (12 in.) in height, that has white flowers in spring, gray-green foliage, and dark purple fruit, 1 cm (0.4 in.) across, in fall. It is suitable for planting as groundcover in a sunny location in well-drained soil.

Pulmonaria
pul-moe-*nay*-ree-a
Lungwort

Pulmonaria mollis (soft lungwort) (Sara Williams)

Pulmonaria is a genus of perennials native to Europe. They are prized for their rather coarse, hirsute foliage. In a number of species, it is spotted with silver, giving rise to its common and botanical names (see Doctrine of Signatures, p. 157). The spring flowers are tubular, with five lobes. In some species, they distinctly change color after opening. The foliage and flowers are an excellent foil for spring-blooming bulbs.

How to Grow
Lungworts grow well in full sun to full shade, preferring soil amended with plenty of organic matter that is not allowed to dry out in the heat of summer. They'll have a tidier appearance if lightly sheared after flowering. Lungworts hybridize freely in the garden, so if other species or cultivars are nearby, the seedlings are likely to be variable. They can be propagated by dividing rhizomes in early spring.

Best Groundcovers & Vines For The Prairies

The Doctrine of Signatures was developed by Swiss physician and alchemist Theophrastus Bombast van Hohenheim (1493–1541), who was also a shoemaker. This theory suggested that God had marked plants useful to man with certain clues or "signatures" that were based on the physical resemblance of the plants to the organs they were able to cure. Thus, *Hepatica*, with its three-lobed, liver-shaped leaves could cure ailments of the liver; walnuts, which looked like the brain, were good for ailments of the psyche; and lungwort, with leaf splotches similar to phlegm, was designed to cure bronchial problems. Bloodroot, with its red roots, was said to cure blood disorders, while goldenrod, which has yellow flowers, was believed to aid jaundice. Joe Pye weed, also called boneset, was used to heal broken bones. The signature? Some species have fused leaves.

Pulmonaria mollis (syn. *P. montana*)
pul-moe-*nay*-ree-a *mol*-lis
Soft lungwort, mountain lungwort

Plant at a Glance
Type: herbaceous perennial
Height/spread: 30 to 45 cm (12 to 18 in.) / 60 cm (24 in.)
Spacing: 30 cm (12 in.)
Light: full sun to full shade
Soil: average to moist; rich in organic matter
Distinguishing features: pink buds that open into blue flowers
Landscape use: small, inaccessible, or inhospitable areas; delineating space and defining property lines; accentuating focal points; shady understory
Propagation: division

In 1976, the well-known English gardener and writer Graham Stuart Thomas described the soft lungwort as "prolific and admirable though seldom seen." It is certainly more underused now in prairie Canada than it was in mainstream England thirty years ago—and that's a shame. It's an excellent and long-lived plant, certainly the most adaptable and durable of the lungworts, and one of the few that is happy in full sun under normal border conditions through the heat of summer. Find a soft lungwort and plant it. You'll not be disappointed.

The genus name is from the Latin *pulmo*, meaning "lung." The blotched leaves of many of the species and cultivars are said to resemble diseased lungs and, according to the medieval Doctrine of Signatures (see above), have the ability to cure them. The common name, lungwort, also reflects this centuries' old belief. The species name, *mollis*, means "soft" and describes the soft, hairy leaves.

Unlike most lungworts, the leaves of the soft lungwort are dark green and lack variegation. Elliptical to lance shaped, they are 20 to 25 cm (8 to 10 in.) in length, soft, hairy, and held on long petioles. They were once used to flavor vermouth. The small, funnel- or bell-shaped flowers, in terminal cymes, are among the earliest of our spring flowers. They change from red to blue as they mature and are attractive to hummingbirds. The 'Royal Blue' cultivar has deep blue-violet flowers and grows to 30 cm (12 in.). Soft lungwort spreads by means of a thick, creeping rootstock.

Pulmonaria saccharata 'Roy Davidson'
pul-moe-*nay*-ree-a sak-a-*rat*-ah
'Roy Davidson' Bethlehem sage

Plant at a Glance
Type: herbaceous perennial
Height/spread: 25 to 30 cm (10 to 12 in.) / 30 to 40 cm (12 to 16 in.)
Spacing: 30 cm (12 in.)
Light: partial shade
Soil: moist; well drained; rich in organic matter
Distinguishing features: sky blue flowers; spotted foliage
Landscape use: small, inaccessible, or inhospitable areas; delineating space and defining property lines; accentuating focal points; shady understory
Propagation: division

The species name *saccharata* means "containing sugar" or "sweet" and was attached to the plant at a time when it was used in herbal medicine. Bethlehem sage has pointed, hairy, elliptical, green leaves, with white spots. The pink flower buds open into sky blue, funnel-shaped flowers in terminal, branched cymes. The cultivar 'Roy Davidson' has lance-shaped, green leaves, with silver spotting. It forms a dense, mounded clump, 25 to 30 cm (10 to 12 in.) in height, and increases from short rhizomes. The foliage stands up in warm weather better than most other *Pulmonaria* cultivars. It makes a beautiful groundcover in dappled shade where the soil is moist.

Cultivars
- 'Margery Fish' has narrow leaves, with even silver spotting. The pink buds open into pale blue flowers.
- 'Spilled Milk' has large, uneven silver patches on its leaves. It is early blooming, with flowers that open pink and age to purple.

Other Species and Hybrids
- *Pulmonaria officinalis* (o-fi-see-*nah*-lis), Jerusalem sage or common lungwort, has hairy, light green, heart-shaped leaves, splotched with white, and red flowers that eventually turn blue. It grows 15 to 30 cm (6 to 12 in.) tall. 'Sissinghurst White' has pure white flowers.
- *Pulmonaria rubra* (*rub*-ra), red lungwort, has coral red flowers and hairy, green, unspotted leaves. It forms 30 cm (12 in.) clumps and is

very early blooming. The cultivar 'David Ward' has pale green leaves, with creamy white edges, and salmon pink flowers. It is prone to sun scorch, so grow it in a shady location.

Rhus glabra
(rus *glab*-ra)
Smooth sumac

Plant at a Glance
Type: deciduous shrub
Height/spread: 3 to 4 m (10 to 13 ft.) / 2 to 3 m (6.5 to 10 ft.) and spreading
Light: full sun to partial shade
Soil: well drained; lean
Distinguishing features: green, pinnately compound leaves that turn orange and red-purple in fall
Landscape use: naturalizing; reclamation; slopes and banks; breaking up large expanses of lawn; transition plantings; back lane plantings; barrier plantings, screening
Propagation: seed; suckers

Native to the eastern portions of the prairies through Ontario, smooth sumac has been valued in the east mainly for its intense fall coloration. Unfortunately, that doesn't always happen on the prairies as the foliage is often killed outright by hard frost. *Rhus glabra* var. *cismontana* (syn. *R. cismontana*), the western smooth sumac, is native to South Dakota, Wyoming, and Montana and is lower growing.

Sumac has been cultivated for almost four centuries. The European species was long used for dyeing, tanning, and basketry. *Rhus* is from the old Latin name *rhoys* that was given to the sumacs of Sicily. The word *glabra* means "smooth" and describes the hairless stems.

Smooth sumac forms an upright, spreading shrub, which is generally leggy, with bare lower branches. New shoots are covered with a blue-gray

Rhus glabra cismontana (smooth sumac) (Hugh Skinner)

bloom. Although it suckers rampantly, it is less aggressive than the staghorn sumac.

The large, 30 to 45 cm (12 to 18 in.) long, attractive leaves are alternate and pinnately compound, with eleven to thirty-one leaflets. Individual leaflets are 5 to 13 cm (2 to 5 in.) long, pointed, lance-like to oblong in shape, with toothed margins. The red rachis that bears the leaflets contrasts well with the dark green, glossy leaflets. Sumacs are valued for their orange red-purple fall color but it develops to its best only in sunny, dry sites.

The greenish yellow flowers in long panicles are dioecious, with male and female flowers on separate plants. The scarlet fruit are borne in dense, hairy clusters on the female plants and persist into winter. The fruit has been used as a dye and as a beverage. Use sumac as a mass planting where the going is tough: for reclamation, on slopes and banks, in poor soils, for naturalizing, or for wildlife plantings.

How to Grow
Sumac grows in any soil as long as it is well drained. It does very well on poor soils in full sun or partial shade and is extremely drought tolerant. It suckers rampantly and is not meant for small or well-manicured landscapes. Propagate by transplanting suckers in early spring or from seed, which requires heat to germinate. Drop the seed in a cup of boiling water for one minute just before spring sowing.

Cultivars
- 'Midi' is a compact form.
- 'Mini' is a very compact cultivar, reaching only 1 m (3.3 ft.).
- 'Morden's' has bright red fruit and is more restrained, growing only to 1.8 m (6 ft.).

Ribes alpinum
rie-beez al-*pie*-num
Alpine currant

Plant at a Glance
Type: deciduous shrub
Height/spread: 1 to 2 m (3.3 to 6.5 ft.) / 1.2 m (4 ft.)
Spacing: 1 m (3.3 ft.)
Light: full sun to partial shade
Soil: well drained
Distinguishing features: dense, upright habit; medium green foliage
Landscape use: delineating space and defining property lines; breaking up large expanses of lawn; transition plantings; barrier plantings; back lane plantings; screening
Propagation: layering; hardwood or softwood cuttings

Best Groundcovers & Vines For The Prairies

Ribes is probably derived from the Arabic word for "acid tasting," or it may be attributed to the Danish "ribs," the name for red currant. Currants are spring-flowering shrubs of the temperate regions. Native to the alpine zones of Europe,

Ribes alpinum (alpine currant) (Brian Baldwin)

alpine currant is a dense, upright shrub, with simple leaves characterized by three- or occasionally five-toothed lobes, like a maple leaf. The light green leaves emerge early in spring and are accompanied by small, greenish yellow flowers. The plants are dioecious. Female plants produce red berries in mid-summer that are eaten by birds. However, it is rare that these plants produce fruit in our landscapes because most clones sold in nurseries are male. It is thought that male plants are less susceptible to rust, which usually affects the fruit.

Alpine currants grow from many upright stems. The bark is yellowish on new stems and later becomes grayish brown, ridged, and shredding. The dense growth is good for hedges or shrubby filler.

How to Grow

Alpine currant develops into a dense, upright plant with minimal pruning or attention and grows well in most soils in sun or partial shade. It transplants easily from bare-root plants in early spring or from container-grown plants any time during the growing season. Alpine currant can be propagated by softwood or hardwood cuttings or by layering.

Other Species and Hybrids

- *Ribes aureum* (or-*ay*-um), golden currant, forms a loose, open shrub with a width and height of 1.5 m (5 ft.). Small, yellow flowers are followed by black fruit. It is exceptionally drought tolerant and suckers readily, making it ideal for a transition planting where conditions are difficult.
- *Ribes oxycanthoides* (ox-ee-can-*thoy*-deez), northern gooseberry, grows to 1 m (3.3 ft.) in height and performs well in shaded locations. Both *R. oxycanthoides* and its cultivar 'Dakota Dwarf' have attractive shiny foliage and form an effective barrier due to their thorns.

Rosa

row-zah

rose

A number of species and cultivars in the genus *Rosa* are hardy plants well adapted to growing as groundcover. They will clothe a slope with attractive pinnately compound foliage, fill a difficult corner along a driveway, or act as a prickly barrier to animals and people. In bloom, they are among the most spectacular of shrubs. Some cultivars develop colorful fruit (hips) and beautiful autumn foliage. *Rosa* is the ancient Latin name for this very large genus of shrubs.

How to Grow

Hardy shrub roses can be planted from bare-root plants in early spring or from container-grown plants throughout the growing season. They grow well on sunny, well-drained sites and benefit from soil enriched with organic matter. Pruning out older canes stimulates new growth and increases the amount of bloom. Rose species can be propagated by planting stratified seed in the spring or by sowing fresh seed in the garden in the fall. Sucker shoots can be transplanted from some cultivars. Most can be started from softwood cuttings.

Rosa pimpinellifolia altaica

(*row*-zah pim-peh-nel-eh-*fow*-lee-ah al-tah-*ic*-ah)

Altai Scotch rose

Plant at a Glance

Type: deciduous shrub

Height/spread: 0.3 to 2.1 m (1 to 7 ft.) / 1 to 2.1 m (3.3 to 7 ft.) or more if suckering

Spacing: 0.6 to 1.2 m (2 to 4 ft.)

Light: full sun to partial shade

Soil: well drained; average to rich in organic matter

Distinguishing features: showy flowers; compound foliage

Landscape use: slopes and banks; delineating space and defining property lines; breaking up large expanses of lawn; transition plantings; barrier plantings; back lane plantings; screening

Propagation: the species from seed; cultivars by suckers or softwood cuttings

Altai Scotch rose is a suckering shrub that grows from numerous upright, thorny stems. Attractive small, bluish green leaves, with nine to thirteen leaflets clothe the plants. Pale yellow flowers appear in early summer, followed by round, dark brown hips in fall. Hybrids can be attractive barrier or

Rosa 'Seager Wheeler' ('Seager Wheeler' rose) (Hugh Skinner)

tall groundcover plants. Planted along a fence in a back lane, many of these would effectively discourage graffiti. They are among the earliest roses to bloom, and although they only bloom in the spring, they produce such an abundance of flowers that it nearly hides the foliage. These large, suckering shrubs should be planted where they have room to develop and spread.

Cultivars
- 'Hazeldean,' blackspot resistant, has deep yellow, double flowers and grows to 2 m (6.5 ft.). Be careful where you plant it—in full bloom, it will stop traffic!
- 'Kakwa', with double, white flowers, grows to 1.2 m (4 ft.). It has a spreading, mounded habit.
- 'Kilwinning' produces medium, golden yellow blooms, a color that combines well with other flowers. It grows to 1.8 m (6 ft.) in height and spreads by suckering.
- 'Seager Wheeler' has fragrant, pale pink, semi-double flowers. It grows to 2 m (6.5 ft.).
- 'Yellow Altai' bears deep yellow, single flowers and is 1.5 m (5 ft.) in height.

Other Species and Hybrids
The following native roses spread by suckering and are recommended as groundcovers. They will grow on difficult well-drained slopes or form an attractive component in a native plant garden.
- *Rosa arkansana* (are-kan-*sah*-nah), prairie rose, is a low-growing shrub and the latest to bloom of our native roses. If it is pruned after the first flush of flowers, it will bloom repeatedly until late summer. Flowers are light to medium rose-pink and 8 cm (3 in.) in diameter. The prairie rose is very drought tolerant and spreads by rhizomes.

- *Rosa nitida* (*nit*-tih-dah), shining rose, is a native of Eastern Canada and has shiny, medium green foliage and 5 cm (2 in.), light rose-pink flowers. It spreads aggressively by rhizomes.

Rosa rugosa hybrids
row-zah roo-*goh*-sah
Rugosa roses

Plant at a Glance
Type: deciduous shrub
Height/spread: 0.3 to 2.1 m (1 to 7 ft.) / 1 to 2.1 m (3.3 to 7 ft.) or more if suckering
Spacing: 0.6 to 1.2 m (2 to 4 ft.)
Light: full sun
Soil: well drained; average to rich in organic matter
Distinguishing features: showy flowers; compound foliage
Landscape use: slopes and banks; delineating space; defining property lines; breaking up large expanses of lawn; transition plantings; barrier plantings; back lane plantings; accentuating focal points; screening
Propagation: the species, from seed; cultivars, by suckers or softwood cuttings

Hybrids of *Rosa rugosa* are ideal for planting on difficult well-drained sites, such as banks and street-side beds. Plants grow from gray, upright, prickly stems and sucker to form colonies. The beautiful medium green, prominently veined foliage is resistant to disease and turns yellow to orange in fall. Flowers range in color from white to dark rose-red. The species has disc-shaped, five-petaled flowers, but most hybrids are semi-double or double flowered, with fifteen to one hundred petals. Most have long bloom periods; flowering begins in late June and continues through August. The showy flowers are followed by orange-red, flattened, round hips, 2 to 4 cm (0.8 to 1.5 in) in diameter. Some hybrid cultivars are sterile and do not produce fruit. The subspecies *Rosa rugosa repens alba* is an aggressive, trailing,

Rosa rugosa hybrid 'Jens Munk' ('Jens Munk' rose) (Hugh Skinner)

In milder climates, climbing roses cover fences, arbors, and walls. On the prairies, plant hardiness has restricted our choices in climbing roses. 'Polstjärnan', a very vigorous plant that originated in Finland, has small, white flowers with a closed center, like a camellia blossom. The root is completely hardy, although the top may show some dieback following hard winters. Wear a suit of armor for pruning this variety with its hooked thorns.

At the other end of the thorniness scale is the completely thornless 'Ames #5' or 'Ames Climber'. This charming shrub has clusters of pale pink, single flowers.

'Prairie Dawn' could be seen as the forerunner of the Explorer Series roses. Its pillar form reaches 2 m (6.5 ft.). It produces clear pink, double flowers over a long period.

Several of the introductions in the Explorer Series from Agriculture Canada have climbing habits.

- 'Captain Samuel Holland' has an arching habit to 2 m (6.5 ft.) and clusters of medium red flowers.
- 'John Cabot' has an arching, upright habit. It produces clusters of medium red flowers on 1.8 m (6 ft.) canes.
- 'John Davis' has beautiful medium pink, double flowers on arching canes, with few thorns. It requires high fertility to produce long canes.
- 'William Baffin' produces clusters of up to thirty semi-double, bright pink flowers. Its canes will grow up to 2.5 m (8 ft.).
- 'William Booth' has a vigorous trailing habit, up to 1.2 m (4 ft.) high, with canes growing to 2 m (6.5 ft.) in length. The flowers are single, medium red, with a lighter eye.

low groundcover plant suitable for stabilizing banks. It produces single, white flowers in early summer.

Cultivars

- 'Aylsham' has shiny foliage and grows to 60 cm (24 in.) in height. It spreads to form an open colony. Flowers are dark rose-red in early summer.
- 'Charles Albanel', an Explorer Series rose, grows to 80 cm (32 in.) Medium rose-red flowers begin in early July and continue until fall.
- 'David Thompson', another Explorer Series rose, has medium-sized, rose-red flowers on a compact plant, 1 m (3.3 ft.) tall, throughout the summer.
- 'Frau Dagmar Hartopp' ('Fru Dagmar Hastrup') is a compact variety, 60 cm (24 in.) tall, with lovely single, pink flowers. It has shiny, dark green foliage and produces attractive round, red hips.
- 'Hansa' is an old prairie garden standard. It grows to 2 m (6.5 ft.) in height and has fragrant, medium, rose-red flowers all summer.
- 'Henry Hudson' is an attractive semi-double, white-flowered cultivar in the Explorer Series. It grows to 1.2 m (4 ft.) in height, with numerous small prickles and attractive fruit in fall.
- 'Jens Munk', an Explorer rose, has fragrant, medium pink, double flowers throughout the summer. It also has hooked, large prickles that

make it an effective barrier plant. It grows to 1.5 m (5 ft.) in height.
- 'Marie Bugnet' is a low-growing, 60-cm (24-in.) cultivar that was developed by Georges Bugnet of Legal, Alberta. The pure-white, semi-double flowers are produced throughout the summer.
- 'Therese Bugnet' grows to 1.8 m (6 ft.) in height and has upright, red stems. It produces medium pink, double flowers all summer.
- 'Will Alderman' is a prolific bloomer, with large, medium pink flowers all summer. It is 60 cm (24 in.) in height.

Salix lanata
say-licks lah-*not*-tah
Woolly willow

Plant at a Glance
Type: deciduous shrub
Height/spread: 30 cm (12 in.) / 60 cm (24 in.)
Spacing: 60 cm (24 in.)
Light: full sun
Soil: evenly moist
Distinguishing features: tiny, felt-like, silver foliage
Landscape use: mixed or perennial border; rock garden; edging; small, inaccessible, or inhospitable areas; accentuating focal points
Propagation: softwood cuttings

Salix is the original Latin name for willow, while *lanata* means "woolly," alluding to the texture of the foliage. Woolly willow is not what you would expect from a willow. While many willows are shrubby rather than tree-like, this one is probably the most ground-hugging of all. Looking down on it, one is struck by the tiny, woolly, gray, felty leaves. Native to Great Britain and Northern Europe, it is perfectly hardy and useful as a groundcover in a mixed border, as edging, and in a rock garden. Unfortunately, you may have to hunt to find it—it hasn't yet reached the horticultural mainstream.

How to Grow
Like other willows, woolly willow likes full sun and even moisture. It is easily propagated by softwood cuttings.

Other Species and Hybrids
- *Salix repens* var. *argentea* (*ree*-penz var. ar-*gent*-ee-ah), dwarf silver willow, is native to the coasts of western Europe. It has superficial similarities of form to *Yucca glauca* when viewed from a distance. Both have silvery foliage and a stiff appearance, are 45 to 60 cm (18 to 24 in.) in height, and are rather vase shaped, but they are very different plants. Whereas the leaves of yucca are stiff, it is the slender, gray branches of

the dwarf silver willow that appear stiff and erect. This willow's oval to elliptical leaves are very tiny, rarely more than 2.5 cm (1 in.) long. They are gray-green on their upper surface and a silky, silvery white beneath. Native to the bogs and moist, sandy soil of Europe and northern Asia, they prefer full sun in well-drained but evenly moist soil. It is sometimes grafted onto a standard of stronger-growing willows and made into an attractive small, weeping tree, but it is generally short-lived when treated this way. It is best used as a groundcover.

Salix lanata (dwarf woolly willow) (Hugh Skinner)

Saponaria ocymoides
sa-po-*nah*-ree-a ok-see-*moi*-deez
Rock soapwort

Plant at a Glance
Type: herbaceous perennial
Height/spread: 10 to 20 cm (4 to 8 in.) / 60 cm (24 in.)
Spacing: 45 cm (18 in.)
Light: full sun
Soil: well drained
Distinguishing features: misty mass of white, trailing flowers
Landscape use: perennial or mixed border; rock garden; over walls; slopes and banks
Propagation: seed

Although individual plants are relatively short-lived (don't count on over three or four years), rock soapworts are prolific self-seeders and can quite happily produce successive generations that collectively act as a groundcover.

Saponaria ocymoides (rock soapwort) (Sara Williams)

They also work well in rock gardens and tumbling over a wall or down a slope.

Both the botanical and common names indicate that the plant's roots and leaves were once used to make soap. *Sapo* is Latin for "soap," while the species name, *ocymoides*, means "resembling basil" (*Ocimum*) and describes the leaves. Native to the Alps and Pyrenees Mountains of southern Europe, it had been introduced to England by the 1500s. John Gerard wrote in his *Historie of Plants* in 1633: "of the great scouring qualitie that the leaves have: for they yield . . . a certain juice when they are bruised which scoureth almost as well as Sope."

Rock soapwort forms a trailing mound of flowers and foliage secured by a deep taproot that makes it difficult to divide or transplant. The tiny, white to pink flowers consist of five petals, each of which is notched. They are formed in loose sprays or cymes from late spring to early summer. Cultivars include 'Splendens' (larger, rose-red flowers), 'Alba' (white flowers), and 'Rosea' (bright rose flowers).

How to Grow
Soapwort requires full sun and well-drained, gritty soil. Shear plants after they bloom in a rock garden, but if your intention is a groundcover, allow them to self-seed.

Schizachyrium scoparium (syn. *Andropogon scoparius*)
skiz-ah-*keer*-ee-um skoe-*par*-ee-um
Little bluestem

Plant at a Glance
Type: ornamental grass
Height/spread: 50 cm (20 in.) / 50 cm (20 in.)
Spacing: 30 cm (12 in.)
Light: full sun
Soil: moist; well drained
Distinguishing features: bluish foliage color, changing to orange in fall
Landscape use: mixed or perennial border; mass planting; prairie restoration; slopes and banks
Propagation: seed; division

Best Groundcovers & Vines For The Prairies

Little bluestem is a warm-season grass that develops tufts of blue-green to intense steely blue foliage once the soil warms in the spring. The species name, *scoparium*, means broom-like and refers to the plant's tufted appearance. As the season progresses, the foliage grows to 40 cm (16 in.), with flowering stems growing to 50 cm (20 in.). As summer turns to fall, the purplish flower heads turn into golden, feathery plumes.

Little bluestem shows spectacular orange or pink fall color that, in a mass planting, will color a hillside. In a more-intimate setting, it is an attractive specimen. Plant little bluestem with other native grasses and perennials. In nature, it grows on moist sites associated with big bluestem and blue grama grass. Despite this, it is quite drought tolerant when grown in the garden.

How to Grow

Little bluestem prefers a sunny location in moist, fertile soil, but it is deep rooted and drought tolerant. Plants should be mowed or burned in the spring to remove the previous year's foliage and renew the plant. Little bluestem can be seeded in spring, planted from plugs, or divided and transplanted before growth starts. Foliage color varies and specimens with superior blue foliage should be propagated by division in early spring.

Scutellaria alpina
skew-te-*lah*-ree-a al-*pie*-na
Alpine skullcap

Plant at a Glance
Type: herbaceous perennial
Height/spread: 15 to 30 cm (6 to 12 in.) / 30 cm (12 in.)
Spacing: 30 cm (12 in.)
Light: full sun to partial shade
Soil: evenly moist; well drained
Distinguishing features: hooded, two-lipped, pastel flowers
Landscape use: perennial or mixed border; rock garden; small, inaccessible, or inhospitable areas; accentuating focal points; shaded understory
Propagation: seed; division

Skullcap forms a dense, mat-like groundcover, with attractive foliage and pastel flowers. Although not often seen in prairie gardens, it should be. Native from the Pyrenees of Spain to Siberia, its common and botanical names are descriptive of the pouch-like covering on the seed capsule. The Latin word *scutella* means "a small dish, saucer or shield," while skullcap refers to the shape of the seed capsule; *alpina*, of course, describes their native habitat.

Another member of the mint family, alpine skullcap has long, dark green leaves that are simple and opposite. The stems are square and erect, growing to 25 cm (10 in.), forming a low mound, and rooting as they go. The

Scutellaria alpina (alpine skullcap) (Hugh Skinner)

root system is rhizomatous. The hooded, two-lipped flowers are in dense, terminal racemes and generally purple on the species. Cultivars are often bicolored in white, yellow, pink, rose, purple, or blue and flower in early summer.

How to Grow

Alpine skullcap is adapted to sun or shade, flowering a bit less in the shade, as long as even moisture is available. Propagate from seed or by division in spring.

Other Species and Hybrids

- *Scutellaria baicalensis* (bie-ka-*len*-sis), Baikal skullcap, is native to the area surrounding Lake Baikal in Russia. It is similar to alpine skullcap but has white or blue flowers with purple markings.

Sedum kamtschaticum 'Variegatum'

see-dum kamt-*sha*-ti-kum var-ee-uh-*gaw*-tum
Variegated Kamchatka sedum

Plant at a Glance

Type: herbaceous perennial
Height/spread: 20 cm (8 in.) / 20 cm (8 in.)
Spacing: 15 cm (6 in.)
Light: full sun
Soil: well drained
Distinguishing features: yellow and red flowers; variegated, fleshy leaves
Landscape use: rock garden; edging; lawn replacement; small, inaccessible, or inhospitable areas; slopes and banks; unifying shrub beds; pavement plantings; back lane plantings; accentuating focal points
Propagation: division; softwood cuttings

Sedum is a large genus of succulent perennials. Its name, derived from Latin, means "to assuage" and originally referred to the healing powers of the *Sempervivums* that were once classified with the sedums. The species name *kamtschaticum* refers to the range of the species on the Kamchatka peninsula, which projects from eastern Siberia between the Sea of Okhotsk and the Bering Sea. The attractive fleshy leaves of the

Best Groundcovers & Vines For The Prairies

cultivar 'Variegatum' are pale green and widely edged with cream. The foliage is topped by cymes of star-shaped flowers that are orange in bud, open yellow, and turn into red seed heads. The plant does not creep, but spreads by branching from the round clump. It is an excellent plant for edging or in the rock garden.

How to Grow
Kamchatka sedum thrives in well-drained soil in full sun or partial shade. It is usually long-lived in the garden. Plants are easily propagated by transplanting divisions in early spring or by rooting softwood cuttings.

Other Species and Hybrids
- *Sedum acre* (*ahk*-er), gold moss sedum, forms a very low, moss-like cover, with creeping stems and small, evergreen leaves. It has bright yellow flowers in twos or threes, each about 1 cm (0.5 in.) across, in early summer. Use with caution as it roots easily from detached pieces and can become a problem weed. You'll soon have acres of it.
- *Sedum reflexum* (re-*fleks*-um), blue stonecrop, blue spruce sedum, is a low-creeping species, with needle-like leaves and contrasting bright yellow flowers in mid-summer.
- *Sedum spurium* (*sper*-ee-um), two row sedum, is a mat-forming plant, with creeping stems and nearly evergreen foliage. The opposite leaves are oval, with flattened bases and toothed margins. Flowers are borne in clusters above the foliage in early summer. Foliage and flowers vary in color, with several cultivars selected and offered, including 'Dragons Blood' (purple-tinted green leaves and deep pink flowers), 'Bronze Carpet' (bronze leaves and pink flowers), 'Ruby Mantle' (wine red leaves and red flowers), var. *album* (pale green leaves and white flowers), and var. *roseum* (medium green leaves and rose-pink flowers). 'Tricolor' has foliage that is variegated with pink and white; remove any foliage that reverts to green to prevent it from taking over. It is not as vigorous and hardy as other *S. spurium* cultivars.

Sedum kamtschaticum 'Variegatum' (variegated kamtschatka sedum) (Hugh Skinner)

Sempervivum tectorum
sem-per-*veev*-um tek-*to*-rum
Hen and chicks, houseleek

Plant at a Glance
Type: evergreen perennial
Height/spread: 5 to 20 cm (2 to 8 in.) / 15 cm (6 in.)
Spacing: 15 cm (6 in.)
Light: full sun
Soil: well drained
Distinguishing features: rosettes of succulent foliage, with smaller "chicks"
Landscape use: rock garden; edging; slopes and banks; lawn replacement; small, inaccessible, or inhospitable areas; pavement plantings; back lane plantings; accentuating focal points
Propagation: division

Sempervivum tectorum (hens and chicks) (Hugh Skinner)

Sempervivum is derived from the Latin word meaning "to live forever"; *tectorum* means "of roofs" and refers to the practice in central Europe of growing *Sempervivum* on the roofs of houses to protect them from lightning and fire. During the Middle Ages, this was sometimes required by law, and you can still find them growing on cottage rooftops in England and continental Europe today.

Sempervivum are grown for their rosettes of thick, fleshy, evergreen foliage and to a lesser extent for their flowers. The leaves are broadly lance shaped and radially arranged on a very short stem. Common forms are glaucous blue-green, with red tips, but many selections and hybrids are offered with varying degrees of red or purple in the leaves. The name "hen and chicks" comes from the plant's habit of producing offsets that surround

Best Groundcovers & Vines For The Prairies

the larger "mother" plant. In favorable conditions, these offsets will form a dense groundcover. The flower heads consist of a flat cluster of star-shaped flowers, rising about 15 cm. (6 in.) on a stalk that is clothed with reduced, spur-like leaves. They vary in color from greenish cream to rose-red, depending on the cultivar. After flowering, the rosette that produces the flower stem dies. Young children are often fascinated by these interesting plants and they are a novel way to introduce children to gardening.

How to Grow
Sempervivum prefer to grow in well-drained soil in full sun but tolerate partial shade. They are easily propagated by removing the offsets and transplanting them in early spring.

Other Species and Hybrids
• *Sempervivum arachnoideum* (a-rak-*noi*-dee-um), cobweb hen and chicks, is noted for the fine hairs that join the leaf tips together. The rosettes are smaller than *S. tectorum* and the flowers are showier, especially in the red-flowered cultivar *S. arachnoideum* 'Rubrum'.

Silene acaulis
si-lean a-*kaw*-lis
Moss campion

Plant at a Glance
Type: evergreen perennial
Height/spread: 5 cm (2 in.) / 25 cm (10 in.)
Spacing: 25 cm (10 in.)
Light: full sun
Soil: well drained; gravelly
Distinguishing features: small, pink flowers; tiny, tufted mounds of soft foliage
Landscape use: rock garden; lawn replacement; small, inaccessible, or inhospitable areas; pavement plantings
Propagation: division

I remember being given my first moss campion by Hugh Skinner some thirty years ago. His parting words were "Remember, it needs good drainage!" Later that same summer, I was hiking in the alpine meadows of the Rocky Mountains and came across them in their native habitat. Far below I could see Banff townsite. There was nothing between the moss campion and the town of Banff but an immense area of good drainage. Take Hugh's advice to heart!

Moss campion has a far-ranging natural distribution through the alpine areas of Eurasia and North America, as well as the north Arctic. *Silene*

Silene acaulis (moss campion) in natural habitat.
(Sara Williams)

is a classical name for *Lychnis*, a closely related genus, while *acaulis* means "stemless" or "with very short stems" and describes the tiny, five-petaled, pink flowers that appear from late spring to early summer. In alpine meadows, moss campions form large, mossy cushions, up to 30 cm (12 in.) in diameter, but they will be somewhat smaller in prairie gardens. The glossy, green foliage appears tufted and consists of tiny, opposite, and linear leaves. Moss campion grows from a deep and fleshy root system and is an ideal pavement plant or groundcover for a rock garden.

How to Grow
Given full sun and gravelly, well-drained soil, moss campion will flourish. Carefully divide the mossy cushions in early spring if you want more plants.

Other Species and Hybrids
- *Silene pedunculata* (pe-dunc-u-*lah*-ta) is slightly taller than *S. acaulis* and said to be more free flowering in gardens.

Smilacina stellata
smy-la-*seen*-ah stel-*la*-tah
Star-flowered Solomon's seal, false Solomon's seal

Plant at a Glance
Type: herbaceous perennial
Height/spread: 25 to 30 cm (10 to 12 in.) / 45 cm (18 in.)
Spacing: 30 cm (12 in.)
Light: shade
Soil: average
Distinguishing features: white, star-like flowers
Landscape use: shady understory
Propagation: division

Found throughout the prairies, generally in low, moist areas, the star-flowered Solomon's seal is amazingly drought tolerant. This was evident when I inadvertently included a small piece of it while transplanting a young Scots pine. This piece flourished in dry shade on sandy soil with no supplemental water,

Best Groundcovers & Vines For The Prairies

forming a sizeable 3 m (10 ft.) in diameter colony, through creeping rhizomes, within a few years. Star-flowered Solomon's seal could be used much more extensively in dry shade as an understory beneath trees.

Smilacina stellata (false Solomon's seal) (Sara Williams)

The small, greenish white flowers are formed in loose, terminal racemes on 30 cm (12 in.) stems in early May. The light green leaves are narrow and sessile, turning gold in the fall.

Called star-flowered Solomon's seal or false Solomon's seal because of its resemblance to *Polygonatum*, the true Solomon's seal, the genus name is derived from its supposed similarity to *Smilax*, a woodland vine. The specific epithet, *stellata*, means "star-like" and describes the flower.

How to Grow

Plant star-flowered Solomon's seal in shade. It does best with even moisture but adapts to drier soil conditions. Propagate through division in spring.

Solidago hybrids
so-li-*dah*-go
Goldenrod hybrids

Plant at a Glance
Type: herbaceous perennial
Height/spread: 25 to 150 cm (10 to 60 in.) / 30 to 60 cm (12 to 24 in.)
Spacing: 30 to 45 cm (12 to 18 in.)
Light: full sun
Soil: well drained
Distinguishing features: plumes of small, yellow flowers
Landscape use: perennial or mixed border; slopes and banks; breaking up large expanses of lawn; transition plantings; back lane plantings; screening
Propagation: seed; division

The genus name *Solidago* is derived from the Greek word meaning "to solidify or make whole" and refers to the plant's reputed wound-healing properties. Of the many species of goldenrod, most are native to North America. Their reputation as a cause of hay fever is unjustified—*Solidago* pollen is heavy and is carried by insects, not wind.

Most native *Solidago* species are too aggressive for use in the garden,

Solidago (goldenrod) (Hugh Skinner)

except in places where they can be naturalized. Hybrids developed in Europe are much more suited to our landscapes. Plants grow in a clump, with unbranched stems bearing alternate, simple leaves that are lance shaped, coarsely toothed, and much longer than wide. The numerous tiny flower heads are borne in various types of branched inflorescences. Individual flower heads consist of a few disc florets, with a single row of yellow or, rarely, white rays.

Both native species and hybrids are a showy part of the late summer and autumn landscape. Hybrid cultivars are particularly striking in the perennial border when combined with early blooming hardy asters.

How to Grow
Goldenrods generally prefer full sun and well-drained soils. They vary in their tolerance for shade and their ability to withstand drought. The species are grown from seed, while hybrid cultivars are easy to propagate by transplanting divisions in early spring.

Cultivars
- 'Cloth of Gold' bears deep yellow flowers on 30 cm (12 in.) stems.
- 'Crown of Rays' grows up to 60 cm (24 in.) tall, with golden yellow flowers held horizontally in clusters.
- 'Golden Fleece' produces masses of golden yellow flowers on 45 cm (18 in.) stems.

Best Groundcovers & Vines For The Prairies

Sorbaria sorbifolia
Sore-*bare*-ree-ah sor-bi-*fow*-lee-ah
Ural false spirea

Plant at a Glance
Type: deciduous shrub
Height/spread: 1.2 m (4 ft.) / 1.2 m (4 ft.)
Spacing: 60 cm (24 in.)
Light: full sun to shade
Soil: moist; well drained
Distinguishing features: white flowers; foliage similar to mountain ash
Landscape use: slopes and banks; transition plantings; barrier plantings; screening
Propagation: suckers; softwood or hardwood cuttings

Sorbaria sorbifolia derives both its genus and species names from the resemblance of the foliage to mountain ash (*Sorbus*). False spirea forms a thicket of slender, upright stems that arise from vigorous rhizomes. Under good growing conditions, it spreads quickly to provide groundcover in shady situations where little else grows, such as along buildings or tree rows. The compound leaves are formed from thirteen to twenty-five lance-shaped leaflets, 5 to 10 cm (2 to 4 in.) long and 1 to 2 cm (0.4 to 0.8 in.) wide, with toothed edges. Plants flower in mid-summer on the previous season's stems. The panicles of small, white flowers are followed by brown seed heads. The hybrid cultivar 'Aurora' is preferred because it doesn't produce seed so it self-cleans after flowering.

Sorbaria sorbifolia 'Aurora' ('Aurora' Ural false spirea) (Sara Williams)

How to Grow
Sorbaria sorbifolia grows in almost any well-drained soil. It prefers partial shade but will grow in full sun. It is easy to plant from bare-root plants in spring or from container-grown plants throughout the growing season. It can also be propagated by transplanting sucker shoots in early spring or from softwood or hardwood cuttings.

Spiraea x *bumalda*
spy-*ree*-ah bew-*mal*-dah
Dwarf bumalda spirea

Plant at a Glance
Type: deciduous shrub
Height/spread: 60 cm (24 in.) / 60 cm (24 in.)
Spacing: 40 cm (16 in.)
Light: full sun to partial shade
Soil: moist; well drained; rich in organic matter
Distinguishing features: pink to white flowers; attractive foliage
Landscape use: mixed border; rock garden; small, inaccessible, or inhospitable areas; delineating space and defining property lines; breaking up large expanses of lawn; directing foot traffic; accentuating focal points
Propagation: suckers; softwood cuttings

The genus *Spiraea* is from the Greek word *speira*, meaning "wreath," and includes numerous species of deciduous shrubs native to the northern hemisphere. Many species and hybrids are grown as garden plants and some are well adapted as groundcovers. The bumalda spirea originated as a hybrid between two Japanese species, *S. japonica* and *S. albiflora*. The resulting hybrid has coarsely toothed, oval, pointed leaves. On many cultivars, the foliage is tinged with red as it emerges in spring, then turns from green to gold, tinged with red, and finally becomes red in autumn. Spirea flowers are produced in flattened corymbs at the ends of the current year's growth. If deadheaded, plants will bloom from mid-summer until fall.

How to Grow
Bumalda spirea grows best in sun but tolerates partial shade. It prefers moist, well drained soil enriched with organic matter. Propagate by removing sucker shoots and transplanting in early spring or by softwood cuttings in early summer. The species is quite free of insect and disease problems but may suffer from iron chlorosis in high pH soils.

Cultivars
• 'Anthony Waterer' is one of the oldest and most winter hardy of the bumalda spirea cultivars. The plant is round and compact, with a

Spiraea 'Goldflame' ('Goldflame' spirea) (Sara Williams)

height of 0.6 m (2 ft.) and a spread of 1 m (3.3 ft). The foliage emerges red and matures to dark green, while the rose-red flowers are in flat terminal clusters.

- 'Crispa' has deeply cut and twisted leaves that emerge red and turn dark green. It has bright rose-pink flowers and is compact and round, with a height of 0.6 m (2 ft.) and a spread of 1 m (3.3 ft.).
- 'Froebelii' is a vigorous selection, growing to 1 m (3.3 ft.). It is similar to 'Anthony Waterer' but has broader leaves and brighter pink flowers.
- 'Goldflame' is a densely mounded shrub, growing to a height of 0.6 m (2 ft.) and a spread of 1 m (3.3 ft.). The leaves emerge reddish and mature to a soft yellow. They become more greenish as the season progresses and turn red in the fall. The flowers are similar to those of 'Anthony Waterer' but smaller.
- 'Gumball' is a compact cultivar, growing to 0.6 m (2 ft.) in height, with a spread of 1 m (3.3 ft.). The dark bluish green leaves are topped by light pink flowers.
- 'Magic Carpet' resembles 'Goldflame' but is more compact, growing 25 to 50 cm (10 to 20 in.) in height.
- 'Mini-Sunglow' has a dwarf mounding form, growing to 0.8 m (2.5 ft.) in height, with a spread of 1 m (3.3 ft.). It has brilliant yellow foliage and pink flowers.
- 'Rosabella' is a very hardy selection that was developed by Frank Skinner. It is compact, growing to 0.5 m (1.5 ft.) in height, and produces large clusters of rose-pink flowers all summer long.

Other Species and Hybrids
- *Spiraea* x *billardi* (bi-lee-*ard*-ee), Billard spirea, is an upright shrub that suckers profusely. It grows to 1.5 m (5 ft.) in height and produces

attractive elongated panicles of deep pink flowers up to 20 cm (8 in.) long. Its suckering habit makes it best suited to planting at the back of a border or the edge of woods.

- *Spiraea japonica* (jah-*pon*-i-kah), Japanese spirea, is a variable species of small, mounded shrubs native to Japan, China, and Korea. The species has dark green foliage but the most popular selection, 'Goldmound,' has bright yellow foliage. 'Goldmound' forms a compact mound (as do all these *S. japonica* cultivars) up to 0.5 m (1.5 ft.) tall and produces small heads of bright pink flowers. 'Little Princess' is 30 cm (12 in.) tall and wide, with blue-green foliage and pink flowers. 'Shirobana' ('Shirobori') is interesting for the deep pink, light pink, and white flowers that it produces simultaneously. It has attractive dark green foliage on plants that are 1 m (3.3 ft.) in height and width.
- 'Summersnow' is a spreading shrub, growing from 0.6 to 0.8 m (2 to 2.5 ft.) in height and spreading 2 to 3 m (6.5 to 10 ft.). A Skinner introduction, it produces flat clusters of white flowers over a long period, beginning in July, and has attractive orange fall color.

Stachys grandiflora (syn. *S. macrantha*)
sta-kis gran-dee-*flor*-ah
Big betony

Plant at a Glance
Type: herbaceous perennial
Height/spread: 30 to 50 cm (12 to 20 in.) / 60 cm (24 in.)
Spacing: 45 cm (18 in.)
Light: full sun to partial shade

Stachys grandiflora (big betony) (Sara Williams)

Best Groundcovers & Vines For The Prairies

Stachys is from a Greek word meaning "an ear of corn," while *grandiflora* means "large flower," both referring to the bloom. Native to the Caucasus Mountains, Asia Minor, and Iran, it was a staple of the medieval pharmacy. Here's what the venerable herbalist John Gerard had to say about it in 1597:

> Betony is good for them that be subject to the falling sickensse, and for those also that have ill heads upon a cold cause. It maketh a man to have a good stomacke and appetite to his meate. It is also good for ruptures, cramps and convulsions: it is a remedy again the biting of mad dogs and venomous serpents, being drunk, and also applied to the hurts, and is most singular against pyson. It is commended against the paine of sciatica, or ache of the huckle bone. There is a conserve made of the floures and sugar good for many thing, and especially for the head-ache.

Soil: average
Distinguishing features: dense whorls of violet flowers
Landscape use: perennial or mixed border; small, inaccessible, or inhospitable areas; delineating space and defining property lines; breaking up large expanses of lawn; directing foot traffic; accentuating focal points
Propagation: division

Big betony is closely related to woolly lambs' ears (*Stachys lanata*); however, it lacks *S. lanata*'s super-soft foliage that begs to be petted and its instinct to die instantly if left to sit in water or poorly drained soil in winter or early spring. What it lacks in cuteness, big betony makes up in durability.

A member of the mint family, it exhibits typical square stems and opposite leaves, forming a medium-sized mound of foliage. The hairy, green leaves are oval to elongated and somewhat heart shaped, with scalloped edges and a wrinkly texture. Small, two-lipped, violet flowers are formed in dense whorls on terminal spikes in early summer. A stoloniferous root system ensures its spread. The most commonly grown cultivar is 'Robusta', which is more vigorous than the species and 60 cm (24 in.) in height.

How to Grow

Given average soil and even moisture, big betony thrives in full sun to partial shade, requiring little maintenance except for deadheading to keep it tidy. Propagation is easiest though division in spring.

Other Species and Hybrids

- *Stachys lanata* (lah-*nah*-ta) (syn. *S. byzantium*, *S. olympica*), woolly lambs' ears, is native from Turkey to northern Iran. It is grown primarily for its soft, silver foliage. The thick, oblong to elliptical basal leaves are a woolly, silver-gray, 10 cm (4 in.) long, and form dense rosettes, with spikes of small, pink flowers held above the foliage. They require full sun and excellent drainage. Among *S. lanata* cultivars are

'Silver Carpet', which is sterile and produces few flowers, and 'Big Ears' (syn. 'Helene von Steine'), which has larger, gray-green leaves, seldom flowers, and is one of the longest-lived lambs' ears. 'Primrose Heron', which has chartreuse leaves in spring, is largely untested on the prairies.

Symphoricarpos albus
sim-for-i-*kar*-pus *al*-bus
Common snowberry

Plant at a Glance
Type: deciduous shrub
Height/spread: 1 to 2 m (3.3 to 6.5 ft.) / 1.2 m (4 ft.)
Spacing: 0.6 m (2 ft.)
Light: full sun to partial shade
Soil: well drained
Distinguishing features: white berries; dense, suckering habit
Landscape use: slopes and banks; transition planting; barrier plantings; screening; shady understory
Propagation: suckers; softwood cuttings

Common snowberry, an upright shrub that grows as numerous slender stems from suckering roots, is native to the eastern edge of the prairie area. The genus name, *Symphoricarpos*, is from Greek words meaning "to bear together" and "fruit," which refers to the clustered fruit that stay on the shrub into the winter. Pink, bell-shaped flowers in spring are followed by berries that ripen to an attractive white but often quickly turn brown from fungus infection.

Symphoricarpos albus (common snowberry) (Sara Williams)

Best Groundcovers & Vines For The Prairies

The simple leaves are oval, bluish green, with wavy margins that may be toothed.

Snowberry is effective for bank stabilization or as a tall groundcover in difficult partially shaded situations under trees. The native dwarf snowberry, *Symphoricarpos albus pauciflora*, which grows to 30 cm (12 in.), makes an effective groundcover but is seldom offered for sale.

How to Grow

Snowberry grows in most soils but does best in heavy soils with adequate moisture. It is easy to transplant from bare-root plants in spring or from container-grown plants any time during the growing season. Snowberry seed is difficult to germinate, but the plant can be propagated by transplanting sucker shoots or rooted from softwood cuttings.

Other Species and Hybrids

- *Symphoricarpos occidentalis* (ox-i-den-*tal*-ez), western snowberry, is a similar upright-growing shrub that is coarser in texture and native throughout the prairies. It is also more drought tolerant than *S. albus*.

Symphytum officinale
sim-*fi*-tum oh-fisz-en-*al*-ay
Comfrey

Plant at a Glance

Type: herbaceous perennial
Height/spread: 1 m (3.3 ft.) / 1 m (3.3 ft.)
Spacing: 1 m (3.3 ft.)
Light: full sun to shade
Soil: average
Distinguishing features: tubular cream to pink or purple flowers; large, hairy leaves
Landscape use: slopes and banks; transition plantings; back lane plantings; screening
Propagation: division

Comfrey is another old-world plant with a long history of folk use. It made its way to North America with the earliest settlers as a medicinal herb and became widely naturalized in many areas. Give careful thought to its placement. Much too aggressive for herbaceous borders, the species is ideal as a groundcover and for naturalizing.

A member of the borage family, it quickly forms large clumps of bold foliage. The 20-cm (8-in.) -wide leaves are alternate, oblong, and covered in hairs. Tubular, nodding flowers, varying from cream to pink to purple, are formed in long, one-sided racemes from June to August. The fleshy

Native from Europe into western Siberia, the genus is derived from the Greek words *sympho*, meaning to "grow together," and *phyton*, "plant," a reference to its reputed healing properties when used as a poultice on wounds. The species name *officinale* indicates that it was used in medicine or sold by apothecaries. It was widely planted in monastic gardens.

Comfrey was used primarily for treating injuries and sprains by applying a paste made from its roots to the afflicted area. The roots contain allantoin, a compound known to cause the proliferation of new cells and there promote healing in connective tissue. In Britain, the red-flowered plants were believed best for healing men and the white-flowered plants for women.

In addition to their medicinal uses, the roots were ground and used as a coffee substitute and the young shoots were prepared like asparagus. The common name, comfrey, is from the medieval English word *cum-frie* and is similar to the French *foie*, meaning "liver," another reference to its use in healing.

Symphytum officinale (comfrey) (Sara Williams)

roots are deep and tuberous. The cultivar 'Goldsmith' has red buds that open into blue flowers and attractive yellow and white variegated foliage. It grows 45 (18 in.) tall and 60 cm (24 in.) wide and lacks the aggressive nature of the species.

How to Grow
Comfrey grows in sun or shade in average soil and is drought tolerant once established. 'Goldsmith' prefers a moister, shadier location. During periods of extreme heat and drought, without irrigation the foliage may sun scorch. Shear or mow to remove dead foliage. To propagate, divide comfrey at any time during the growing season, although it's less of a chore in spring while the plant is still small.

Thymus serpyllum
ty-mus ser-*pil*-lum
Creeping thyme

Plant at a Glance
Type: evergreen perennial or sub-shrub
Height/spread: 5 cm (2 in.) / 30 cm (12 in.)
Spacing: 20 cm (8 in.)
Light: full sun
Soil: well drained; lean to average
Distinguishing features: prolific purple flowers; tiny, fragrant, dark green leaves
Landscape use: rock gardens; edging; lawn replacement; small, inaccessible, or inhospitable areas; slopes and banks; unifying shrub beds; pavement plantings; accentuating focal points
Propagation: seed; division; softwood cuttings
Photo: page 79

Thymes are low-growing, fragrant members of the mint family. The genus and common names are their ancient Greek names. Thyme bears tiny, round to oval, opposite leaves on fine stems that lie close to the ground. They tolerate limited foot traffic and release their pungent odor when crushed. Creeping thyme blooms in early summer with small, two-lipped flowers in terminal clusters. The most common forms have pink or purple flowers; however, the variety *albus* has white flowers and *coccineus* red flowers. The stems root where they touch the ground, making thyme an ideal groundcover between stepping stones.

Remember scale—here is a perfect groundcover for a smaller space. Thyme makes a dense cover that can be mowed and will withstand some foot traffic. Plant a bed where you can roll in it and savor its fragrance!

How to Grow
Thymes grow best on lean to average, well-drained soils. They should be planted in an open, sunny location where they won't be overgrown by more aggressive plants. Thymes are easily propagated by transplanting divisions in the spring. They may also be grown from seed or from softwood cuttings in the summer.

Other Species and Hybrids
- *Thymus* x *citriodorus* (sit-ree-o-*dor*-us), lemon-scented thyme, is a group of hybrid cultivars that grow to 15 cm (6 in.) high. The foliage has the sharp odor of lemon and some of the cultivars have variegated foliage. They are less winter hardy than creeping thyme and should either be planted where they have snow cover or be given winter protection.
- *Thymus pallasianus* (syn. *T. odoratissimus*) pal-*as*-ee-an-us, Ukrainian

thyme, is a sub-shrub that grows to 15 cm (6 in.) in height, with mauve pink flowers and hirsute foliage.

- *Thymus pseudo lanuginosus* (syn. *T. serpyllum lanuginosis*) (soo-doh-lan-u-gee-*no*-sis), woolly thyme, has pubescent, gray, woolly foliage and pink flowers.

Tradescantia virginiana (syn. *T.* x *andersonia*)
tra-des-*kan*-shee-a vir-gin-ee-*an*-ah
Spiderwort

Plant at a Glance
Type: herbaceous perennial
Height/spread: 45 to 60 cm (18 to 24 in.) / 30 cm (12 in.)
Spacing: 40 cm (16 in.)
Light: full sun to shade
Soil: evenly moist; rich in organic matter
Distinguishing features: three-petaled, blue, purple, pink, or white flowers; grassy foliage
Landscape use: small, inaccessible, or inhospitable areas; accentuating focal points; shady understory
Propagation: division

Tradescantia virginiana (spiderwort) (Brian Baldwin)

With attractive grassy foliage, a fleshy but determined root system, and a long flowering period, spiderwort is an ideal groundcover. Native to a large area of eastern North America, it was introduced from the Virginia Colony to England by John Tradescant the Elder, the head gardener at Hatfield House in England and later for the royal family. By 1632, Tradescant was growing it in his own garden near London. The common name arises from the resemblance of the long, narrow foliage to the legs of a spider.

Plants soon form dense clumps of long, arching leaves, with parallel veins that clasp the base of the erect, but somewhat fleshy stems. Like daylilies,

Best Groundcovers & Vines For The Prairies

individual flowers are open only for a day, but the plants flower freely for up to eight weeks in late spring and early summer. Flowers of the species are blue-purple or pink, but cultivars bear pink, white, purple, or blue flowers. The small flowers have three distinct petals and are formed in umbels in the axils of leaf-like bracts.

How to Grow
Spiderworts grow in sun to light shade, given even moisture and soil well amended with organic matter. They may need to be cut back if they appear untidy after flowering. Newer cultivars may benefit from mulch where snow cover is lacking in winter. Divide spiderwort in early spring.

Cultivars
Most of the cultivars are hybrids of several species, including *Tradescantia virginiana,* and are more correctly listed as *T. andersonia.* What has been sold in garden centers as *T. virginiana* has survived and established itself as a good groundcover on the prairies. However, many of the newer cultivars now being sold are largely untested. They are all similar in size to the species.
- 'Concord Grape' has a compact habit, frosty blue foliage, and small, purple flowers.
- 'Isis' bears Oxford blue flowers.
- 'Osprey' has large, white flowers, with violet-blue stamen filaments.
- 'Red Cloud' has rose-red flowers.
- 'Snowcap' produces white flowers.
- 'Zwanenburg Blue' has large, royal blue flowers.

Veronica incana
ve-*ron*-i-ka in-*kan*-a
Woolly speedwell

Plant at a Glance
Type: herbaceous perennial
Height/spread: 30 to 45 cm (12 to 18 in.) / 30 cm (12 in.)
Spacing: 45 cm (18 in.)
Light: full sun to partial shade
Soil: well drained
Distinguishing features: blue flowers; silver foliage
Landscape use: perennial or mixed border; rock garden; edging; small, inaccessible, or inhospitable areas; unifying shrub bed; pavement plantings; accentuating focal points
Propagation: division

The genus name, *Veronica,* comes from the Latin root *vera,* meaning "true," and the Greek word *icon,* meaning "an image," thus it is a true likeness. Saint

Veronica incana (woolly speedwell) with *Cerastium tomentosum* (snow-in-summer) (Sara Williams)

Veronica is said to have used her handkerchief to wipe Christ's brow as he carried the cross to Calvary. He returned it to her imprinted with a perfect likeness of his face. The species name, *incana*, means "hoary" or "gray" and describes the foliage; the common name, speedwell, is a reference to its easy cultivation. The word "speed" at one time meant to "thrive."

Blue flowers combine with soft silver foliage to give woolly speedwell a calm and inviting appearance. Add drought tolerance, a slowly spreading rhizomatous root system, and little if any maintenance and you have an almost perfect groundcover. Woolly speedwell works equally well toward the front of a herbaceous border, in a rock garden, or as edging.

The silver-gray leaves are opposite, oblong, and about 8 cm (3 in.) long, while the stem leaves are more lance shaped. Dense, 15-cm (6-in.) -tall spikes of lavender-blue flowers bloom for about four weeks in late June and early July. The cultivar 'Rosea' is similar but has pink flowers.

How to Grow
Plant woolly speedwell in full sun to partial shade in well-drained soil. Propagate through division from spring to mid-summer.

Other Species and Hybrids
- *Veronica austriaca* (ow-stree-*ah*-ka) (syn. *V. teucrium*), Austrian speedwell, has tufts of deeply cut, dark green foliage that grow to 45 cm (18 in.) tall and 60 cm (24 in.) wide. Short spikes of deep blue flowers bloom in early summer. 'Rosea' has pink flowers.
- *Veronica gentianoides* (gen-tee-a-*noi*-deez), gentian speedwell, differs from most of the shorter species because of its broad, fleshy leaves that form dark green, tufted rosettes. The pale, icy blue flowers are in loose racemes that grow to 25 cm (10 in.) in summer.

Best Groundcovers & Vines For The Prairies

- *Veronica pectinata* (pek-ti-*nah*-ta), comb speedwell, is low, mat-forming, and fairly drought tolerant and prefers full sun and well-drained soil. It is somewhat similar to *V. whitleyi*. It's useful in a rock garden, as a pavement planting, and among early minor bulbs. Although it has a woody base, comb speedwell roots at stem nodes as it spreads, soon forming a dense mat of trailing stems, 5 cm (2 in.) tall and 30 cm (12 in.) wide. The lovely blue flowers, with white centers, bloom for two to three weeks in late May to early June. The gray, woolly foliage is finely cut and pubescent. 'Rosea' has pink flowers.
- *Veronica prostrata* (pros-*trah*-ta), creeping speedwell or harebell speedwell, forms a dense mat of gray, pubescent, horizontal stems that have tiny, linear leaves and pale blue flowers in early summer. 'Rosea' is a pink form. 'Trehane' is 15 to 20 cm (6 to 8 in.) tall and has yellow-chartreuse foliage and bright blue flowers. It benefits from afternoon shade through the heat of summer.
- *Veronica repens* (*re*-penze), creeping veronica, forms an extremely low mat and tolerates both partial shade and limited foot traffic. It shows dieback in harsh winters without snowcover, but it quickly recovers. 'Alba' is a white form.
- *Veronica whitleyi* (*whit*-lee-i), Whitley's veronica, is low and mat forming and grows 5 to 10 cm (2 to 4 in.) tall and 45 cm (18 in.) wide, with tiny, gray-green, incised leaves and little blue flowers in spring. Its origin is a mystery, though probably British. It is tough and long lasting, heat and drought tolerant, and perfect for well-drained soils in full sun. Use it as a groundcover where its diminutive stature is in keeping with its placement, such as pavement plantings, in rock gardens, or among minor spring bulbs such as squills, *Tulipa tarda*, or *Puschkinia*.

Vinca herbacea
vin-ka er-*bay*-see-ah
Herbaceous periwinkle

Plant at a Glance
Type: herbaceous perennial
Height/spread: 5 cm (2 in.) / 50 cm (20 in.)
Spacing: 20 cm (8 in.)
Light: full sun to partial shade
Soil: moist; well drained
Distinguishing features: blue flowers; trailing stems; dark green leaves
Landscape use: rock garden; lawn replacement; small, inaccessible, or inhospitable areas; unifying shrub beds; pavement plantings; accentuating focal points; shady understory
Propagation: division; softwood cuttings

Herbaceous periwinkle is a vigorous and rapidly spreading groundcover. Numerous slender, green stems emerge in spring and give rise to opposite, lance-shaped, dark green leaves. Stems grow stacked on each other to provide dense groundcover. The plants are covered with purplish blue, star-shaped flowers in July.

Both the genus name, *Vinca*, and the common name, periwinkle, are derived from *pervinca*, the ancient Latin name for the plant. The species name, *herbacea*, indicates that it sheds its leaves over winter, unlike the evergreen *V. minor*.

How to Grow
Herbaceous periwinkle is adaptable to a variety of conditions, from full sun to partial shade. It is easy to propagate from divisions taken in early spring or can be rooted from softwood cuttings in early summer.

Other Species and Hybrids
- *Vinca minor*, common periwinkle, is less winter hardy than herbaceous periwinkle but will grow in protected situations and develop into a dense, evergreen groundcover. Cultivars that are offered include *V. minor* var. *alba*, with white flowers, var. 'Variegata' with white-edged leaves and blue flowers, and 'Sterling Silver', with silver-edged leaves and white flowers. Plant common periwinkle in shaded and sheltered locations on the prairies.

Vinca herbacea (herbaceous periwinkle) (Hugh Skinner)

Viola Canadensis (western Canada violet)
(Sara Williams)

Viola canadensis
(syn. *V. rugulosa, V. canadensis* var. *rugulosa*)
vi-*ol*-lah can-a-*den*-sis
Western Canada violet, wood violet

Plant at a Glance
Type: herbaceous perennial
Height/spread: 20 cm (8 in.) / 30 cm (12 in.)
Spacing: 30 cm (12 in.)
Light: shade
Soil: average
Distinguishing features: white flowers; heart-shaped foliage
Landscape use: naturalizing; unifying shrub beds; back lane plantings; accentuating focal points; shady understory
Propagation: division

The western Canada violet, native to the woodlands of the prairie provinces, is all one could ask for in terms of a hardy, enduring, and attractive groundcover for dry or moist shade. It is especially suited for naturalizing under trees.

The stoloniferous root system, with numerous slender, white roots, soon forms a dense, low mat. The heart-shaped leaves, pointed at the apex, have long petioles. Fragrant, white flowers, with distinct purple-pink veins, appear in late spring and early summer. The flowers have five petals, one with a distinct spur, and a yellow eye.

The common name, violet, is from the Latin *viola*. The species name, *canadensis*, indicates part of its natural range.

How to Grow

Western Canada violet has simple needs: shade, average soil, and average moisture. Propagate through division in spring.

Waldsteinia ternata
wald-*stin*-ee-uh ter-*na*-tah
Siberian barren strawberry

Plant at a Glance
Type: evergreen perennial
Height/spread: 10 to 15 cm (4 to 6 in.) / 30 cm (12 in.) to indefinite
Spacing: 30 cm (12 in.)
Light: full sun to full shade
Soil: average
Distinguishing features: bright yellow flowers; glossy foliage
Landscape use: naturalizing; lawn replacement; small, inaccessible, or inhospitable areas; unifying shrub beds; back lane plantings; accentuating focal points; shady understory
Propagation: division

Waldsteinia ternata (siberian barren strawberry) (Sara Williams)

Best Groundcovers & Vines For The Prairies

Waldsteinia is an attractive and effective but sadly underused groundcover, deserving much greater attention. The common name, Siberian barren strawberry, speaks volumes to its appearance, as well as its hardiness and adaptability. It looks very much like a strawberry but bears no fruit, thus, the common name. Honoring Count Franz Adam Waldstein-Wartenburg (1759–1823), an Austrian botanist, *Waldsteinia* is native from central Europe into Siberia and Japan. The small, bright yellow flowers, formed in clusters, have five petals and bloom from late spring to early summer. As the specific epithet *ternata* implies, the glossy leaves are ternate, in clusters of three, and irregularly toothed. The plants quickly form a low, dense, weed-suppressing mat by means of fibrous rhizomes and are excellent for naturalizing.

How to Grow
Siberian barren strawberry grows in sun or shade in a range of soils. It spreads at a faster pace when given even moisture but is very drought tolerant. Propagate through division in spring or summer.

Vines

Celastrus scandens
sel-*as*-trus *scan*-dens
American bittersweet vine

Plant at a Glance
Type: woody vine
Climbing mechanism: twining stems
Pruning: only to control form
Height/spread: 6 m (20 ft.) / 1.5 m (5 ft.)
Light: full sun
Soil: well drained
Distinguishing features: brilliant yellow fall color; orange and scarlet seeds
Landscape use: fences or walls
Propagation: seed; layering; softwood cuttings

American bittersweet vine is native to eastern parts of the prairie region and can be found growing in well-drained soil at the edge of woods. At one time, street vendors in Winnipeg, Manitoba, sold bunches of the colorful fruit to use as decorations. The species is usually dioecious, so it is necessary to have both male and female plants to produce these fruit.

Celastrus is the ancient Greek name for the genus; *scandens* means "climbing." The vine climbs by twining around shrubs and trees and can choke small trees if allowed to climb on them. The woody stems have smooth, gray bark and can grow to 5 to 8 cm (2 to 3 in.) in diameter. The shiny green, oval to oblong leaves are 5 to 10 cm (2 to 4 in.) long and turn bright yellow in autumn. Clusters of small, yellowish white flowers appear in June and produce the brilliant orange fruit that open to reveal a scarlet seed in September.

American bittersweet vine makes a lush covering for a fence. To ensure fruit production, buy plants that have been propagated by cuttings from plants of known sex.

How to Grow
Plant American bittersweet vine in a sunny location with good drainage. It tolerates dry conditions and poor soil and requires pruning only to control size and direct growth. To start plants from seed, sow in the fall after collection or cold stratify seeds (see p. 33) and sow them in the spring. They may also be propagated by softwood cuttings taken in early summer or by layering vines.

Clematis
clem-*ah*-tis or *clem*-ah-tis
Clematis

Clematis, "the queen of vines," is a varied genus that includes many members with spectacularly beautiful flowers. The genus name, *Clematis,* is derived from an ancient Greek word for "climbing plants." Taxonomists have divided this genus into a number of groups, some of which are adapted to growing in prairie gardens. Most species are native to the edge of woodlands and grow best where roots are shaded but stems and foliage can grow up into the sunlight.

How to Grow
Plant clematis where the roots can be shaded or mulched and where the vines can grow into full sun. They grow best in well-drained soil that is rich in organic matter. Plants are normally purchased as container-grown shoots. It is important to encourage development of a crown below ground (see p. 32 for planting tips). Plant clematis where they can be trained on a fence or other structure or grow up through a shrub or tree. Alternatively, choose a location where they can run along the ground as a groundcover. Most species climb by twining leaf petioles and require a minimum of encouragement. A few, such as *Clematis integrifolia* hybrids, need more direction and support to climb. Different groups of clematis vary in their pruning requirements (see p. 38).

Clematis alpina, C. koreana, C. macropetala (*atragene* group)
cle-*mat*-is al-*pie*-na; cle-*mat*-is cor-ee-*an*-ah; cle-*mat*-is mac-row-*pet*-al-a
Alpine clematis, Korean clematis, bigpetal clematis

Plant at a Glance
Type: woody vine
Climbing mechanism: twining leaf petioles
Pruning: Group A (see p. 38, "Pruning Clematis")
Height/spread: 3 m (10 ft.) / 1.5 m (5 ft.)
Light: full sun, with shaded roots
Soil: well drained; rich in organic matter
Distinguishing features: showy flowers; dense, hardy vines
Landscape use: fences or walls; arbors; accent; groundcover
Propagation: division; layering; softwood cuttings

Clematis alpina, C. koreana, and *C. macropetala* fall into a group that was formerly identified as the genus *Atragene* and they have similar characteristics. They begin to grow early in spring and flower on the previous

Clematis alpina 'Ruby' ('Ruby' alpine clematis) (Hugh Skinner)

year's vines soon after growth starts. They are winter-hardy vines that climb by twining the petioles and the rachis of the compound leaves. The flowers are formed from colored sepals, not petals, and sometimes have large, colored, petal-like stamens. Plants covered with hundreds of flowers give a spectacular display. Flowers may be bell shaped as in *C. alpina* and *C. koreana* cultivars or a "spider" form, made up of many long, narrow petaloids, as in a number of the *C. macropetala* hybrids. Most bloom in late spring or early summer and some may have a second bloom period in late summer.

Most of the clematis in this group have bi-ternately compound leaves, with each leaf composed of three groups of three leaflets. The margins of the broadly lance-shaped leaflets are coarse toothed and sometimes lobed. Petioles are angular and twist around any available stem, stick, or wire. Stems are angular and become woody as they mature. The species and cultivars recommended here are hardy; vines will survive to the top and require only minor pruning to train them. Use them to cover an arbor, fence, or wall or allow them to creep on a slope and act as groundcover.

Clematis alpina, alpine clematis, has small, white, pink, or blue, bell-shaped flowers in early spring. It includes 'Ruby' (deep pink, bell-shaped flowers), 'Willy' (pale pink flowers with a darker edge), and 'Pamela Jackman' (medium blue flowers).

C. koreana, Korean clematis, has bell-shaped, purple or white flowers in late spring. It has coarser foliage than either *C. alpina* or *C. macropetala* and it is generally less winter hardy than these species. The dark purple

Clematis alpina 'Willy' ('Willy' alpine clematis) (Hugh Skinner)

cultivar 'Brunette' did not survive in Hugh's Manitoba garden, although a number of seedlings of the species did.

C. macropetala, bigpetal clematis, has flowers that are formed from a number of long, thin, colored sepals; some cultivars display large stamenoids in a central boss. Their main flush of bloom is in spring, with many cultivars re-blooming in late summer and some of the newest cultivars blooming repeatedly throughout summer. A number of cultivars

Clematis macropetala 'Lagoon' ('Lagoon' big petal clematis) (Sara Williams)

have been developed on the Canadian prairies, most notably by Frank Skinner and Stan Zubrowski, and these are well adapted to prairie growing conditions.

Clematis macropetala 'Rosy O'Grady' ('Rosy O'Grady' bigpetal clematis) (Hugh Skinner)

Cultivars
- 'Blue Bird', developed by F. L. Skinner, bears medium blue flowers on a very vigorous plant.
- 'Doctor F.L. Skinner' was developed by Stan Zubrowski and has deep purple flowers.
- 'Joe Zary' was developed by Stan Zubrowski. It has purple flowers formed from many narrow, spidery sepals and blooms throughout the summer.
- 'Lagoon' (syn. 'Blue Lagoon') grows to 2.5 m (8 ft.) tall and has deep blue flowers. It was developed by George Jackman and Sons of Woking, England.
- 'Markham's Pink' is an English cultivar. The flowers are darker in color and the vine is less vigorous than 'Rosy O'Grady'.
- 'Rosy O'Grady' was developed by Frank Skinner. It bears rosy pink flowers with pale centers.
- 'White Swan', developed by F. L. Skinner, is a vigorous cultivar that has relatively large, white flowers with narrow petals.

Clematis tangutica, C. serratifolia (*orientalis* group)

cle-*mat*-is tan-*gewt*-ick-ah; cle-*mat*-is ser-rat-ih-*fol*-i-uh

Golden clematis, serrate-leafed clematis

Plant at a Glance

Type: woody vine
Climbing mechanism: twining leaf petioles
Pruning: Group A, B (see p. 38, "Pruning Clematis")
Height/spread: 4 m (13 ft.) / 2 m (6.5 ft.)
Light: full sun, with shaded roots
Soil: well drained
Distinguishing features: yellow, bell-shaped flowers; silver seed heads
Landscape use: fences or walls; arbors; groundcover
Propagation: seed

Clematis tangutica 'Bill McKenzie' ('Bill McKenzie'
bigpetal clematis) (Sara Williams)

Clematis tangutica gets its species name from Gansu, NW China, that is part of its natural range. Its common name, golden clematis, describes the golden yellow, bell-shaped blooms that grace the plant from July until September. The flowers are followed by round seed heads, with long, silvery hairs. Grow it on a wall or fence or let it climb high into a tree. Prune it back hard periodically (yearly or every second year) to encourage bloom on the lower part of the vine. 'Bill MacKenzie' is a vigorous cultivar that blooms prolifically from June to September.

Clematis serratifolia, serrate-leafed clematis, has small, bell-shaped, yellow flowers, with purple anthers in the fall. The species spreads by underground stolons. It is effective as a groundcover on a slope but sometimes becomes a problem weed in the garden. Serrate-leafed clematis can provide dense

Best Groundcovers & Vines For The Prairies

cover on a fence or it can grow up into a tree. The 'Golden Cross' hybrid has cross-shaped, sterile, yellow flowers that bloom from August until October and does not produce unwanted seedlings. It spreads much less aggressively than the species.

Clematis viticella
cle-mat-*is vit-i*-sell-*ah*
Italian clematis and hybrids

Plant at a Glance
Type: herbaceous vine
Climbing mechanism: twining leaf petioles
Pruning: Group C (see p. 38, "Pruning Clematis")
Height/spread: 2 to 3 m (6.5 to 10 ft.) / 0.6 to 1.2 m (2 to 4 ft.)
Light: full sun, with shaded roots
Soil: well drained; rich in organic matter
Distinguishing features: spectacular flowers in a wide range of colors
Landscape use: fences or walls; accent
Propagation: division; layering; softwood cuttings

Clematis viticella is native to southern Europe and western Asia. This slender vine has leaves that are singly pinnate, with five leaflets, or bi-ternate, with smooth, broadly lance-shaped to oval leaflets. The flowers of the species are rose to purple, broadly bell shaped, and formed from four colored sepals. It blooms in late summer. *C. viticella* has been widely used in the development of some of our showiest hybrid clematis.

Clematis viticella 'Etoile Violet' ('Etoile Violet' Italian clematis)
(Hugh Skinner)

These eye-catching vines will break up the expanse of a blank wall and are especially useful where there is a narrow space available for planting. Use them on fences to provide a splash of color, grow them up through an ornamental obelisk, or allow them to scramble through a shrub to provide an unexpected burst of bloom.

Some cultivars require covering and heat from building foundations, but others survive in protected garden situations and grow vigorously year after year. The vines die back to near ground level each year. They should be pruned back before growth elongates in the spring. New vines grow back quickly, with bloom beginning in mid-summer and often continuing until fall.

Clematis viticella 'Mme. Julia Correvon'
('Mme. Julia Correvon' Italian clematis) (Sara Williams)

Cultivars
- 'Etoile Violet' originated in France in 1885. Its medium-sized, bluish purple flowers are produced in profusion from July to September.
- 'Mme. Julia Correvon' has abundant bright wine-red flowers from July to September. It originated in France around 1900.
- 'Polish Spirit' was raised by Brother Stefan Franczak in Poland in 1984. Blooming from July to September, its deep purple flowers are larger than many others of this group.
- 'Purpurea Plena Elegans', a cultivar from the sixteenth century, produces deep purple, double flowers from July to September.
- 'Venosa Violacea' has purple flowers, with a white stripe down the center of each tepal. It blooms from early summer to early autumn.

Other Species and Hybrids
Clematis x *jackmanii* (jack-*man*-ee-i) and other large-flowered clematis originated as hybrids between *C. lanuginosa* and *C. viticella* (or, according to some authorities, *C. hendersonii*) in the nursery of George Jackman and

Sons of Woking, England, in 1860. When these seedlings flowered in 1862, they were named after the owners of the nursery. These are now known as the Jackmani group and are the most widely grown clematis in North America. These lovely vines are tender on the prairies, thus, they require a protected location or heat from the foundation of a building and an ample covering of mulch. Many prairie gardeners are willing to make the effort to grow them because of their spectacular flowers. The cultivars listed below are among the most winter hardy of the group.

Clematis x *jackmanii* (Jackman clematis)
(Hugh Skinner)

- 'Comtesse de Bouchaud' was developed in France and introduced in 1900. It has pink flowers from July to September.
- 'Hagley Hybrid' (syn. 'Pink Chiffon') was developed in the United Kingdom in 1945. Its large, pale pink flowers are produced from July to September.
- 'Jackmanii' has splendid large, deep purple flowers that account for its long popularity. It should be grown near a foundation and protected from the most severe winters.
- 'John Huxtable' has large, white flowers, with creamy yellow stamens.

Clematis integrifolia (in-teg-ri-*fol*-ee-ah) is a herbaceous perennial but has been bred with *C. viticella* to produce hybrids that climb to 2 m (6.5 ft.) if provided with a suitable trellis. On the prairies, these very hardy and

Clematis integrifolia hybrid 'Blue Boy'
('Blue Boy' clematis) (Hugh Skinner)

vigorous hybrids die back to near ground level over winter, but grow back quickly in the spring and bloom from late June or early July until late summer. They are not aggressive or weedy and can be allowed to ramble through a large shrub to provide unexpected bloom.

- 'Aljonushka' was raised in Ukraine and named in 1969. It produces elegant clear rose-pink flowers, consisting of four long, curved tepals, from June to September. It grows from 1.5 to 2 m (5 to 6.5 ft.) in height.
- 'Blue Boy', developed by F. L. Skinner in the 1950s, is long-lived and very hardy. It produces medium purple-blue, bell-shaped flowers from early July to September.

Other Species and Hybrids

- *Clematis* x *jouiniana* 'Praecox' (*zhoo*-awn-ee-awn-uh *pray*-cox) is a vigorous herbaceous plant. Use it as a groundcover, over a stump to form a mound, or against a fence. Clusters of small, blue-scented flowers are produced in foamy abundance in late summer. Prune vines back in spring (Group C).
- *Clematis ligusticifolia* (li-gus-tick-i-*foe*-lee-ah), Western virgin's bower, is native to the southern part of the prairies. A vigorous hardy vine, it rambles over shrubs and trees in its native habitat. Its leaves are pinnately compound, formed by five to seven broadly lance-shaped leaflets.

Best Groundcovers & Vines For The Prairies

Plants are dioecious, with white flowers borne in terminal and axial clusters (cymes) in mid-summer. The seed heads, consisting of numerous hairy seeds, with a long plume attached to each seed, are only produced if both male and female plants are present. This species and hybrids such as 'Prairie Traveler's Joy' form dense perennial cover for fences or arbors. These are extremely vigorous and aggressive vines that can smother shrubs or small trees if allowed to climb on them. Prune to remove damaged vines, control, or shape the plant (Group A).

- *Clematis recta* (*reck*-tah) is a herbaceous clematis that will scramble into shrubs and can also be tied to a fence or grown through taller peony-type hoops. It produces numerous small, white flowers in early summer that are pleasantly fragrant. 'Purpurea' has deep purple foliage in the spring that turns to bluish green after the plant flowers. *Clematis* 'Pamela', a hybrid of *C. recta*, grows to 1.8 m (6 ft.). Its numerous small, white flowers are produced from June to September. Plants are herbaceous. Prune back tops in early spring (Group C).

- *Clematis texensis* (tek-*sen*-sis) produces bell-shaped flowers of a unique red color in late summer. The vines die back to ground level over winter and should be pruned back in spring (Group C). It requires a protected location in prairie gardens, but the species and its cultivars are worthy of trial. Try 'Duchess of Albany'.

Humulus lupulus
hum-ew-lus *lu*-pew-lus
Common hops

Plant at a Glance
Type: herbaceous vine
Climbing mechanism: twining shoots
Pruning: remove dead foliage and vines at ground level each year in late fall or early spring
Height/spread: 4 to 7 m (13 to 23 ft.) / 1 m (3.3 ft.)
Spacing: 2 m (6.5 ft.)
Light: full sun to light shade
Soil: well drained
Distinguishing features: scale-like cones; pinnately compound foliage
Landscape use: summer screening
Propagation: suckers; division

The name of the genus, *Humulus*, is derived from the Latin word *humus*, meaning "soil" and alluding to its occasional prostrate form. The specific epithet *lupulus* means "a small wolf" and indicates the vine's ability to smother small shrubs and trees as it climbs over them. Native to the prairies, including Saskatchewan's Qu'Appelle Valley, hops climbs by twining shoots. Its greenish white flowers are small and inconspicuous. Because it is dioecious, male and female flowers are on separate plants and one of each is required for fruit production. The catkin-like cones contain compounds that are used to flavor beer. They are ready to use when the scales are paper-like and springy to the touch and the centers are dark yellow when cut.

The large, opposite leaves are palmately compound, each of the three to seven leaflets having toothed margins. The cultivar 'Aurea' has attractive yellow foliage and is fully hardy but slightly less vigorous. Place it in full sun for best color.

Humulus lupulus (common hops) (Sara Williams)

Keep in mind this plant's herbaceous nature when placing it in the garden. Because hops dies back to ground level each fall, it does not provide cover during the winter. In addition, it takes about a month to get where it's going each spring. On the more positive side, gardeners often cut the rope-like vines at ground level each November and use them as bases for seasonal wreaths. Left in place, the vines with cones are an interesting feature in the winter landscape.

How to Grow
Hops is a herbaceous vine that seems to thrive on neglect. Given full sun to light shade and well-drained soil, it is virtually foolproof, as well as drought tolerant, once established. Prune off the previous season's growth in late fall or early spring. Hops is very easily propagated by division or suckers during the growing season.

Best Groundcovers & Vines For The Prairies

Lonicera x *brownii* 'Dropmore Scarlet Trumpet'

lah-*nis*-er-ah *brow*-nee-i

'Dropmore Scarlet Trumpet' honeysuckle

Plant at a Glance

Type: woody vine
Climbing mechanism: twining stems
Pruning: seldom required
Height/spread: 3 m (10 ft.) / 1 m (3.3 ft.)
Spacing: 2 m (6.5 ft.)
Light: full sun to partial shade
Soil: evenly moist; well drained; rich in organic matter
Distinguishing features: scarlet-orange, trumpet-shaped flowers
Landscape use: fences or walls; arbors; accent
Propagation: layering; softwood cuttings

The genus *Lonicera* honors Adam Lonitzer (1528–1586), a German naturalist and herbalist. One of the best known of Dr. Frank Skinner's many introductions, 'Dropmore Scarlet Trumpet' honeysuckle was introduced in 1950, a hybrid of *L. sempervirens* and *L. hirsuta*. The village of Dropmore, Manitoba, was once the nearest post office to Skinner's Nursery.

The bright red, trumpet-shaped flowers are two-lipped, with an orange interior. Sterile and in clusters, they bloom from June until frost. The oval to oblong leaves are opposite and 8 cm (3 in.) in length, with the two pairs below the flower clusters united at their bases on the stem. The vine clings by a twining stem and requires the support of a trellis. 'Mandarin',

Lonicera x brownii 'Dropmore Scarlet Trumpet' ('Dropmore Scarlet Trumpet' honeysuckle) (Sara Williams)

introduced by the University of British Columbia Botanical Garden, has not proved hardy in zone 2b.

How to Grow
Place 'Dropmore Scarlet Trumpet' in full sun to partial shade in evenly moist soil well amended with organic matter. Prune only to remove damaged stems or control growth. Propagate by layering or through softwood cuttings in early summer.

Parthenocissus quinquefolia
par-then-o-*sis*-us kwing-kwee-*fo*-lee-uh
Virginia creeper

Plant at a Glance
Type: woody vine
Climbing mechanism: tendrils
Pruning: only to control size
Height/spread: 15 to 20 m (50 to 65 ft.) / 3 m (10 ft.)
Spacing: 2.5 m (8 ft.)
Light: full sun to full shade
Soil: average
Distinguishing features: red fall foliage
Landscape use: fences or walls; arbors; groundcover for slopes and banks; summer screening
Propagation: suckers; layering; softwood cuttings

Virginia creeper is most admired for its brilliant scarlet fall foliage. Hardy, fast growing, and vigorous, it is also heavy and requires adequate support and sufficient space. It serves a multitude of purposes: as a groundcover, especially on slopes or banks; softening a large expanse of fence or wall; over a large arbor or gazebo; or hiding a neighbor's old shed or ugly garage. (It's not difficult to plant at night by flashlight.) It climbs by tendrils.

The genus name echoes the common name: *parthenos* is the Greek word for "virgin" and *kissos* means "ivy." It was first introduced to England from the Virginia colony in 1629. The species name describes the foliage, *quinque*, meaning "five," and *folia*, "leaf," thus, the five leaflets that make up the compound leaf.

The large leaves are 5 to 15 cm (2 to 6 in.) across and palmately compound, each with five toothed leaflets. The inconspicuous flowers are followed by small, blue berries that resemble grapes.

How to Grow
Drought tolerant once established, Virginia creeper grows in sun or full shade in most soils. Leafhoppers are sometimes present, and powdery

Best Groundcovers & Vines For The Prairies

Parthenocissus quinquefolia (Virginia creeper)
(Brian Baldwin)

mildew can be a problem during periods of high humidity if air circulation is poor. Pruning may be required when the vigorous growth starts to block windows or doors or otherwise gets out of hand. Propagate through softwood cuttings in early summer or by layering or suckers in early spring.

Other Species and Hybrids

- *Parthenocissus quinquefolia* var. *engelmannii* (en-gel-*man*-ee-i), Engelmann's ivy, differs from the species in a few ways. It has smaller leaflets, is less susceptible to powdery mildew, and climbs by holdfasts, which are small discs on the end of each tendril that secret a resinous cement. This characteristic enables Engelmann's ivy to adhere to bricks or other hard surfaces without support, but it has been known to damage wood. It may not be as hardy as Virginia creeper in the colder regions of the prairies.

Vitis riparia

vi-tis ree-*pare*-ee-ah

Riverbank grape, Manitoba grape

Plant at a Glance

Type: woody vine

Climbing mechanism: tendrils

Pruning: to remove damaged stems and control growth

Height/spread: 6 m (20 ft.) / 3 m (10 ft.)

Spacing: 3 m (10 ft.)

Light: full sun to partial shade

Soil: well drained

Distinguishing features: large, palmately lobed leaves

Landscape use: fences or walls; arbors; groundcover on slopes and banks

Propagation: seed; softwood or hardwood cuttings

Vitis is the classical name given to grapes; *riparia* means "riverbank," an indication of its natural habitat. Riverbank grape is native to the prairies as far north and west as Riding Mountain in Manitoba. It works well as a ceiling for a large pergola or arbor, covering a large expanse of wall or fence, or as a groundcover on a slope or bank.

Opposite each large, palmately lobed leaf is a tendril by which it clings for support. Male and female flowers, both inconspicuous, are on separate plants; one of each is needed for fruit production. The small, dark blue grapes are good for jelly, wine, or feeding birds.

Vitis riparia (riverbank grape) (Brian Baldwin)

Best Groundcovers & Vines For The Prairies

How to Grow

Riverbank grape grows vigorously in full sun to partial shade in a range of soils, but does better with even moisture. For maximum fruit production, give it full sun. Leafhoppers are sometimes a problem, and powdery mildew can occur under conditions of poor air circulation. If grape vines are being grown to produce fruit, severe pruning will promote fruit production. Lateral branches should be pruned back to two to three nodes to produce fruit clusters with good size that will be exposed to sun and ripen well. Otherwise, prune riverbank grape vines in early spring to remove damaged vines and control growth. Propagate by sowing fresh seed in the fall or cold-stratified seed (see p. 33) in spring or by taking hardwood cuttings in early spring or softwood cuttings in early summer.

Glossary

adpressed: pressed together

allelopathic: producing a chemical compound that suppresses the growth of other plants

axillary: in the axil of a leaf where the petiole attaches to the stem

bi-ternately compound: made up of three groups of three

bloom: a powdery or waxy substance on fruit or leaves that gives them a whitish appearance

boss: a circular prominence

calcareous: containing calcium or limestone

calyx: the outermost parts of a flower, individually called sepals; they are usually leaf-like and green but may be colored and petaloid (petal-like)

clone: a group of plants propagated by vegetative or asexual means, all individuals being genetically identical

corolla: a whorl, or whorls, of petals forming the inner envelope of a flower

corona: a crown-like process at the top of the tube formed from the corolla of a flower

corymb: a flat-topped or convex flower cluster in which the outer flowers open first

cruciform: cross shaped

cultivar: a variety developed in cultivation that has stable characteristics that can be maintained when the cultivar is propagated

cutting: a plant shoot cut off for vegetative propagation

cyme: a flat-topped flower cluster in which the central flowers open first

deadhead: remove flowers that have faded

dioecious: male and female flowers are on separate plants

farina: a white, meal- or flour-like powder on leaves

glaucous: covered with a bluish white bloom

hardwood cutting: cutting made from the previous season's woody growth; usually taken in winter or early spring

heeled-in: temporarily covering the roots of dormant plants with soil to store them

hirsute: covered with coarse, stiff hairs

holdfast: a specialized organ of attachment used by vines

lanceolate: lance shaped, tapering to a point

layer: a shoot laid on the ground to take root without being detached from the mother plant

monoecious: male and female flowers are separate but on the same plant

palmately compound: a compound leaf in which the leaflets radiate from one point

pappus: bristle-like calyx limb borne on the ovary and persisting on the fruit

pedicel: the stalk supporting a single flower in an inflorescence

petal: one part of the corolla of a flower

petaloid: appearing like a petal

petiole: the leaf stalk

pinnately compound: a compound leaf with leaflets coming off either side of a central stem or rachis

pip: rhizome piece with a bud

provenance: the origin, or documented source, of a plant

pubescent: covered with short, soft hairs

raceme: a flower cluster in which individual flowers are arranged singly on distinct, nearly equal pedicels along a central axis

rachis: an axis bearing flowers or leaflets

rhizome: a creeping or underground root-like stem, producing roots from its lower side and shoots or leaves from its upper side

rosette: a flower-like cluster of leaves

sepal: individual leaf or part of the calyx

sessile: without stalks

softwood cutting: cutting made from the current season's growth before it has matured

specific epithet: the second term of the Latin name of a plant that, combined with the genus name, designates a species

spike: a flower cluster in which numerous flowers are arranged along a common axis

stamenoid: a sterile stamen

stolon: a trailing branch that roots at intervals

stool: to send up shoots or suckers

stratify: to layer seeds with moist medium for pre-germination treatment

suckers: shoots arising from the below-ground portion of a stem or a root near, or at a short distance from, the trunk of a tree or the main stem of a shrub

tendril: a slender, leafless, coiling organ that curls around stems, a fence, or other support to hold up a climbing plant

tepal: combination of petals and sepals

tomentose: covered with matted, woolly hairs

umbel: an umbrella-like inflorescence that has a number of pedicels radiating from near the top of a short axis

whorl: a set of leaves that is distributed in a circle around a stem on the same plane

Bibliography

Aden, Paul. *The Hosta Book*. Portland, OR: Timber Press, 1988.

Allen, David E., and Gabrielle Hatfield. *Medicinal Plants in Folk Tradition*. Portland, OR: Timber Press, 2004.

American Hosta Society. *The Genus Hosta, List of Registered Cultivars*. Indianapolis, IN: Priority Press, 1993.

Armitage, Allan M. *Herbaceous Perennial Plants*. Athens, GA: Varsity Press, 1989.

Bailey, L. H. *Manual of Cultivated Plants*. rev. ed. New York: Macmillan Publishing Co., 1949.

Bailey, L. H. *The Standard Cyclopedia of Horticulture*. 2nd ed. New York: The Macmillan Company, 1917.

Bailey, Liberty Hyde. *Hortus Third*. New York: Macmillan Publishing Co., 1976.

Bean, W. J. *Trees and Shrubs Hardy in the British Isles*. 3rd ed. London, UK: John Murray, 1924.

Bond, Sandra. *Hostas*. London, UK: Wardlock, 1994.

Britton, L. N., and Hon. Addison Brown. *An Illustrated Flora of the Northern United States, Canada and the British Possessions*. 2nd ed. New York: Charles Scribner's Sons, 1913.

Budd, Archibald C., and Keith F. Best. *Wild Plants of the Canadian Prairies*. Ottawa, ON: Information Canada, 1964.

Clausen, Ruth Rogers, and Nicolas H. Eckstrom. *Perennials for American Gardens*. New York: Random House, Inc., 1989.

Cole, Trevor J. *Ground Covers and Climbing Plants*. Ottawa, ON: Agriculture Canada #1698, 1980.

Coombes, Allen J. *Dictionary of Plant Names*. Portland, OR: Timber Press, 1985.

Darke, Rick. *Color Encyclopedia of Ornamental Grasses*. Portland, OR: Timber Press, 1999.

Dirr, Michael A. *Manual of Woody Landscape Plants, Their Identification, Ornamental Characteristics, Culture, Propagation and Uses*. 5th [rev.] ed. Champaign, IL: Stipes Publishing, L.L.C., 1998.

Feltwell, John. *Clematis for all Seasons*. Willowdale, ON: Firefly Books Ltd., 1999.

Flanagan, June. *Native Plants for Prairie Gardens*. Calgary, AB: Fifth House Ltd., 2005.

Gerard, John. *Gerard's Herbal: The History of Plants*. New York: Crescent Books, 1985.

Heger, Mike, and John Whitman. *Growing Perennials in Cold Climates*. Chicago: Contemporary Books, 1998.

Hyam, Roger, and Richard Pankhurst. *Plants and Their Names, A Concise Dictionary*. Oxford, UK: Oxford University Press, 1995.

Jelitto, Leo, and Wilhelm Schacht. *Hardy Herbaceous Perennials*. Portland, OR: Timber Press, 1990.

Kirkpatrick, Betty. *Brewer's Concise Phrase and Fable*. London, UK: Cassell & Co., 2000.

Knowles, Hugh. *Woody Ornamentals for the Prairies*. Edmonton, AB: University of Alberta, Faculty of Extension, 1995.

Krussman, Gerd. *Manual of Cultivated Conifers*. Portland, OR: Timber Press, 1985.

MacKenzie, David S. *Perennial Ground Covers*. Portland, OR: Timber Press, 1997.

Marles, Robin J., Christina Clavelle, Leslie Monteleone, Natalie Tays, and Donna Burns. *Aboriginal Plant Use in Canada's Northwest Boreal Forest*. Vancouver, BC: UBC Press/Natural Resources Canada, Canadian Forest Service, 2000.

Mickel, John T. *Ferns for American Gardens*. Portland, OR: Timber Press, 2003.

Mikolajski, Andrew. *Hostas*. London, UK: Lorenze Books, 1997.

Looman, J., and K. F. Best. *Budd's Flora*. Hull, QC: Agriculture Canada, Canadian Government Publishing Centre, 1979.

Merriam-Webster's Geographic Dictionary. 3rd ed. Springfield, MA: 1997.

Paterson, Allen. *Plants for Shade and Woodland*. Markham, ON: Fitzhenry and Whiteside Limited, 1987.

Phillips, Roger, and Martin Rix. *Perennials*. New York: Random House, 1991.

Reinhardt, Thomas A., Martina Reinhardt, and Mark Moskowitz. *Ornamental Grass Gardening*. Los Angeles, CA: H.P. Books, 1989.

Rydberg, Per Axel. *Flora of the Prairies and Plains of Central North America*. New York: The New York Botanical Garden, 1932.

Rice, Graham. *Hardy Perennials*. Portland, OR: Timber Press, 1995.

Rose, Nancy, Don Selinger, and John Whitman. *Growing Shrubs and Small Trees in Cold Climates*. Chicago: Contemporary Books, 2001.

Shosteck, Robert. *Flowers and Plants, An International Lexicon with Biographical Notes*. New York: Quadrangle/The New York Times Book Company, 1974.

Skinner, Hugh, and Sara Williams. *Best Trees and Shrubs for the Prairies*. Calgary, AB: Fifth House Ltd., 2004.

Stearn, William T. *Stearn's Dictionary of Plant Names for Gardeners*. London, UK: Cassell Publishers Limited, 1996.

Still, Steven M. *Manual of Herbaceous Ornamental Plants*. Champaign, IL: Stipes Publishing L.L.C, 1988.

Thomas, Graham Stuart. *Perennial Garden Plants*. London, UK: J.M. Dent & Sons, 1976.

Toop, Edgar W., and Sara Williams. *Perennials for the Prairies*. Edmonton, AB, Saskatoon, SK: University of Alberta, Faculty of Extension, University of Saskatchewan, Extension Press, 1991.

USDA, ARS, National Genetics Resources Program, *Germplasm Resources Information Network* (GRIN), online database, National Germplasm Resources Laboratory, Beltsville, Maryland, URL: http://www.ars-grin.gov/cgi-bin/pgs/html/pl?104191 (accessed 15 November 2006).

Valleau, John M. *Heritage Perennials: Perennial Gardening Guide*. Abbottsford, BC: Valleybrook International Ventures Inc., 2003.

Vance, F. R., J. R. Jowsey, and J. S. McLean. *Wild Flowers Across the Prairies*. Saskatoon, SK: Western Producer Prairie Books, 1984.

Vance, F. R., J. R. Jowsey, J. S. McLean, and F. A. Switzer. *Wildflowers Across the Prairies*. 3rd ed. Vancouver, BC: Greystone Books, 1999.

Williams, Sara. *Creating the Prairie Xeriscape*. Saskatoon, SK: University of Saskatchewan, Extension Press, 1997.

Wyman, Donald. *Wyman's Gardening Encyclopedia*. New York: The Macmillan Company, 1972.

Wyman, Donald. *Wyman's Gardening Encyclopedia*. New York: Macmillan Publishing Co., 1986.

Index

In this index, numbers appearing in Roman bold type indicate main entries in the book.

Achillea (yarrow) 8, 16, **44–47**
Achillea millefolium (common yarrow) 10, 13, 14, 16, 17, 19, 22, **44–45**, 'Cerise Queen' 45, 'Colorado' 45, 'Fire King' 45, 'Galaxy' 45, 'Summer Pastels' 45, 'Terracotta' 45; *A. ptarmica* (sneezewort, sneezeweed) **46**, 'Ballerina' 46, 'Perry's White' 46, 'The Pearl' ('Boule de Neige') 46; *A. tomentosa* (woolly yarrow) 18, 20, **47**
Aegopodium podograria 'Variegatum' (goutweed, bishop's goutweed) 6, 10, 16, 17, 23, 28, **47–49**
Ajuga pyramidalis (pyramidal bugleweed) 'Metallica Crispa' 50; *A. reptans* (bugleweed, carpet bugle) 5, 6, 8, 12, 20, 23, 28, **49–50**, 'Alba' 50, 'Bronze Beauty' 50, 'Burgundy Glow' 50, 'Caitlin's Giant' 50; *A.* x *tenorii* 'Chocolate Chip' 49, 50
Alchemilla (lady's mantle) 12, 14, 20, **50–51**; *A. alpina* (alpine lady's mantle) 51; *A. erythropoda* (dwarf lady's mantle) 51; *A. mollis* (common lady's mantle) 6, 33, **50–51**
alpine clematis (*Clematis alpina*) 38, **196–97**
alpine currant (*Ribes alpinum*) **160–61**
alpine forget-me-not (*Brunnera macrophylla*) 6, 23, **70–71**
alpine lady's mantle (*Alchemilla alpina*) 51

alpine skullcap (*Scutellaria alpina*) **169–70**
Altai Scotch rose (*Rosa pimpinellifolia altaica*) **162–64**
alumroot (*Heuchera* Morden hybrids) 4, 9, 15, 21, **114–15**
Alyssum saxatile (see *Aurinia saxatilis*)
American bittersweet vine (*Celastrus scandens*) 24, **195**
American ostrich fern (*Matteuccia struthiopteris*) 6, 9, 14, 19, 21, 22, 23, **130–31**
Anaphalis margaritacea (pearly everlasting) 5, 9, 33, **52**
Andropogon gerardii (big bluestem) 5, 10, 22, **52**; *A. scoparius* (see *Schizachyrium scoparium*)
Anemone (windflower) 5, 9, 17, 20, 23, **53–55**; *A. canadensis* (Canada anemone) 54; *A. multifida* (cutleaf anemone) 54; *A. sylvestris* (snowdrop anemone, windflower) **54–55**, 'Flore Pleno' 55
Antennaria (pussytoes) 3, 8, 9, 12, 18, 20, **55–56**; *A. parvifolia* (small-leaved pussytoes) 56; *A. plantaginifolia* (plantain-leaved pussytoes) 56; *A. rosea* (pink pussytoes) **55–56**
aphids, 40
Arabis alpina (syn. *A. caucasica*, *A. alpina* subsp. *caucasica*) (rock cress, mountain rock cress) 3, 8, 9, 18, 20, **56–57**, 'Flore Plena' 57, 'Rosabella' 57, 'Rosea' 57, 'Snow Peak' 57, 'Snowball' 57, 'Variegata' 57

Aralia nudicaulis (wild sarsaparilla) 5, 23, **58**

arctic phlox (*Phlox borealis*) 8, 10, **145–47**

Arctostaphylos uva-ursi (bearberry) 8, 9, 20, 23, 28, 34, **59**, 'Vancouver Jade' 59

Argentina anserina (see *Potentilla anserina*)

Aronia melanocarpa (black choke-berry) 13, **59–60**, 'Autumn Magic' 60

Arrhenatherum bulbosum 'Variegatum' (variegated tuber oat grass) 9, 14, 17, 23, **61**

arrow broom (*Genista sagittalis*) 104

Artemisia 3, **62–63**; *A. ludoviciana* (artemisia, wormwood, ghost plant, silver sage) 10, 16, 17, **62–63**, 'Silver Frost' 63, 'Silver King' 63, 'Silver Queen' 63, 'Valerie Finnis' 63; *A. stelleriana* 'Silver Brocade' 8, 9, 63

Asarum canadense (Canadian ginger, wild ginger) 6, 8, 9, 20, 23, **63–64**

Asperula odorata (see *Galium odoratum*)

Astilbe 6, 13, 20, 23, **65–66**; *A. chinensis* 'Pumila' **65–66**; *A. simplicifolia* 'Sprite' (dwarf astilbe) 22, **65**

Aurinia saxatilis (syn. *Alyssum saxatile*) (basket-of-gold) 3, 8, 9, 18, 20, **66–67**, 'Ball of Gold' 67, 'Citrinum' 67, 'Compactum' 67

Austrian speedwell (*Veronica austriaca*) 188

Baikal skullcap (*Scutellaria baicalensis*) 170

basket-of-gold (*Aurinia saxatilis*) 3, 8, 9, 18, 20, **66–67**

bearberry (*Arctostaphylos uva-ursi*) 8, 9, 20, 23, 28, 34, **59**

bedstraw (*Galium odoratum*) 20, 22, 23, **102**

bee balm (*Monarda* hybrids) 10, 14, 15, 19, **133–35**

bellflower (*Campanula*) **73–75**

Bergenia cordifolia (heart-leaved bergenia, pigsqueak) 4, 5, 9, 12, 13, 14, 16, 17, 20, 23, **67–68**, 'Baby Doll' 68, 'Bressingham Ruby' 68, 'Bressingham White' 68

betony (*Stachys*) 10, 14, 15, 19, **180–82**

big betony (*Stachys grandiflora*) 5, **180–81**

big bluestem (*Andropogon gerardii*) 5, 10, 22, **52**

bigflower dragonhead (*Dracocephalum grandiflorum*) 5, **90–91**

bigpetal clematis (*Clematis macropetala*) 196–99

bigroot perennial geranium (*Geranium macrorrhizum*) 5, 13, 107

Billard spirea (*Spiraea* x *billardi*) 179

bishop's goutweed (*Aegopodium podograria*) 6, 16, 17, 23, 28, **47**

black chokeberry (*Aronia melanocarpa*) 13, **59–60**

bloody cranesbill (*Geranium sanguineum*) 107

blue fescue (*Festuca glauca*) 4, 9, 14, 15, 18, 20, 39, 62, **98–99**

blue grama grass (*Bouteloua gracilis*) 4, 9, 11, 28, **68**

blue lyme grass (*Elymus arenarius*) 4, 11, 16, **92–93**

blue spruce sedum (*Sedum reflexum*) 171

blue stonecrop (*Sedum reflexum*) 171

boneset (*Eupatorium maculatum*) 5, 13, 15, 19, 22, **95–97**

Best Groundcovers & Vines For The Prairies

Bouteloua gracilis (blue grama grass) 4, 9, 11, 27, **68**

Bromus inermis 'Skinner's Golden' ('Skinner's Golden' brome grass) 4, 9, 11, 16, 17, 22, **69–70**

broom (*Cytisus*) 13, **86–87**; (*Genista*) 15, **103–104**

Brunnera macrophylla (alpine forget-me-not) 6, 23, **70–71**, 'Hadspen Cream' 71, 'Langtrees' 71, 'Variegata' 71

bugleweed (*Ajuga reptans*) 5, 6, 8, 12, 20, 23, 28, **49–50**

bunchberry (*Cornus canadensis*) 5, 23, **83–84**

Calamagrostis x *acutiflora* 'Karl Foerster' (syn. *C.* x *acutiflora* 'Stricta') ('Karl Foerster' feather reed grass) 13, 14, 18, **71–72**

Campanula (bellflower) **73–75**; *C. cochlearifolia* (syn. *C. pusilla)* (dwarf bellflower, fairy thimble) 9, 12, 18, 20, **73–74**, 'Alba' 74, 'Elizabeth Oliver' 74, 'Miranda' 74; *C. glomerata* (clustered bellflower, Danesblood bellflower) 9, 13, 14, 16, 17, 18, **74–75**, 'Superba' 75, 'Superba Alba' 75; *C. persicifolia* (peach-leaved bellflower) 9, 13, 14, 23, **75**, 'Alba' 75, 'Alba Flore-pleno' 75, 'Chettle Charm' 75, 'Moerheimii' 75, 'Telham Beauty' 75

Canada anemone (*Anemone canadensis*) **54**

Canadian ginger (*Asarum canadense*) 6, 8, 9, 20, 23, **63–64**

Caragana 4, 13, 14, 22, **76–77**; *C. arborescens* 'Pendula' (weeping caragana) 11, **76–77**; *C. pygmaea* (pygmy caragana) 19, 77

Carex (sedge) **77–79**; *C. muskingumensis* (palm sedge) 5, 20, **77–78**; *C. pennsylvanica* (sun-loving sedge) 4, 8, 9, 11, **78**

Carolina phlox (*Phlox carolina*) 146

carpet bugle (*Ajuga reptans*) 5, 6, 8, 12, 20, 23, 28, **49–50**

catmint (*Nepeta*) 12, 15, 16, 17, 21, 22, **135–36**

Caucasian catmint (*Nepeta* x *faasenii*) 136

Celastrus scandens (American bittersweet vine) 24, **195**

Cerastium tomentosum (snow-in-summer) 4, 8, 9, 11, 12, 17, 18, 20, **79–80**

Cheddar pinks (*Dianthus gratianopolitanus*) 88

Chelone (turtlehead) 9, 20, **80–81**; *C. glabra* (white turtlehead) 81; *C. lyonii* (pink turtlehead) 81; *C. obliqua* (pink turtlehead) 23, **80–81**

Chrysanthemum zawadskii subsp. *zawadskii* 'Clara Curtis' (syn. *Dendranthema zawadskii* 'Clara Curtis') ('Clara Curtis' chrysanthemum) 9, 13, **81–82**

cinquefoil (*Potentilla*) **149–153**

Clematis 11, **196–205**; *C. alpina* (alpine clematis) 38, 196, 197; *C. alpina, C. koreana, C. macropetala* (atragene group) **196–99**; *C. integrifolia* 203, 'Aljonushka' 204, 'Blue Boy' 204; *C. koreana* (Korean clematis) 197, 198; *C. ligusticifolia* (western virgin's bower) 204, 'Prairie Traveller's Joy' 205; *C. macropetala* (big-petal clematis) 196–99, 'Blue Bird' 199, 'Doctor F. L. Skinner' 199, 'Joe Zary' 199, 'Markham's Pink' 199, 'Lagoon' 199, 'Rosy O'Grady' 199, 'White Swan' 199; *C. recta* 205, 'Purpurea' 205, 'Pamela' 205; *C. serratifolia* (serrate-leaved clematis) 200, 'Golden Cross' 201; *C. tangutica* (golden clematis) 5, 200, 'Bill MacKenzie' 38, 200; *C. tangutica, C. serratifolia* (orientalis group) **200–201**; *C. texensis* 205, 'Duchess of Albany' 205; *C. viticella* (Italian clematis) 38, **201–202**, 'Etoile Violet' 202, 'Mme. Julia Correvon' 202, 'Polish Spirit' 202, 'Purpurea Plena Elegans' 202, 'Venosa Violacea' 202; *C.* x *jackmanii* 202-203, 'Comtesse de Bouchaud' 203, 'Hagley Hybrid' (syn. 'Pink Chiffon') 203, 'Jackmanii' 203, 'John Huxtable' 203; *C.* x *jouiniana* 'Praecox' 204

cliffgreen (*Paxistima canbyi*) 6, 8, 10, 21, 23, 27, **141**

climbing roses 165

clustered bellflower (*Campanula glomerata*) 9, 13, 14, 16, 17, 18, **74–75**

comb speedwell (*Veronica pectinata*) 189

comfrey (*Symphytum officinale*) 4, 11, 16, 17, 22, **183–84**

common golden juniper (*Juniperus communis* 'Depressa Aurea') **120–21**

common hops (*Humulus lupulus*) 4, 5, **205–206**

common lady's mantle (*Alchemilla mollis*) 5, 33, **50–51**

common lungwort (*Pulmonaria officinalis*) 158

common snowberry, (*Symphoricarpos albus*) 16, **182–83**

common yarrow (*Achillea millefolium*) 10, 13, 14, 16, 17, 19, 22, **44–45**

Convallaria majalis (lily-of-the-valley) 6, 9, 11, 15, 17, 20, 23, 27, **82–83**, 'Rosea' 83

coral bells (*Heuchera* Morden hybrids) 4, 9, 15, 21, **114–15**

Cornus canadensis (bunchberry, dwarf dogwood) 5, 23, **83–84**

Coronilla varia (crown vetch) 4, 9, 11, 17, **84–85**

Cotoneaster adpressus (creeping cotoneaster) 86; *C. adpressus* var. *praecox* (Nan Shan cotoneaster) 86; *C. horizontalis* 'Perpusillus' (ground cotoneaster) 6, 9, 20, **85–86**

cottage pinks (*Dianthus plumarius*) 89

cowslip primrose (*Primula veris*) 153

cranesbill (*Geranium* x *cantabrigiense*) 6, **105–107**

creeping baby's breath (*Gypsophila repens*) 4, 9, 11, **108–109**

creeping cotoneaster (*Cotoneaster adpressus*) 86

creeping forget-me-not (*Omphaloides verna alba*) 5, 10, 12, 21, 23, **136–37**

creeping Jenny (*Lysimachia nummularia*) 8, 9, 12, 21, 23, **127–28**

creeping juniper (*Juniperus horizontalis*) **121–22**

creeping Oregon grape (*Mahonia repens*) 5, 9, 23, **129**, 130

creeping speedwell (*Veronica prostrata*) 189

creeping thyme (*Thymus serpyllum*) **185**

crown vetch (*Coronilla varia*) 4, 9, 11, 17, **84–85**

currant (*Ribes*) 14, 15, 16, 17, 19, 22, **160–61**

cutleaf anemone (*Anemone multifida*) 54

cuttings 30, 32, 35, 36, 79, 54, 84, 86, 88, 89, 91, 94, 95, 96, 97, 103, 108, 109, 119, 121, 122, 123,

Best Groundcovers & Vines For The Prairies

131, 132, 134, 135, 136, 141, 142, 143, 144, 150, 151, 160, 161, 162, 164, 166, 170, 171, 177, 178, 182, 183, 185, 189, 190, 195, 196, 201, 207, 208, 209, 210, 211, 213, 214

Cypress spurge (*Euphorbia cyparissias*) 4, 9, 11, 17, **97–98**

Cytisus (broom) 13, **86–87**; *C. decumbens* (prostrate broom) 4, 11, **86–87**; *C. purpurea* var. *procumbens* (dwarf purple broom) 87

Danesblood bellflower (*Campanula glomerata*) 9, 13, 14, 16, 17, 18, **74–75**

Dasiphora fruticosa spp. *floribunda* (see *Potentilla fruticosa*)

dead nettle (*Lamiastrum galeobdolon*) 6, 8, 9, 11, 12, 14, 15, 17, 21, 22, 23, **124–25**

Dendranthema zawadskii 'Clara Curtis' (see *Chrysanthemum zawadskii* subsp. *zawadskii* 'Clara Curtis')

Dianthus (pinks) 4, 8, 9, 12, **88–89**; *D. deltoides* (maiden pinks) 89; *D. gratianopolitanus* (Cheddar pinks) **88–89**, 'Tiny Rubies' 18, 88; *D. plumarius* (cottage pinks) 89

Diervilla lonicera (dwarf bush honeysuckle) 4, 5, 11, 13, 15, 16, 19, 22, 23, **89–90**

division 33, 44, 46, 47, 49, 50, 51, 52, 53, 54, 56, 58, 61, 62, 63, 64, 65, 67, 68, 69, 70, 71, 73, 74, 75, 77, 78, 79, 80, 81, 82, 84, 87, 88, 90, 91, 92, 93, 96, 97, 98, 99, 100, 102, 104, 105, 106, 107, 110, 111, 112, 113, 114, 116, 125, 126, 127, 130, 131, 132, 133, 134, 135, 136, 137, 138, 140, 141, 142, 143, 144, 145, 146, 147, 148, 150, 153, 157, 158, 168, 169, 170, 171, 172, 173, 174, 175, 176, 181, 183, 185,

186, 187, 188, 189, 190, 191, 192, 193, 196, 201, 205, 206

double lilac geranium (*Geranium pratense* 'Plenum Violaceum') 107

Dracocephalum (dragonhead) 4, 9, 11, **90–91**; *D. grandiflorum* (bigflower dragonhead) 5, **90–91**; *D. ruyschianum* (Russian dragonhead) 91; *D. sibericum* 'Souvenir d'Andre Chaudron' (syn 'Blue Beauty') (syn. *Nepeta siberica* 'Souvenir d'Andre Chaudron') 91

'Dropmore Blue' catmint (*Nepeta* x 'Dropmore Blue') 4, 10, 14, **135–36**

'Dropmore Scarlet Trumpet' honeysuckle (*Lonicera* x *brownii* 'Dropmore Scarlet Trumpet') 24, **207–208**

Drummond avens (*Dryas drummondii*) 91

Dryas 4, 8, 9, 11, **91–92**; *D. drummondii* (Drummond avens) 91; *D. octopetala* (mountain avens) 28, 33, **91**; *D.* x *suendermannii* (Suendermann avens) 92

dusty miller primrose (*Primula auricula*) 154

dwarf astilbe (*Astilbe simplicifolia* 'Sprite') 22, **65**

dwarf baby's breath (*Gypsophila repens*) 4, 9, 11, **108–109**

dwarf bellflower (*Campanula cochlearifolia*) 9, 12, 18, 20, **73–74**

dwarf bumalda spirea (*Spiraea* x *bumalda*) **178–79**

dwarf bush honeysuckle (*Diervilla lonicera*) 4, 5, 11, 13, 15, 16, 19, 22, 23, **89–90**

dwarf dogwood (*Cornus canadensis*) 5, 23, **83–84**

dwarf lady's mantle (*Alchemilla erythropoda*) 51

dwarf purple broom (*Cytisus purpurea* var. *procumbens*) 87

dwarf sandcherry (*Prunus pumila*) 155

dwarf Siberian meadowsweet (*Filipendula palmata* 'Nana') 100

dwarf silver willow (*Salix repens* var. *argentea*) 14, 15, 166–67

dwarf snowberry (*Symphoricarpos albus pauciflora*) 183

dwarf Solomon's seal (*Polygonatum falcatum*) 149

dwarf Turkestan burning bush (*Euonymus nanus* var. *turkestanicus*) 5, 19, 28, **94–95**

Elymus arenarius (syn. *Leymus arenarius*) (blue lyme grass) 4, 11, 16, **92–93**

Engelmann's ivy (*Parthenocissus quinquefolia* var. *engelmannii*) 209

Erigeron speciosus (Oregon fleabane) 5, 9, 13, 15, **93–94**, 'Azure Beauty' 94, 'Azure Fairy' 94, 'Double Beauty' 94, 'Pink Jewel' 94, 'Prosperity' 94, 'Quakeress' 94

Euonymus (burning bush) 11, 13, 15, 19, **94–95**; *E. nanus* (dwarf narrow-leafed burning bush) 23, 95; *E. nanus* var. *turkestanicus* (dwarf Turkestan burning bush) 5, 19, 28, **94–95**

Eupatorium maculatum (syn. *E. purpureum, E. purpureum* subsp. *maculatum)* (Joe Pye weed, boneset) 5, 13, 15, 19, 22, **95–97**, 'Atropurpureum' 97, 'Gateway' 97; *E. purpureum* 97

Euphorbia cyparissias (Cypress spurge) 4, 9, 11, 17, **97–98**

European liverleaf (*Hepatica nobilis*) 113

European meadowsweet (*Filipendula ulmaria* 'Flora Plena') 22, **99–100**

evergreen candytuft (*Iberis sempervirens*) 4, 9, **118–19**

everyman's gentian (*Gentiana septemfida*) 105

fairy thimble (*Campanula cochlearifolia*) 9, 12, 18, 20, **73–74**

false Solomon's seal (*Smilacina stellata*) 5, 23, **174–75**

false sunflower (*Heliopsis helianthoides*) (syn. *H .scabra, H. helianthoides* subsp. *scabra*) 4, 13, 15, 17, 19, 22, **110–11**

fertilizer 7, 28, 29, 38, 39, 44

Festuca glauca (syn. *F. ovina* var. *glauca, F. cinerea* var. *glauca*) (blue fescue) 4, 9, 15, 18, 20, **98–99**

Filipendula (meadowsweet) 5, 6, 13, 15, 23, **99–100**; *F. ulmaria* (European meadowsweet) 'Flora Plena' 22, **99–100**, 'Aurea' 100, 'Variegata' 100; *F. palmata* 'Nana' (dwarf Siberian meadowsweet) 100

fleeceflower (*Persicaria*) 23, **143–44**

Fragaria (strawberry) 20, **100–101**; *F. virginiana* (wild strawberry) 4, 5, 8, 9, 11, 17, **100–101**; *F. ananassa* x *Potentilla palustris* x 'Pink Panda' ('Pink Panda' strawberry potentilla) 12, 101

Galium odoratum (syn. *Asperula odorata*) (sweet woodruff, bedstraw) 20, 22, 23, **102**

Genista (broom) 15, **103–104**; *G. lydia* (Lydia broom) 13, 20, **103–104**; *G. sagittalis* (arrow broom) 104

gentian speedwell (*Veronica gentianoides*) 188

Gentiana (gentian) 8, 9, 20, **104–105**; *G. acaulis* (stemless gentian) 23, **104–105**; *G. paradoxa* 105; *G. septemfida* (everyman's gentian) 105; *G. septemfida lagodechiana* 105

Geranium 8, 9, 11, 15, 17, 19, 20, 22, 23, **105–107**; *G. macrorrhizum* (bigroot geranium) 5, 13, 107; *G. pratense* 'Plenum Violaceum' (double lilac geranium) 107; *G. sanguineum* (bloody cranesbill) 107; *G.* x 'Johnson's Blue' 13, 107; *G.* x *cantabrigiense* (perennial geranium, cranesbill) 6, **105–107**, 'Biokova' 106, 'Cambridge' 106

germination 30, 33, 37, 39

Geum urbanum (syn. *G. urbanum* var. *sibiricum*) (Siberian avens, wood avens) 9, 20, **107–108**

ghost plant (*Artemisia ludoviciana*) 10, 16, 17, **62–63**

giant Solomon's seal (*Polygonatum commutatum*) 149

gold moss sedum (*Sedum acre*) 171

golden clematis (*Clematis tangutica*) 5, 200

golden currant (*Ribes aureum*) 161

goldenrod hybrids (*Solidago* hybrids) 4, 11, 15, 16, 17, 22, **175–76**

goutweed (*Aegopodium podograria*) 6, 16, 17, 23, 28, **47**

ground cotoneaster (*Cotoneaster horizontalis* 'Perpusillus') 6, 9, 20, **85–86**

Gypsophila repens (dwarf baby's breath, creeping baby's breath) 4, 9, 11, **108–109**, 'Alba' 109, 'Rosea' 109, 'Rosyveil' 109

harebell speedwell (*Veronica prostrata*) 189

heart-leaved bergenia (*Bergenia cordifolia*) 4, 5, 9, 12, 13, 14, 16, 17, 20, 23, **67–68**

Heliopsis helianthoides (syn. *H. scabra*, *H. helianthoides* subsp. *scabra*) (false sunflower, rough heliopsis) 4, 13, 15, 17, 19, 22, **110–11**, 'Golden Plume' 111, 'Loraine Sunshine' 111, 'Summer Sun' 111

Hemerocallis (daylily) 5, 6, 9, 19, 22, **111–12**, 'Bertie Ferris' 112, 'Happy Returns' 112, 'Hyperion' 112, 'Kwanso' 112, 'Pardon Me' 112, 'Stella d'Oro' 112; *H. fulva* (orange daylily, tawny daylily) 11, 14, 15, 16, 17, **111–12**; *H. lilioasphodelus* (syn. *H. flava*) (lemon daylily) 112

hen and chicks (*Sempervivum tectorum*) **172–73**

Hepatica 6, 23, **113**; *H. nobilis* (hepatica, European liverleaf) **113**; *H. transsylvanica*, 113

herbaceous periwinkle (*Vinca herbacea*) 8, 13, 18, 21, 24, **189–90**

Heuchera Morden hybrids (coral bells, alumroot) 4, 9, 15, 21, **114–15**, 'Brandon Pink' 115, 'Brandon Glow' 115, 'Northern Fire' 115, 'Ruby Mist' 115

Himalayan fleeceflower (*Persicaria affinis*) 10, 14, 15, 19, 21, **143–44**

Hood's phlox (*Phlox hoodii*) 146

Hosta 6, 8, 9, 14, 15, 21, 23, **115–18**, 'August Moon' 116, 'Blue Boy' 117, 'Bold Ribbons' 117, 'Francee' 117, 'Gingko Craig' 117, 'Gold Standard' 117, 'Golden Tiara' 117, 'Halcyon' 117, 'Honeybells' 117, 'Invincible' 117, 'Lancifolia' 117, 'Lemon Lime' 117, 'Paul's Glory' 117, 'Pearl Lake' 117, 'Royal Standard' 117, 'Sagae' 117, 'Shade Fanfare' 117, 'Sum and Substance' 117; *H. fortunei* 117;

H. sieboldiana 117; *H. sieboldii* 117; *H. undulata* 117, 'Albo-marginata' 117

houseleek (*Sempervivum tectorum*) **172–73**

Humulus lupulus, (common hops) 4, 5, **205–206**, 'Aurea' 206

Iberis sempervirens (evergreen candytuft) 4, 9, **118–19**

Italian clematis (*Clematis viticella*) 38, **201–202**

Japanese spirea (*Spiraea japonica*) 180

Japanese spurge (*Pachysandra terminalis*) 6, 8, 10, 21, 23, **137–38**

Jerusalem sage (*Pulmonaria officinalis*) 158

Joe Pye weed (*Eupatorium maculatum*) 5, 13, 15, 19, 22, **95–97**

Juniperus (juniper) 4, 9, 11, 14, 15, 16, 19, 21, **120–24**; *J. communis* 'Depressa Aurea' (common golden juniper) **120–21**; *J. horizontalis* (creeping juniper) 8, 28, 34, **121–23**, 'Andorra' (var. 'Plumosa') 122, 'Bar Harbour' 122, 'Blue Chip' 122, 'Dunvegan Blue' 122, 'Hughes' 122, 'Prince of Wales' 122, 'Waukegan' 123, 'Wiltonii' 123; *J. sabina* (savin juniper) **123–24**, 'Arcadia' 123, 'Blue Danube' 124, 'Broadmoor' 124, 'Buffalo' 124, 'Calgary Carpet' 124, 'Skandia' 164, var. *tamariscifolia* 124

'Karl Foerster' feather reed grass (*Calamagrostis* x *acutiflora* 'Karl Foerster') 13, 14, 18, **71–72**

Korean clematis (*Clematis koreana*) 197, 198

lady's mantle (*Alchemilla*) 12, 14, 20, **50–51**

Lamiastrum galeobdolon (yellow archangel, dead nettle) 6, 8, 9, 11, 12, 14, 15, 17, 21, 22, 23, **124–25**

Lamium maculatum (spotted dead nettle) 6, 8, 9, 12, 14, 15, 17, 21, 22, 23, **126–27**, 'Album' 127, 'Aureum' 127, 'Beacon's Silver' 127, 'Chequers' 127, 'Pink Pewter' 127, 'Red Nancy' 127, 'Shell Pink' 127, 'White Nancy' 127

layering 28, 33, 35, 84, 95, 122, 151, 195, 196, 201, 207, 208, 209

lemon-scented thyme (*Thymus* x *citriodorus*) 185

Leymus arenarius (see *Elymus arenarius*)

lily-of-the-valley (*Convallaria majalis*) 6, 9, 11, 15, 17, 20, 23, 27, **82–83**

little bluestem (*Schizachyrium scoparium*) 5, 10, 11, **168–69**

Lonicera x *brownii* 'Dropmore Scarlet Trumpet' ('Dropmore Scarlet Trumpet' honeysuckle) 24, **207–208**

lungwort (*Pulmonaria*) 6, 10, 14, 15, 21, 23, **156–59**

Lydia broom (*Genista lydia*) 13, 20, **103–104**

Lysimachia nummularia (creeping Jenny, moneywort) 8, 9, 12, 21, 23, **127–28**; *L. punctata* (yellow loosestrife) 9, 14, 15, 128

madwort (*Aurinia saxatilis*) 3, 8, 9, 18, 20, **66–67**

Mahonia repens (creeping Oregon grape) 5, 9, 23, **129**, 130

maiden pinks (*Dianthus deltoides*) 89

Manitoba grape (*Vitis riparia*) 11, 24, **210**

mat penstemon (*Penstemon caespitosus*) **142–43**

Matteuccia struthiopteris (syn. *M. struthiopteris* var. *pensylvanica*, *M. pensylvanica*) (ostrich fern, American ostrich fern) 6, 9, 14, 19, 21, 22, 23, **130–31**

Microbiota decussata (Russian cypress, Siberian cypress) 5, 9, 14, 21, **131–32**

Molinia caerulea variegata (variegated moor grass) 21, **132–33**

Monarda hybrids (monarda, wild bergamot, bee balm, Oswego tea) 10, 14, 15, 19, **133–35**, 'Marshall's Delight' 135, 'Petite Delight' 135, 'Petite Wonder' 135

moneywort (*Lysimachia nummularia*) 8, 9, 12, 21, 23, **127–28**

moss campion (*Silene acaulis*) 8, 10, 18, **173–74**

moss phlox (*Phlox subulata*) 8, 10, 146

mountain lungwort (*Pulmonaria mollis*) **157–58**

mountain rock cress (*Arabis alpina*) 3, 8, 9, 18, 20, **56–57**

mulch 31, 32, 33, 37, 38, 196

mulching 30, 37, 39

nailwort (*Paronychia capitata*) 1, 4, 8, 10, 18, **139–40**

Nan Shan cotoneaster (*Cotoneaster adpressus* var. *praecox*) 86

Nepal cinquefoil (*Potentilla nepalensis*) 153

Nepeta (catmint) 12, 15, 16, 17, 21, 22, **135–36**; *N.* x 'Dropmore Blue' ('Dropmore Blue' catmint) 4, 10, 14, **135–36**; *N.* x *faasenii* (Caucasian catmint) 136; *N. siberica* 'Souvenir d'Andre Chaudron' (see *Dracocephalum sibericum* 'Souvenir d'Andre Chaudron')

nitrogen 28, 39, 44

northern gooseberry (*Ribes oxycanthoides*) 161

obedient plant (*Physostegia virginiana*) 5, 10, 14, 15, **147**

Omphalodes verna alba (creeping forget-me-not) 5, 10, 12, 21, 23, **136–37**

orange daylily (*Hemerocallis fulva*) 11, 14, 15, 16, 17, **111–12**

orangespot potentilla (*Potentilla alpestre*) 152

Oregon fleabane (*Erigeron speciosus*) 5, 9, 13, 15, **93–94**

ostrich fern (*Matteuccia struthiopteris*) 6, 9, 14, 19, 21, 22, 23, **130–31**

Oswego tea (*Monarda* hybrids) 10, 14, 15, 19, **133–35**

Pachysandra terminalis (Japanese spurge) 6, 8, 10, 21, 23, **137–38**

palm sedge (*Carex muskingumensis*) 5, 20, **77–78**

Panicum virgatum (switch grass) 10, 14, 15, **138–39**

Paronychia capitata (syn. *P. nivea*) (whitlowwort, nailwort) 1, 4, 8, 10, 18, **139–40**

Parthenocissus quinquefolia (Virginia creeper) 5, 11, 24, 33, **208–209**; *P. quinquefolia* var. *engelmannii* (Engelmann's ivy) 209

Paxistima canbyi (cliffgreen, paxistima) 6, 8, 10, 21, 23, 27, **141**

peach-leaved bellflower (*Campanula persicifolia*) 9, 13, 14, 23, **75**

pearly everlasting (*Anaphalis margaritacea*) 5, 9, 33, **52**

Penstemon 10, 18, 21, **142–43**; *P. caespitosus* (mat penstemon) **142–43**; *P. davidsonii* var. *menziesii* 143; *P. fruticosus* 'Purple Haze' 143

perennial alyssum (*Aurinia saxatilis*) 3, 8, 9, 18, 20, **66–67**
perennial geranium (*Geranium* x *cantabrigiense*) 6, **105–107**
periwinkle (*Vinca*) 10, **189–90**
Persicaria (fleeceflower) 23, **143–44**; *P. affinis* (syn. *Polygonum affine*) (Himalayan fleeceflower) 10, 14, 15, 19, 21, **143–44**; *P. bistorta superba* (superb European bistort) 144
pH 28
Phalaris arundinacea 'Picta' (ribbon grass) 6, 10, 14, 15, 17, 23, 33, **144–45**
Phlox 18, 21, **145–47**; *P. borealis* (arctic phlox) 8, 10, **145–47**, 'Rubies Choice' 147; *P. carolina* (Carolina phlox) 'Bill Baker' 146; *P. hoodii* (Hood's phlox) 146; *P. subulata* (moss phlox) 8, 10, 146
phosphorous, 52
Physostegia virginiana (obedient plant) 5, 10, 14, 15, **147**, 'Bouquet Rose' 147, 'Miss Manners' 147, 'Summer Snow' 147, 'Variegata' 147
pigsqueak (*Bergenia cordifolia*) 4, 5, 9, 12, 13, 14, 16, 17, 20, 23, **67–68**
'Pink Panda' strawberry potentilla (*Fragaria* x *ananassa* x *Potentilla palustris* 'Pink Panda') 101
pink pussytoes (*Antennaria rosea*) **55–60**
pink turtlehead (*Chelone obliqua, C. lyonii*) 23, **80–81**
pinks (*Dianthus*) 4, 8, 9, 12, **88–89**
plantain-leaved pussytoes (*Antennaria plantaginifolia*) 56
Polygonatum 14, 18, 23, 29, 32, 35, **148–49**; *P. commutatum* (syn. *P. giganteum*) (giant Solomon's seal) 149; *P. falcatum*

(dwarf Solomon's seal) 149; *P. multiflorum* (syn. *P. x hybridum*) (Solomon's seal) **148–49**; *P. odoratum* var. *pluriforum* 'Variegatum' (variegated Solomon's seal) 149
Polygonum affine (see *Persicaria affinis*)
potassium 39
Potentilla (cinquefoil) 4, 11, 16, 17, 21, 23, **149–53**; *P. alpestre* (orangespot potentilla) 152; *P. anserina* (syn. *Argentina anserina*) (silverweed) 8, 10, **150**; *P. fruticosa* (syn. *Dasiphora fruticosa* spp. *floribunda*) (shrubby cinquefoil, potentilla) 15, 19, 22, **151–52**, 'Abbotswood' 151, 'Coronation Triumph' 151, 'Goldfinger' 152, 'Katherine Dykes' 152, 'Mango Tango' ('Uman') 152, 'McKay's White' 152, 'Orange Whisper' 152, 'Pink Beauty' 152, 'Primrose Beauty' 152, 'Snowbird' 152, 'Yellow Gem' 152; *P. megalantha* (woolly cinquefoil) 153; *P. nepalensis* (Nepal cinquefoil) 153; *P. tridentata* (syn. *Sibbaldiopsis tridentata*) (three-toothed cinquefoil) 153
prairie rose (*Rosa arkansana*) 163
Primula (primrose) 21, 23, **153–54**; *P. auricula* (dusty miller primrose) 154; *P. veris* (cowslip primrose) **153–54**
prostrate broom (*Cytisus decumbens*) 4, 11, **86–87**
pruning 37, 38, 209, 211
Prunus pumila (dwarf sandcherry) 155
Prunus tenella (Russian almond) 4, 11, 16, 17, 19, 22, **155**
Pulmonaria (lungwort) 6, 10, 14, 15, 21, 23, **156–59**; *P. mollis*

(syn. *P. montana*) (soft lungwort, mountain lungwort) **157–58**; *P. officinalis* (Jerusalem sage, common lungwort) 158; *P. rubra* (red lungwort) 158; *P. saccharata* (Bethlehem sage) 'Margery Fish' 158, 'Roy Davidson' **158**, 'Spilled Milk' 158

pussytoes (*Antennaria*) 3, 8, 12, 18, 20, **55–56**

pygmy caragana (*Caragana pygmaea*) 19, 77

pyramidal bugleweed (*Ajuga pyramidalis*) 50

red lungwort (*Pulmonaria rubra*) 158

rhizomes, 2, 27, 42, 57, 60, 63, 69, 70, 78, 83, 96, 99, 104, 107, 112, 113, 116, 129, 131, 139, 141, 145, 148, 155, 163, 164, 175, 177, 193

Rhus glabra (smooth sumac) 11, 15, 16, 17, 19, 22, **159–60**, 'Midi' 160, 'Mini' 160, 'Morden's' 160

ribbon grass (*Phalaris arundinacea* 'Picta') 6, 10, 14, 15, 17, 23, 33, **144–45**

Ribes (currant) 14, 15, 16, 17, 19, 22, **160–61**; *R. alpinum* (alpine currant) **160–61**; *R. aureum* (golden currant) 161; *R. oxycanthoides* (northern gooseberry) 161

riverbank grape (*Vitis riparia*) 1, 24, **210**

rock cress (*Arabis alpina*) 3, 8, 9, 18, 20, **56–57**

rock soapwort (*Saponaria ocymoides*) 4, 11, **167–68**

Rosa (rose) 4, 5, 11, 14, 15, 16, 17, 19, 21, 22, **162–66**; *R. arkansana* (prairie rose) 163; *R. nitida* (shining rose) 164; *R. pimpinellifolia altaica* (Altai Scotch rose) **162–64**; 'Hazeldean' 163, 'Kakwa' 163,

'Kilwinning' 163, 'Seager Wheeler' 163, 'Yellow Altai' 163; *R. rugosa* hybrids (rugosa roses) 33, **164–66**; 'Aylsham' 165, 'Charles Albanel' 165, 'David Thompson' 165, 'Frau Dagmar Hartopp' ('Fru Dagmar Hastrup') 165, 'Hansa' 165, 'Henry Hudson' 165, 'Jens Munk' 165, 'Marie Bugnet' 166, 'Therese Bugnet' 166, 'Will Alderman' 166; roses, climbing, 'Ames #5' 165, 'Ames Climber' 165, 'Captain Samuel Holland' 165, 'John Cabot' 165, 'John Davis' 165, 'Polstjärnan' 165, 'Prairie Dawn' 165, 'William Baffin' 165, 'William Booth' 165

'Roy Davidson' Bethlehem sage (*Pulmonaria saccharata* 'Roy Davidson') **158**

Rugosa roses (*Rosa rugosa* hybrids) 33, **164–66**

rough heliopsis (*Heliopsis helianthoides*) (syn. *H .scabra*, *H. helianthoides* subsp. *scabra*) 4, 13, 15, 17, 19, 22, **110–11**

Russian almond (*Prunus tenella*) 4, 11, 16, 17, 19, 22, **155**

Russian cypress (*Microbiota decussata*) 5, 9, 14, 21, **131-32**

Russian dragonhead (*Dracocephalum ruyschianum*) 91

Salix (willow) 10, 21, **166–67**; *S. lanata* (woolly willow) **166**; *S. repens* var. *argentea* (dwarf silver willow) 14, 15, **166–67**

Saponaria ocymoides (rock soapwort) 4, 11, **167–68**

Savin juniper (*Juniperus sabina*) **123–24**

Schizachyrium scoparium (syn. *Andropogon scoparius*) (little bluestem) 5, 10, 11, **168–69**

Scutellaria 10, 21, 23, **169–70**;
  S. alpina (alpine skullcap) **169–70**;
  S. baicalensis (Baikal skullcap) 170
sedge (*Carex*) **77–79**
Sedum (stonecrop) 4, 8 10, 11,
  17, 18, 21, **170–71**; *S. acre*
  (gold moss sedum) 171;
  S. kamtschaticum 'Variegatum'
  (variegated Kamchatka sedum)
  170–71; *S. reflexum* (blue
  stonecrop, blue spruce sedum)
  171; *S. spurium* (two row
  sedum) 171, 'Bronze Carpet'
  171, 'Dragon's Blood' 171, 'Ruby
  Mantle' 171, 'Tricolor' 171, var.
  album 171, var. *roseum* 171
Sempervivum 4, 8, 10, 17, 18,
  21, **172–73**; *S. arachnoideum*
  (cobweb hen and chicks) 173,
  'Rubrum' 173; *S. tectorum* (hen
  and chicks, houseleek) **172–73**
serrate-leafed clematis (*Clematis
  serratifolia*) 200
shining rose (*Rosa nitida*) 164
shrubby cinquefoil (*Potentilla
  fruticosa*) 15, 19, 22, **151–52**
Sibbaldiopsis tridentata (see
  Potentilla tridentata)
Siberian avens (*Geum urbanum*) 9,
  20, **107–108**
Siberian barren strawberry
  (*Waldsteinia ternata*) 5, 8, 10, 13,
  17, 21, 24, **192–93**
Siberian cypress (*Microbiota
  decussata*) 5, 9, 14, 21, **131–32**
Silene acaulis (moss campion) 8, 10,
  18, **173–74**; *S. pedunculata* 174
silver sage (*Artemisia ludoviciana*)
  10, 16, 17, **62–63**
silverweed (*Potentilla anserina*) 8,
  9, 10, 149, **150**
'Skinner's Golden' brome grass
  (*Bromus inermis* 'Skinner's
  Golden') 4, 9, 11, 16, 17, 22,
  69–70

small-leaved pussytoes (*Antennaria
  parvifolia*) 56
Smilacina stellata (star-flowered
  Solomon's seal, false Solomon's
  seal) 5, 23, **174–75**
smooth sumac (*Rhus glabra*) 11, 15,
  16, 17, 19, 22, **159–60**
sneezewort, sneezeweed (*Achillea
  ptarmica*) **46**
snowdrop anemone (*Anemone
  sylvestris*) **54–55**
snow-in-summer (*Cerastium
  tomentosum*) 4, 8, 9, 11, 12, 17,
  18, **79–80**
soft lungwort (*Pulmonaria mollis*)
  157–58
Solidago hybrids (goldenrod
  hybrids) 4, 11, 15, 16, 17, 22,
  175–76, 'Cloth of Gold' 176,
  'Crown of Rays' 176, 'Golden
  Fleece' 176
Solomon's seal (*Polygonatum
  multiflorum*) **148–49**
Sorbaria sorbifolia (Ural false
  spirea) 4, 11, 16, 19, 22, **177–78**
speedwell (*Veronica*) 4, 8, 10, 12, 18,
  21, **187–89**
spiderwort (*Tradescantia
  virginiana*) 10, 21, 24, **186–87**
Spiraea 4, 5, 10, 14, 15, 19, 21,
  'Summersnow' 180; *S. japonica*
  (Japanese spirea) 180,
  'Goldmound' 180, 'Little
  Princess' 180, 'Shirobana'
  ('Shirobori') 180; *S.* x *billardi*
  (Billard spirea) 179; *S.* x
  bumalda **178–79**, 'Anthony
  Waterer' 178, 'Crispa' 179,
  'Froebelli' 179, 'Goldflame' 179,
  'Gumball' 179, 'Magic Carpet'
  179, 'Mini-Sunglow' 179,
  'Rosabella' 179
spotted dead nettle (*Lamium
  maculatum*) 6, 8, 9, 12, 14, 15, 17,
  21, **126–27**

Stachys (betony) 10, 14, 15, 19,
180–82; *S. grandiflora* (syn.
S. macrantha) (big betony) 5,
180–81, 'Robusta' 181; *S. lanata*
(syn. *S. byzantium, S. olympica*)
(woolly lambs' ears) 4, 21, 181,
'Big Ears' (syn. 'Helene von
Steine') 182, 'Primrose Heron'
182, 'Silver Carpet' 182
star-flowered Solomon's seal
(*Smilacina stellata*) 5, 23, **174–75**
stemless gentian (*Gentiana acaulis*)
23, **104–105**
stolons, stoloniferous 2, 27, 42, 50,
78, 97, 101, 126, 137, 143, 150,
200, 215
stonecrop (*Sedum*) 4, 8, 10, 11, 17,
18, 21, **170–71**
stratification 33, 69
strawberry (*Fragaria*) 20,
100–101
sucker, suckering 27, 33, 60, 92, 95,
129, 155, 160, 162, 164, 178, 183,
206, 208, 209, 215
Suendermann avens (*Dryas* x
suendermannii) 92
sun-loving sedge (*Carex
pennsylvanica*) 4, 8, 9, 11, **78**
superb European bistort (*Persicaria
bistorta superba*) 144
sweet woodruff (*Galium odoratum*)
20, 22, 23, **102**
switch grass (*Panicum virgatum*)
10, 14, 15, **138–39**
Symphoricarpos 4, 5, 11, 19,
22, 24; *S. albus* (common
snowberry) 16, **182–83;** *S. albus
pauciflora* (dwarf snowberry)
183; *S. occidentalis* (western
snowberry) 183
Symphytum officinale (comfrey)
4, 11, 16, 17, 22, **183–84,**
'Goldsmith' 184
tawny daylily (*Hemerocallis fulva*)
11, 14, 15, 16, 17, **111–12**

three-toothed cinquefoil (*Potentilla
tridentata*) 153
Thymus (thyme) 8, 10, 11, 12,
18, 21, **185–86**; *T. pallasianus*
(Ukrainian thyme) 186;
T. serpyllum (creeping thyme)
185; *T. pseudolanuginosis* (woolly
thyme) 186; *T.* x *citriodorus*
(lemon-scented thyme) 185
Tradescantia virginiana (syn. *T.* x
andersonia) (spiderwort) 10, 21,
24, **186–87**, 'Concord Grape'
187, 'Isis' 187, 'Osprey' 187,
'Red Cloud' 187, 'Snowcap' 187,
'Zwanenburg' 187
two row sedum (*Sedum spurium*)
171
Ukrainian thyme (*Thymus
pallasianus*) 186
Ural false spirea (*Sorbaria
sorbifolia*) 4, 11, 16, 19, 22,
177–78
variegated Kamchatka sedum
(*Sedum kamschaticum*
'Variegatum') **170–71**
variegated moor grass (*Molinia
caerulea variegata*) 21, **132–33**
variegated Solomon's seal
(*Polygonatum odoratum* var.
pluriflorum 'Variegatum') 149
variegated tuber oat grass,
(*Arrhenatherum bulbosum*
'Variegatum') 9, 14, 17, 23, **61**
Veronica (speedwell) 4, 8, 10, 12,
18, 21, **187–89**; *V. austriaca*
(syn. *V. teucrinum*) (Austrian
speedwell) 188; *V. gentianoides*
(gentian speedwell) 188;
V. incana (woolly speedwell)
187–88; *V. pectinata* (comb
speedwell) 189, 'Rosea' 189;
V. prostrata (creeping speedwell,
harebell speedwell) 189, 'Rosea'
189, 'Trehane' 189; *V. whitleyi*
(Whitley's veronica) 189

Vinca (periwinkle) 10, **189–90**;
    V. herbacea (herbaceous peri-
    winkle) 8, 13, 18, 21, 24, **189–90**;
    V. minor common periwinkle)
    190, 'Sterling Silver' 190, var.
    alba 190, 'Variegata' 190
Viola canadensis (syn. *V. rugulosa*,
    V. canadensis var. *rugulosa*)
    (western Canada violet, wood
    violet) 5, 13, 17, 21, 24, **191–92**
Virginia creeper (*Parthenocissus
    quinquefolia*) 5, 11, 24, 33,
    208–209
Vitis riparia (riverbank grape,
    Manitoba grape) 11, 24, **210**
Waldsteinia ternata (Siberian
    barren strawberry) 5, 8, 10, 13,
    17, 21, 24, **192–93**
weeping caragana (*Caragana
    arborescens* 'Pendula') 11, **76–77**
western Canada violet (*Viola
    canadensis*) 5, 13, 17, 21, 24,
    191–92
western snowberry (*Symphoricarpos
    occidentalis*) 182
western virgin's bower (*Clematis
    ligusticifolia*) 204
white turtlehead (*Chelone glabra*) 81
Whitley's veronica (*Veronica
    whitleyi*) 189
whitlowwort (*Paronychia capitata*)
    1, 4, 8, 10, 18, **139–40**

wild bergamot (*Monarda* hybrids)
    10, 14, 15, 19, **133–35**
wild ginger (*Asarum canadense*) 6,
    8, 9, 20, 23, **63–64**
wild sarsaparilla (*Aralia nudicaulis*)
    5, 23, **58**
wild strawberry (*Fragaria virginiana*)
    4, 5, 8, 9, 11, 17, **100–101**
willow (*Salix*) 10, 21, **166–67**
windflower (*Anemone sylvestris*)
    54–55
wood avens (*Geum urbanum*) 9,
    20, **107–108**
wood violet (*Viola canadensis*) 5,
    13, 17, 21, 24, **191–92**
woolly cinquefoil (*Potentilla
    megalantha*) 153
woolly speedwell (*Veronica incana*)
    187–88
woolly thyme (*Thymus
    pseudolanuginosis*) 186
woolly willow (*Salix lanata*) **166**
woolly yarrow (*Achillea tomentosa*)
    18, 20, **47**
wormwood (*Artemisia ludoviciana*)
    10, 16, 17, **62–63**
yarrow (*Achillea*) 8, 16, **44–47**
yellow archangel (*Lamiastrum
    galeobdolon*) 6, 8, 9, 11, 12, 14, 15,
    17, 21, 22, 23, **124–25**
yellow loosestrife (*Lysimachia
    punctata*) 9, 14, 15, 128

Best Groundcovers & Vines For The Prairies